THE REPRESENTATION OF SPEECH IN THE PERIPHERAL AUDITORY SYSTEM

To Valerij Kozhevnikov

THE REPRESENTATION OF SPEECH IN THE PERIPHERAL AUDITORY SYSTEM

Proceedings of the Symposium on the Representation of Speech in the Peripheral Auditory System held in Stockholm, Sweden on May 17-19, 1982.

Editors

Rolf Carlson and **Björn Granström**

1982

ELSEVIER BIOMEDICAL PRESS
AMSTERDAM · NEW YORK · OXFORD

ISBN 0-444-80447-1

Published by:
Elsevier Biomedical Press B.V.
P.O. Box 211
1000 AE Amsterdam, The Netherlands

Sole distributors for the USA and Canada:
Elsevier Science Publishing Company Inc.
52 Vanderbilt Avenue
New York, N.Y. 10017

Printed in The Netherlands

INTRODUCTORY REMARKS*

In the past hearing research and speech research seem to have been pursued relatively independently. On the international scene there have recently been indications of a development towards greater interaction between the two fields. It appears possible to draw attention to a few of the reasons why having a cross-disciplinary meeting on the auditory processing of speech seems justified at the present stage.

We find such motivations in both applied and basic work. Consider technical applications of speech research, for instance. According to current predictions for the 80´ies speech technology appears to face extremely favorable prospects. A lot of efforts is now being devoted to improving techniques for automatic voice response and automatic speech recognition - applications that are today becoming commercial realities. Aids for the handicapped are being developed as a result of the evolution of hardware and signal processing techniques. Active steps are being taken in clinical work to develop tests of hearing that measure not only sensory but also functional performance, in particular those aspects that determine a person's ability to perceive speech.

With regard to basically oriented research, we note that physiological studies on animals have progressed to a state that enables the study of how speech sounds are coded in the auditory nerve. Also psycho-acoustic techniques are being applied to speech-like stimuli.

Finally, let us mention that the goal of accounting for speech perception under normal as well as disturbed conditions is a strong driving force for current, more theoretically oriented work in experimental psychology and phonetics.

We may ask whether such developments are indications of the fact that before long we will be taking significant steps towards the implementation of, what our colleagues in Leningrad have called, an auditory speech spectrograph that will portray speech

----

* The essentials of this introduction were read by Björn Lindblom as a key-note paper at the opening of the symposium.

in auditorily more realistic ways than our present sound analyzers. In other words, shall we get access to displays more similar to the manner in which the ear presents speech to the CNS?

Some of us are no doubt inclined to view such visions with a great deal of pessimism. For instance, the sheer magnitude of such an undertaking might give sufficient reason for scepticism. Or we might subscribe to a rather extreme version of a perceptual theory that claims that "speech is special" and that the exploration of hearing by means of non-speech-like stimuli, and often with the aid of animal preparations, will accumulate information largely irrelevant to the understanding of human speech perception. We could conceivably raise still further objections by arguing that our limited understanding of speech perception is not primarily due to the lack of information on how the ear processes speech. Rather it reflects to a far greater extent the need to pursue further the quest for invariance in the acoustic signal itself, or to describe the operation of the non-peripheral, so-called top-down mechanisms that listeners invoke.

On the other hand, to the optimists the idea of an auditory spectrograph may still be rather utopian but represents a genuine worth-while long-term goal. They offer the hope that the "information-bearing" elements of speech will stand out much more clearly in auditory displays than they do in our present acoustic representations. Consequently, the classical speech research issues of invariance and segmentation might be considerably illuminated by the development of better auditory models. As a result significant insights into the perception of speech by the hard of hearing might be obtained and technical applications, such as the recognition of speech, considerably facilitated.

During the meeting these issues received ample exposure. Another topic closely related to the theme of the conference is cochlear implants. One discussion session was devoted to this issue. Even though the implantation is rapidly getting into clinical practise the general concensus was that we still are quite far from being able to define an optimal prosthesis on solid scientific grounds. It seems, however, equally clear that we have now reached a point in time when we are ready to approach the research topics productively in an interdisciplinary context.

ACKNOWLEDGMENTS

We want to acknowledge the Swedish Council for Research Planning and Coordination for making this symposium possible. We also want to thank all people at the Conference Secretariat of the Wenner-Gren Center and the Department of Speech Communication and Music Acoustics who helped in organizing and carrying out the symposium. Our special thanks are due to Si Felicetti who also assisted in editing this book.

DEDICATION

During the past year we were reached by the news of the tragic and untimely death of a pioneer in auditory modeling and cross-disciplinary speech and hearing research: Valerij Kozhevnikov. We want to dedicate this book to his memory.

CONTENTS

© 1982 Elsevier Biomedical Press
The Representation of Speech in the Peripheral
Auditory System, R. Carlson and B. Granström eds.

STRUCTURE AND FUNCTION OF THE HEARING ORGAN: RECENT INVESTIGATIONS OF MICROMECHANICS AND ITS CONTROL

ÅKE FLOCK
Department of Physiology II, Karolinska institutet, S-104 01
Stockholm 60, Sweden

INTRODUCTION

The fundamentals of structure and function of the hearing organ is well described in a number of textbooks (1,3,4), review articles (2) and conference proceedings (5-7). The present synopsis is intended to review work carried out at our laboratory during recent years, to give references to published articles and to preview unpublished work that is now in press or in progress.

The framework of our topic is micromechanics. Since a number of years we have strived to obtain physiological measurements of the mechanical properties of inner ear sensory organs at a cellular level. This has been done by micromanipulation on isolated sense organs under microscopical observation at high magnification, initially on organs of the vestibular system, more recently on the organ of Corti in the guinea pig. Our interest has been aimed especially at the mechanoreceptor structures of the sensory cells; the stereocilia and the cuticular plate. In parallel electron microscopy has been used to examine the fine structure of this region. This has been combined with immunofluorescence techniques to identify and localize specific proteins in the sensory and supporting elements

MICROMECHANICAL PROPERTIES OF SENSORY HAIRS

Vestibular system. Initial work was performed on the crista ampullaris of the semicircular canal in the frog (8,9). This organ can be maintained in a microscope chamber permitting insertion of a microprobe to manipulate the sensory hairs which are viewed in profile through differential interference contrast optics. The main finding was that the sensory hairs exhibit considerable stiffness, to the point of being brittle, and that the stereocilia within the bundle of each sensory cell are connected to one another. A method was developed which allowed quantitative

calibrated stimuli to be delivered to selected sensory hairs (10).
This consisted of a pulse of fluid ejected from a micropipette
aimed at the sensory hair region. The fluid pulse was of short
duration and caused the sensory hairs to swing away, to return
spontaneously by inherent elasticity. The motion was filmed and
hair deflection was recorded frame by frame on a projecting screen.
It was found that the motion pattern could vary from one hair to
the next, some sensory hairs are slow in their response properties,
others return to zero position quite rapidly, while still others
have intermediate time constants. It was observed in the microscope that hair bundles with different motion patterns varied in
structure. This was confirmed by scanning electron microscopy
revealing the presence of at least 3 different bundle types. Fast
hair bundles have tall, thick and numerous stereocilia accompanying the kinocilium, slow bundles have a kinocilium joined at the
base by fes slender short stereocilia. One concludes that in this
organ the structural arrangement of stereocilia within the sensory hair bundle determines the mechanical response characteristics. On this basis it was natural to inquire about mechanical
properties of sensory hair bundles in the mammalian hearing
organ, because inner and outer hair cells in the organ of Corti
have a rather elaborate structure.

Organ of Corti. A technique was developed for the isolation
and maintenance of individual coils of guinea pig organ of Corti
in a tissue fluid chamber allowing quantitative micromanipulation
(11). When the fluid pulse stimulus was applied to sensory hair
bundles of inner and outer hair cells it was found that organ of
Corti stereocilia are much stiffer than those of the crista
ampullaris. Even at the highest velocity available, sensory hairs
could barely be seen to move. This velocity was large enough to
cause slight motion of the whole surface of the organ due to
viscous drag. Occational bundles that did move were considered
damaged during the dissection procedure. Another method was therefore developed to obtain absolute values of compliance for organ
of Corti sensory hairs. A fibre of quartz glass, 1-2 um in dia-
meter and 400-700 um long, was glued to the tip of a glass
probe. The fibre was pushed against a selected sensory hair dis-
placing it 1 um. The amount of bending (=displacement) of the

glass fibre that was required was measured and this value was used to calculate the stiffness of the sensory hair in dynes/cm. This was done statistically on a large number of cells. It was found that the stereocilia within the rows of sensory hairs of outer as well as inner hair cells are joined laterally to one another. The stereocilia are fragile and fracture at the junction with the hair cell surface when displaced in excess of about 2 um. They do not arch but pivot at the base. Quantitative measurements of stiffness were obtained for the different rows and for 3 different coils. It was found that the stiffness is not constant for either of these dimensions: the stiffness increases from apex to base, measuring 0.94 ± 0.35 d/cm in turn 4 and 3.48 ± 0.38 d/cm in turn 2 (outer hair cells of the first row). There is also a gradation of stiffness in the radial direction, stiffness decreasing from row 1 towards row 3. On this basis we conclude that the sensory hairs are tuned and are likely to contribute to frequency selectivity of the organ of Corti through their mechanical coupling to the tectorial membrane. Electron microscopy was used to measure the height of the stereocilia in the different coils and in the different rows. It was found that for the 3 rows of outer hair cells there is a match between stereociliary height and hair stiffness so that the torque force at the ciliary base is approximately constant. It was also found that there is systematic change in height between the different coils, however, not sufficient to account for the stiffness variation.

Another significant observation was made in experiments where the sensory hair was moved in the excitatory or inhibitory direction (excitatory=stereocilia moving towards the centriole). The sensory hairs were found to differ for the two directions of applied force; the stiffness in the excitatory direction exceeded that in the inhibitory by a factor of proximately 2. Consequently the sensory hairs have asymmetric, nonlinear stiffness properties, at least at this magnitude of displacement. This observation may relate to nonlinear properties in mechanics as well as in neural responses noted by several investigators (12, 13,1,14). Nonlinear phenomena in the organ of Corti have been attributed to an essential and vulnerable "second filter" located at some critical position in the hearing organ. Our findings hint that it may be related to the sensory hairs.

ACTIN AND CONTROL OF SENSORY HAIR MOTION

Responsible for the stiffness properties of the stereocilia is an internal core of filaments of the protein actin which traverses each stereocilium longitudinally and inserts as a rootlet in the cuticular plate (Fig. 1, ref. 15a). This protein is best

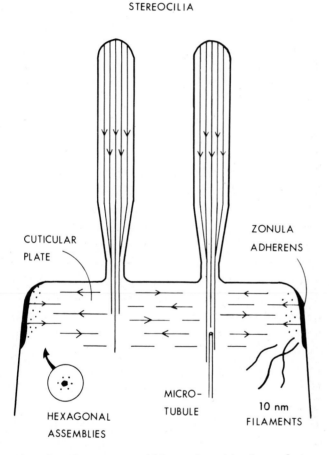

STEREOCILIA

CUTICULAR
PLATE

ZONULA
ADHERENS

HEXAGONAL
ASSEMBLIES

MICRO-
TUBULE

10 nm
FILAMENTS

Fig. 1. The stereocilia and cuticular plate contain filaments of actin, a protein that in many cell types participates in mechanical or motile functions (from ref. 15a).

known from skeletal muscle fibres where it participates, together with other proteins, in the contractile process. In other cell types it serves in mechanical support functions, or in different forms of contraction-like processes. The presence of this protein in the mechanoreceptor region of inner

ear sensory cells led to the question of whether the mechanical
behaviour of the sensory hairs could be affected by conditions
that would induce contraction in muscle cells. Experiments to
test this question were carried out on the isolated crista
ampullaris in the frog (15b) using the jet stimulating technique.
It was found that sensory hair motion became severely restricted
in media that contained ATP and Ca-ions as compared to media composed to induce relaxation. Furthermore it was found that calcium-
ionophore (a substance that allows Ca-ions to pass across cell
membranes) had a similar effect. These findings suggest the
possibility that the sensory cells in the ear possess some
mechanism by which the mechanical properties, and the sensitivity of the organ, can be physiologically controlled. An interesting finding in this context is that of Siegel and Kim (16) who
found that stimulation of the efferent nerve fibres to outer
hair cells in the organ of Corti cause a change in the nonlinear
behaviour of acoustically and electrophysiologically recorded responses. This implies that efferent innervation possibly controls
organ of Corti mechanical properties through a contraction-like
mechanism in the sensory hair region, exerting its influence
through coupling to the tectorial membrane. Highly interesting
in relation to motile processes is also the phenomenon originally described by Kemp (17) as stimulated acoustic emissions. Related spontaneous oto-acoustical emissions (18) are tones generated in some structure of the inner ear which exhibits the critical
nonlinear behaviour referred to above.

MECHANICAL STRUCTURE OF CORTI'S ORGAN: BIOCHEMICAL COMPOSITON
OF THE CYTOSKELETON
    Another line of investigation includes the search for con-
tractile and cytoskeletal proteins in the organ of Corti through
immuno-histochemical methods (19,20). This technique involves
the production of highly specific antibodies against purified
proteins. The antibodies are applied to thin, frozen sections
(o.2-1 um) and their binding sites are revealed by fluorescent
markers. In this way the identity and localization of the
various proteins can be studied. It has been found that different sets of proteins reside in the sensory and the supporting

elements. The Deiters' cells and inner and outer pillar cells
are traversed by mechanically rigid cables built up by micro-
tubules, composed of the protein tubulin, intermixed with filaments of actin. These cables provide a mechanical framework
within the organ of Corti, supporting mainly the three outer
hair cells like the arches of a dome. The inner hair cell is
conspicuously excluded from this mechanical frame. It is significant to note here that inner hair cells receive about 95% of
the sensory innervation of the organ of Corti. For outer hair
cells the efferent innervation is dominating. One wonders, regarding the total picture, if the inner hair cell system is mainly sensory perhaps the outer hair cell assembly serves a "motor"
function.

   The biochemical makeup of the sensory cell mechanoreceptor
region is unique in the sense that a protein named fimbrin exists
exclusively in this region where it occurs in conjunction with
actin (Fig. 2, ref. 20).

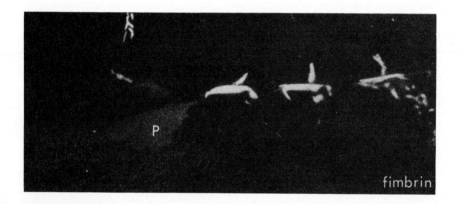

Fig. 2. Fimbrin is exclusively located in the mechanosensitive
region of the receptor cells (from ref. 20).

In vitro experiments have shown that this protein is capable of
forming cross-links between actin filaments which are stable in
Ca-environment (21,22). Although its function is yet obscure the
presence of fimbrin in this region indicates a correlation to

mechano-sensory function. From a clinical point of view it is of interest to note that loss of form of the cuticular plate and disarray of sensory hairs is seen in relation to some forms of heriditary deafness (23). The defect appears to involve the actin containing structure in this region (24).

SUMMARY

Mechanical analysis of speech, and other modalities of sound, in the peripheral auditory sense organ involves several steps of processing. Some of these may be passive in that they rely on physical properties of the basilar membrane or sensory hairs. Other steps involve more complex mechanisms which are nonlinear and may exhibit active components injecting energy into the system. These are possibly under physiological control, at the mechanical input end or through efferent nerve fibres. If this turns out to be true a new aspect of auditory function is that of a motor capacity at the periphery involved in mechanical sensitivity and its modulation. This function may serve an important role in the perception of speech.

REFERENCES

1. Dallos, P. (1973b) The Auditory Periphery: Biophysics and Physiology, Academic, New York, p. 566.

2. Dallos, P. (1981) Cochlear physiology, Am. Rev. Psychol. 32, pp. 153-190.

3. Green, D.M. (1976) An Introduction to Hearing, Hillsdale, NJ, Erlbaum, p. 353.

4. Picles, J.O. (1982) An introduction to the physiology of hearing, Academic Press, London, pp. 1-341.

5. Evans, E.F. (1972) Does frequency sharpening occur in the cochlea? Symp. Hearing Theory, IPO, Eindhoven, pp. 27-34.

6. Bielsen, E. (1980) Neurophysiological mechanisms in hearing, Elsevier/North-Holland Biomedical Press, Amsterdam, pp. 1-250.

7. Naunton, R.F. and Fernández, C. (1978) Evoked Electrical Activity in the Auditory Nervous System, Academic, New York, p. 588.

8. Flock, Å., Flock, B. and Murray, E. (1977) Studies on the Sensory Hairs of Receptor Cells in the Inner Ear. Acta Otolaryngol. 83, pp. 85-91.

9. Flock, Å. (1977) Physiological properties of sensory hairs in ear, in: Evans, E.F. and Wilson, J.P. (Eds.), Psycho-physics and physiology of hearing, Academic Press, London, pp. 15-25.

10.   Orman, S. and Flock, Å. (1981) Micromechanics of the hair
       cell stereociliary bundles in the frog crista ampullaris,
       in: Lim, D.J. (Ed.), Abstracts of the fourth midwinter re-
       search meeting, Ass. Res. Otolaryngol., pp. 30-31.

11.   Strelioff, D. and Flock, Å. (1982) Mechanical properties of
       hair bundles of receptor cells in the guinea pig cochlea.
       Soc. Neurosci., Abst. 8.

12.   Le Page, E.L. and Johnston, B.M. (1980) Basilar membrane
       mechanics in the guinea pig cochlea. Details of nonlinear
       frequency response characteristics. J. Acoust. Soc. Am.
       67. p. 45.

13.   Rhode, W.S. (1971) Observations of the vibration of the ba-
       silar membrane in squirrel monkeys using the Mössbauer tech-
       nique, J. Acoust. Soc. Am. 49, pp. 1218-1231.

14.   Evans, E.F. (1975a) The sharpening of cochlear frequency
       selectivity in normal and abnormal cochlea, Audiology, 14,
       pp. 419-444.

15a.   Flock, Å., Cheung, H.S., Flock, B. and Utter, G. (1981)
       Three set of actin filaments in sensory cells of the inner
       ear. Identification and functional orientation determined by
       gel electrophoresis- immunofluorescence and electron
       microscopy, J. Neurocytol, 10, pp. 133-147.

15b.   Orman, S. and Flock, Å. (1981) Stiffness measurements of
       stereociliary bundles in frog crista ampullaris, Soc.
       Neurosci, Abst. 7, 175.6.

16.   Siegel, J.H. and Kim, D.O. (1971) Efferent neural control
       of cochlear mechanics? Olivocochlear bundle stimulation
       affects cochlear biomechanical nonlinearity. Hearing Res.
       6, pp. 171-182.

17.   Kemp, D.T. (1978) Stimulated acoustic emissions from with-
       in the human auditory system, J. Acoust. Soc. Am. 64,
       pp. 1386-1391.

18.   Zurek, P.M. (1981) Spontaneous narrowband acoustic signals
       emitted by human ears. J. Acoust. Soc. Am. 69, pp. 514-523.

19.   Flock, Å., Hoppe, Y. and Xu Wei (1981) Immunofluorescence
       localization of proteins in semithin 0.2-1 μm frozen sec-
       tions of the ear. Arch. Otorhinolaryngol. 233 pp. 55-66.

20.   Flock, Å., Bretscher, A. and Weber, K. (1982) Immunohisto-
       chemical localization of several cytoskeletal proteins in
       inner ear sensory and supporting cells. Hearing Res. 7,
       75-89.

21.   Glenney, J., Kaulfus, P., Matsudaira, P. and Weber, K.
       (1981) F-actin binding and bundling properties of fimbrin,
       a major cytoskeletal protein of microvillus core filaments,
       J. Biol. Chem. 256, pp. 9283-9288.

22.   Bretscher, A. (1981) Fimbrin is a cytoskeletal protein
       that cross-links F-actin *in vitro*, Proc. Natl. Acad. Sci.
       75, pp. 6849-6853

23.   Ernstson, S. (1971) Cochlear morphology in a strain of the
       waltzing guinea pig. Acta Otolaryngol. 71. pp. 469-482.

24.   Sobin, A. and Flock, Å. (1981) Sensory hairs and filament
       rods in vestibular hair cells of the waltzing guinea pig.
       Acta Otolaryngol. 91, pp. 247-254.

© 1982 Elsevier Biomedical Press
The Representation of Speech in the Peripheral
Auditory System, R. Carlson and B. Granström eds.

ON THE DISSOCIATION OF AUDITORY AND PHONETIC PERCEPTION

MICHAEL STUDDERT-KENNEDY
Queens College and Graduate Center, City University of New York and Haskins
Laboratories, 270 Crown Street, New Haven, CT. 06510, U.S.A.

My charge for this meeting is to review some facts about speech perception
that might seem to be explicable, or not explicable, by reference to a peripheral representation of the speech signal. Since many later speakers will
surely report what they think can be explained, I shall confine my remarks to
what I think cannot.

Let me state, at the outset, that my view is, in the current jargon, uncom-
promisingly "bottom up." Whatever "top down" processes may contribute to
speech perception (and, in my view, it is very little) I shall not consider it
here. In other words, my initial and unequivocal assumption is that all information necessary to support the perception of speech is present in the
acoustical signal and in its peripheral auditory representation. Of course,
much remains to be learned about the acoustic structure of speech and about
its auditory transformations. But, beyond that, lies the deeper question of
what the acoustic structure means. What does it refer to? Certainly, it con-
veys information, but information about what? We lack insight into the nature
of the perceptual object, and therefore of the mechanism by which raw audition
becomes speech perception.

There is nothing biologically unsound here. On the contrary, all animals
live in the same terrestial world and are exposed, or could be exposed, to
the same patterns of radiant or mechanical energy, but they differ in their
capacities to use those patterns for information about the world. Indeed, as
von Uexküll (28) suggested many years ago, the interlocking of animal and
environment, that is, the peculiar fit of each species to its niche, is a de-
finition of that species. We might do well in our study of speech to take a
leaf from the ethologist's notebook.

Consider, for example, the barn owl and the extraordinary precision with
which it can localize sources of sound (4,8). All the information necessary
for localization is present in the peripheral sensory arrays, properly viewed.

But the physiologist contemplating those arrays could never discover their import, if he were not guided by the ethologist's knowledge of how the owl lives. Moreover, even when the physiologist has guessed that the changing auditory patterns provide a map, he still cannot understand how they do so in isolation, because the map only emerges from a central, midbrain comparison of input from the two ears (4). For speech perception a double input is not necessary, but we do need a central mechanism to read the phonetic import of the auditory array.

In what follows, I will do four things:
    --cite evidence that auditory and phonetic perception are
      distinct processes that can be dissociated experimentally;
    --infer from certain experimental results something about how
      phonetic perception uses auditory information;
    --illustrate how phonetic perception may be engaged, or dis-
      engaged, ontogenetically and experimentally;
    --speculate briefly on the biological function of phonetic
      perception.

Briefly, my broad hypotheses are: that phonetic perception is a specialized mode of auditory localization, in which we use sound to inform ourselves about the positions and changes in position of a speaker's articulatory apparatus; that the phonetic percept is an abstract buffer intermediate between the auditory array and the articulatory mechanisms necessary to reproduce that array; and that one function of phonetic perception is to faciliate language learning.

THE DISSOCIATION OF AUDITORY AND PHONETIC PERCEPTION

Twenty years ago, Fant (6) drew a distinction between the speech signal and its linguistic message. He illustrated compellingly the discrepancy between the sound segments of the acoustic event and the phonemic segments of its percept. He emphasized that the two levels are not contradictory, but "different aspects" of the same event. I propose to follow Fant's lead, extending his description of the signal upstream into the auditory system and his description of the linguistic message downstream into phonetics. In other words, I shall distinguish between two qualitatively different aspects of a single percept: auditory and phonetic. I shall argue that the two perceptual modes are different, active, "attentional" modes of scanning the signal for information.

Duplex perception. The distinction can be demonstrated experimentally in
an effect, discovered by Rand (20), recently elaborated and dubbed "duplex
perception" by Liberman and his colleagues (12,15): two different percepts,
one auditory, the other phonetic, arise simultaneously when the acoustic con-
stituents of a synthetic syllable are separated and presented dichotically.
Figure 1 displays a 9-step continuum of patterns sufficient to induce the
effect, taken from Mann, Madden, Russell and Liberman (15). If the base
(bottom left) is presented alone, it is usually heard as [da]; if one of the
isolated transitions (bottom right) is presented alone, it is heard as a non-
speech "chirp." If the two patterns are presented dichotically in appropriate temporal alignment, the listener hears a fused syllable (either [da] or
[ga], depending on which transition is presented) and, at the same time, a
non-speech chirp perceptually identical to the chirp heard in isolation. If,
now, the patterns are presented for discrimination in pairs of stimuli, separated by three steps along the continuum, with instructions to attend on
one series of trials to the speech percepts and on the other series of trials
to the non-speech chirps, the results for a typical subject are those of
Figure 2: for the non-speech judgments, a more-or-less continuous descending
function, for the speech judgments, a discrimination function peaked at the
phoneme boundary in the fashion typical of categorical perception (11). We
thus have clear behavioral evidence for perception of a single acoustic event
in two different perceptual modes at the same time.

Audio-visual adaptation. A second, perhaps even more compelling demonstration of the dissociation derives from an effect discovered by McGurk and
MacDonald (16). They demonstrated that listeners' perceptions of a speech
sound presented over a loudspeaker could be changed, if they simultaneously
watched a videotape of a speaker producing another sound. For example, presented with audio [ga] and video [ba], a subject will typically report a
cluster [bga] or [gba]. On the other hand, presented with the reverse arrangement, audio [ba] and video [ga], a subject will typically report a sort
of auditory-articulatory blend [da]. Notice that, in this instance, the phonetic percept corresponds to neither visual nor auditory pattern. The effect
is not well understood, but evidently arises from a process by which two continuous sources of information, acoustic and optical, are actively combined
at an abstract level at which each has already lost its distinctive sensory
quality (for fuller discussion, see Summerfield (27).

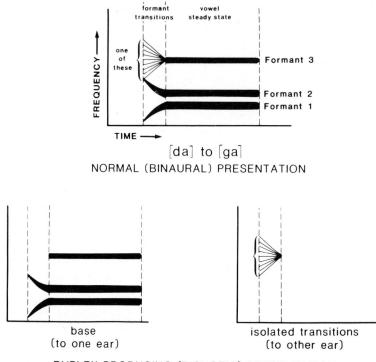

formant transitions | vowel steady state

one of these

Formant 3

Formant 2
Formant 1

FREQUENCY →

TIME →

[da] to [ga]

NORMAL (BINAURAL) PRESENTATION

base
(to one ear)

isolated transitions
(to other ear)

DUPLEX-PRODUCING (DICHOTIC) PRESENTATION

Fig. 1. Schematic representation of the stimulus patterns used to study the integration of formant transitions (from (15)).

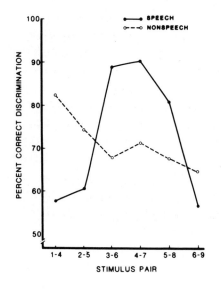

Fig. 2. Discriminability of formant transitions when, on the speech side of the duplex percept, they supported perception of stop consonants and when, on the nonspeech side, they were perceived as chirps (from (15)).

Roberts and Summerfield (24) took advantage of this phenomenon to test the nature of speech adaptation, and in so doing demonstrated dissociation of auditory and phonetic processes. Adaptation, it will be recalled, is a form of perceptual contrast, induced by prolonged exposure to some fixed pattern of energy. The most familiar example comes from color vision. If we stare for several minutes at a circle of red light and then look away at a neutral background, we will see a circle of a somewhat unsaturated, complementary green. A similar effect can be demonstrated in speech. First, a baseline is established by asking subjects to identify items along a synthetic speech continuum, stretching from, say [bɛ] to [dɛ]. Next, subjects are exposed to repeated presentations (typically, over a hundred presentations at a rate of about two per second) of one or the other endpoints of the continuum. Finally, subjects are again asked to identify items drawn from the continuum. The last two steps are repeated as often as is necessary to obtain a reliable adapted identification function. On this function, subjects typically report fewer instances of the class of items on which they have been "satiated" or "adapted" than they did before they were adapted. In other words, the category boundary is shifted toward the end of the continuum to which the subject has been repeatedly exposed.

Roberts and Summerfield's ingenious twist on this paradigm was to expose subjects to an audio-visual adaptor, audio [bɛ], video [gɛ], intended to be perceived phonetically as [dɛ]. In the event, six of their twelve subjects perceived the adapting pattern as either [dɛ] or [ðɛ], four as [klɛ], one as [flɛ], one as [ma]. Not a single subject perceived the phonetic event corresponding to the auditory event actually presented, namely [bɛ]. Yet every single subject displayed a significant shift of his [bɛ ⇌ dɛ] boundary toward [bɛ]. In other words, the procedure effectively dissociated auditory and phonetic processes. Subjects' only conscious percepts were phonetic, but their auditory systems demonstrated, by their response to adaptation, that they were simultaneously registering the acoustic signal presented over the loudspeaker.

I take these two experimental procedures of duplex perception and audio-visual adaptation to demonstrate unequivocally the "on-line" dissociation of auditory from phonetic perception. Moreover, following Summerfield (27),

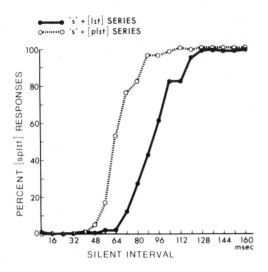

Fig. 3. Effect of silent interval on the perception of [slIt] vs. [splIt] for the two settings of the labial transition cue. (Reprinted from (7) by permission of the Psychonomic Society, Inc.)

I take the results of the audio-visual adaptation study to demonstrate that the support for phonetic perception is information about the common source of acoustic and optical information, namely, articulatory dynamics.

THE USE OF AUDITORY INFORMATION FOR PHONETIC PERCEPTION

A commonplace in discussions of speech perception is that the information for particular phonetic segments is often widely scattered, both temporally and spectrally, through the signal (13). Again, Fant (6) remarked that a single segment of sound may carry information about several segments of the message and a single segment of the message may draw information from several segments of the sound. For an example of the latter, consider the work of Bailey and Summerfield (1). They showed that perceived place of articulation of a stop consonant, induced artificially by inserting a brief silence between [s] and a following vowel (as in [si] and [su]), depends in English on the duration of the silence, on spectral properties at the offset of [s] and on the relation between these properties and the following vowel. One function of the phonetic mode is apparently to integrate, or to exploit the integration of, such diverse auditory properties into a coherent percept.

Support for this hypothesis comes from two recent experiments. The first was done by Fitch, Halwes, Erickson and Liberman (7), who demonstrated the perceptual equivalence of two distinct cues to a voiceless stop in a fricative-stop-liquid cluster: silence and rapid spectral change. They constructed two synthetic syllables [plIt] and [lIt], the first differing from the second only in having initial transitions appropriate to a labial stop. If a brief band-passed noise, sufficient to cue [s], was placed immediately before these syllables, both were heard as [slIt], but if small interval of silence, long enough to signal a stop closure, was introduced between [s] and the vocalic portion, both were heard as [splIt]. What is of interest is that the silent interval necessary to induce the stop percept was shorter when the vocalic portion carried labial transitions than when it did not. Figure 3 displays the perceptual effect of systematically manipulating the duration of the silent interval before each of the two syllables: the procedure titrates the initial transition **and shows** that it is equivalent to roughly 25 msec of silence.

On the face of it, there would seem to be no psychoacoustic grounds for this spectral-temporal equivalence. However, Delgutte (this volume, Figure 4), testing the output of his model of the peripheral auditory system for an analogous equivalence between the rise-time of friction noise and the duration of preceding silence in the fricative-affricate distinction (studied by Repp, Liberman, Eccardt and Pesetsky (22)) finds that these different cues do have similar effects on the response of his model: "...both a decrease in rise time and a longer silence duration increase the amplitude of the peak in discharge rate at the onset of frication."

Nonetheless, it seems that listeners are only able to make use of this auditory information, if they are listening in the speech mode. This is the implication of a study by Best, Morrongiello and Robson (2) using "sine-wave speech" (21). Best and her colleagues constructed a sound from three sine waves modulated to follow the path of the center frequencies of the three formants of a naturally spoken syllable [dei], in two forms: one form had a relatively long initial F_1 transition ("strong" [deI]), one had a relatively short initial F_1 transition ("weak" [deI]).

16

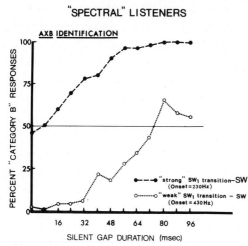

"SPECTRAL" LISTENERS

AXB IDENTIFICATION

- ●——● "strong" SW₁ transition–SW (Onset=230Hz)
- ○·····○ "weak" SW₁ transition – SW (Onset = 430Hz)

Figs. 4, 5 and 6.
Effect of silent interval on "identification" of sine-wave analogues of "say-stay" stimuli. (Reprinted from (7) with permission.)

Figs. 4 and 5 are for those who perceived them as non-speech, divided, according to their reports of what the sounds were like, into those who were apparently attending to the transition cue (Figure 4, "Spectral" listeners) and those who were apparently attending to the silence cue (Fig. 5, "temporal" listeners). Fig. 6 is for the subjects who perceived the sounds as speech ("say-stay" listeners)).

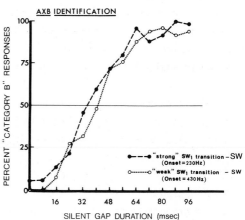

"TEMPORAL" LISTENERS

AXB IDENTIFICATION

- ●——● "strong" SW₁ transition–SW (Onset=230Hz)
- ○·····○ "weak" SW₁ transition – SW (Onset = 430Hz)

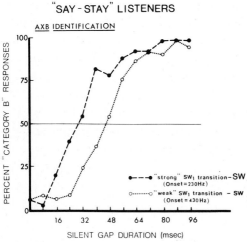

"SAY-STAY" LISTENERS

AXB IDENTIFICATION

- ●——● "strong" SW₁ transition–SW (Onset=230Hz)
- ○·····○ "weak" SW₁ transition – SW (Onset = 430Hz)

Given a perceptual set for speech, some listeners identify these sounds as [deI] and [eI], while others hear them as different non-speech chords. If a suitable patch of noise is placed immediately before these sounds, they can be heard as [sei]; if a sufficient silent interval is introduced between noise and sine waves, a so-called "speech" listener will hear [steI], and he will hear it with a shorter interval before "strong" [deI] than before "weak" [deI].

On this basis, Best et al. constructed two continua, analogous to those of the earlier experiments, varying silent interval in combination with one or other of the [deI] syllables. To obtain identification functions without an explicit request for identification, they used an AXB procedure. In this procedure A and B are endpoints of a synthetic continuum, X a variable item from the continuum, to be judged on each trial as "more like A" or "more like B." Thus, despite the bizarre quality of their stimuli, Best and her colleagues obtained identification functions and assessed the perceptual equivalence of silence and formant transitions in a manner analogous to that of the earlier [slIt - splIt] studies.

Their fifteen listeners divided themselves neatly into three groups of five. The results are displayed in Figures 4, 5 and 6. One group (the "spectral" listeners of Figure 4), though not entirely insensitive to the temporal variations, tended to hear a pattern with the short F_1 transition as more like the [seI] end of the continuum and a pattern with the long F_1 transition as more like the [steI] end of the continuum. A second group (the "temporal" listeners of Figure 5) disregarded spectral differences and based its judgments on the duration of the silent interval. Only the five "speech" listeners of Figure 6 were sensitive to the integrated auditory pattern and displayed the expected perceptual equivalence of silence duration and spectral change.

Evidently, one aspect of phonetic function is a capacity either to integrate or to make use of an auditorily integrated pattern of, temporally and spectrally distributed acoustic properties, to arrive at a unified phonetic percept.

ONTOGENETIC ENGAGEMENT AND DISENGAGEMENT OF THE PHONETIC MODE

Let us turn now to the development of the phonetic mode. I will describe a small set of interconnecting studies that converge on a view of
phonetic perception as a specialized mechanism of attention that normally begins to be differentiated from general auditory perception during
the first year of life.

We begin with the well-known observation that native speakers of
Japanese typically cannot discriminate English [r] from English [l]. In
fact, Miyawaki, Strange, Verbrugge, Liberman, Jenkins and Fujimura (19)
formally demonstrated this fact in an experimental test. Subsequently
Eimas (5) showed that 4-6 month old, prelinguistic English infants discriminated between, but not within, the [r] and [l] categories very much
as English-speaking adults do. Although comparable tests have not, so
far as I know, been done on Japanese infants, presumably they would behave like the English infants. We might then reasonably infer that learning the sound system of a language involves, among other things, not only
learning to tell the difference between sounds that are put to linguistic
use, but also learning to disregard differences between sounds that are
not.

In fact, Werker and her colleagues have evidence of precisely this (30).
Their initial finding was that 7-month old Canadian English infants, tested in a head-turning   paradigm, could discriminate between natural,
non-English contrasts in Hindi that English-speaking adults could not.
Werker (29) followed this up by tracking the decline of discriminative
capacity over the second half of the first year of life. She used a
conditioned head-turning paradigm to test three groups of infants on two
non-English sound contrasts: Hindi voiceless, unaspirated retroflex vs.
dental stops and Thompson (Interior Salish, an American Indian language)
voiced glottalized velar vs. glottalized uvular stops. On the Hindi contrast, the number of infants successfully discriminating were: 11/12 at
6-8 months, 8/12 at 8-10 months, 2/10 at 10-12 months; for the Thompson
contrast the results were essentially the same. (An infant was only
classified as having failed to discriminate, if it had successfully discriminated an English contrast both before and after the failure on a

non-English contrast.) Finally Werker (29) reports longitudinal data
for six Canadian-English infants on the same two non-English contrasts.
All six discriminated both contrasts at 6-8 months, but by 10-12 months
none of them could make the discriminations. By contrast, the one
Thompson and two Hindi infants so far tested at 10-12 months could all
make the called-for discriminations in their own language.

   Is infant loss of discriminative capacity a permanent loss, followed
by neural atrophy, or can it be reversed? MacKain, Best and Strange
(14) addressed this question in a study of native Japanese speakers.
They constructed a [rak-lak] series on the Haskins Laboratories ØVE IIIc
synthesizer (see Figure 7). They then tested 10 American English speakers and 12 native Japanese speakers, divided into two groups on the basis
of their experience with English. On the average, experienced Japanese
speakers (n=5) and inexperienced Japanese speakers (n=7), respectively,
had been spending either more than half of their time for over two years
or about a quarter of their time for less than one year speaking English,
and were taking either eight hours or less than one hour of English instruction a week. Figure 8 summarizes the results of an identification
test and two types of discrimination test. The native American English
speakers display standard categorical perception with consistent identification functions and discrimination peaks at the category boundary.
By contrast, the inexperienced Japanese listeners display more-or-less
chance performance across the board, while the experienced Japanese
identify the syllables very much as the American English do, and display
moderate discrimination peaks at the category boundary.

   The final experiment in the series is an ongoing study by Catherine
Best and myself, intended to assess how far either auditory or phonetic
perception of the same acoustic pattern can be induced by instructional
set. We constructed a sine-wave three-formant analog continuum, modeled
on a [ra-la] series (similar to that of Figure 7), by varying only the
sine-wave analog of F_3 from a steady pattern [la] to an upglide [ra].
One group of subjects (the music group) was informed that they would
hear computer-made violin-like sounds and was given several examples of
the isolated, endpoint F_3 analogs to be identified as "steady" or "upglide." Then, in a training series, the lower two endpoint sine waves

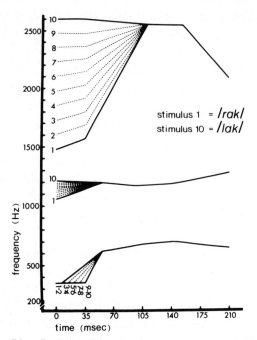

Fig. 7. Schematic spectrogram representations of the 10 stimuli in the synthetic [rak] - [lak] series. (Reprinted from (14) with permission).

SUMMARY OF RESULTS

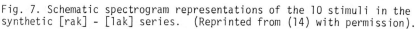

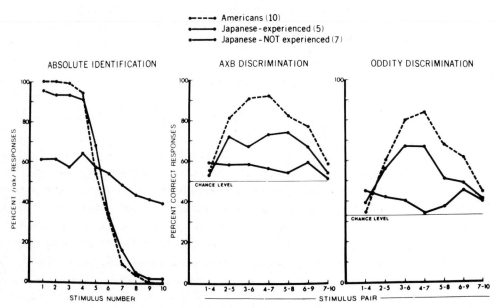

Fig. 8. Comparison of Americans, Experienced Japanese and Not-experienced Japanese results on three tests. (Reprinted from (14) with permission.).

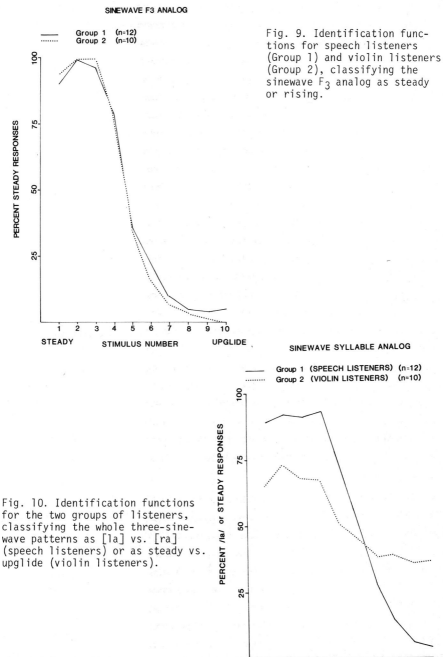

SINEWAVE F3 ANALOG

Group 1 (n=12)
Group 2 (n=10)

Fig. 9. Identification functions for speech listeners (Group 1) and violin listeners (Group 2), classifying the sinewave F_3 analog as steady or rising.

PERCENT STEADY RESPONSES

STEADY   STIMULUS NUMBER   UPGLIDE

SINEWAVE SYLLABLE ANALOG

Group 1 (SPEECH LISTENERS) (n=12)
Group 2 (VIOLIN LISTENERS) (n=10)

PERCENT /la/ or STEADY RESPONSES

Fig. 10. Identification functions for the two groups of listeners, classifying the whole three-sinewave patterns as [la] vs. [ra] (speech listeners) or as steady vs. upglide (violin listeners).

/la/
STEADY   STIMULUS NUMBER   /ra/
UPGLIDE

were gradually added to the upper endpoint waves until subjects were
hearing the full chord. Finally, subjects were tested on the whole
series with instructions to listen for the upper element of each musical chord and to identify it as either "steady" or "upglide". By contrast, the speech group was first played full, synthetic ØVE IIIc endpoint patterns to identify as [la] or [ra]. Then, in a training series,
the synthetic formants were gradually faded out, while the sine-wave
chord was faded in. Finally, subjects were tested on the whole series
with instructions to identify each sine-wave syllable as [ra] or [la].
Subsequently, both groups were tested on the series of isolated F_3 analogs and instructed to identify them as "steady" or "upglide".

Figure 9 displays the results of this last test. Both groups classify the isolated F_3 sine-wave analogs quite consistently, with a 50%
boundary around stimulus 5, close to the midpoint of the series. Figure
10 displays the results of the full-chord test. The speech listeners
are quite consistent, with a 50% boundary shifted away from the midpoint
of the series toward stimulus 6. The violin listeners, on the other
hand, give a sloping function close to chance (similar, in fact, to the
identification function of the inexperienced Japanese listeners in the
left panel of Figure 8). Thus, although both groups of listeners were
well able to classify the varying F_3 analog in isolation, only the speech
listeners were able to use the F_3 sine-wave information to classify the
full pattern.

Evidently, the phonetic mode begins to be engaged for some sounds and
disengaged for others during the second six months of life. Subsequently,
with appropriate acoustic materials and instruction it may be reengaged
for certain sounds on which discrimination has been lost, or disengaged
for certain other sounds on which discrimination has been retained.

A POSSIBLE BIOLOGICAL FUNCTION OF THE PHONETIC MODE

The distinction between auditory and phonetic perception is not new
(10) and by now has substantial support from studies of hemispheric
specialization in both normal and pathological populations. Some years
ago, Donald Shankweiler and I concluded from the results of a dichotic

study of normals that "...while the general auditory system common to both hemispheres is equipped to extract the auditory parameters of a speech signal, the dominant hemisphere may be specialized for the extraction of linguistic features from those parameters"(26, p. 579).

Subsequently, Levy (9) and Zaidel (31,32) reached a similar conclusion on the basis of studies of split-brain patients, individuals whose two cerebral hemispheres have been surgically separated for control of epilepsy. Levy showed that only the left hemisphere can carry out the phonological analysis needed to recognize written rhymes; Zaidel showed that, while the right hemisphere may have a sizeable auditory and visual lexicon, only the left hemisphere can carry out the auditory-phonetic analysis necessary to identify synthetic nonsense syllables or the phonological analysis necessary to read new words. Moreover, dissociation of auditory discrimination and phonetic classification is commonplace among certain types of aphasic patients, suffering from left hemisphere lesions. For example, Blumstein, Cooper, Zurif and Caramazza (3), and Riedel (23) have described patients who could discriminate between syllables differing in the acoustic correlates of voice onset time or in medial vowel duration, but could not use these acoustic properties to classify the syllables phonetically.

We may gain some insight into the biological function of this dissociation, if we remember that the single most securely established specialization of the left hemisphere in over 90% of the population is for motor control of the right hand and of the speech apparatus. Whatever the perceptual capacities of the right hemisphere, studies of aphasics (17), of split-brain patients (32) and of the effects of sodium amytal injection (18; Borchgrevink, this volume) agree that the right hemisphere is essentially mute.

A plausible hypothesis then is that phonetic processes emerged phyletically, within the hominid line, in close association with the motor processes of the left hemisphere. The phonetic percept is then an abstract, sensorimotor link between the sounds of speech and the motor controls necessary to reproduce them. One source of ethological support for this hypothesis comes from the phenomenon of dialect. Every child, uninstructed and without effort, learns the dialect of his peers. This seems to call for, on the one hand, recognition of subtle details of temporal and spectral structure of the kind we have been discussing and, on the other, the discovery of precise patterns of articulator place-ment and interarticulator timing necessary to reproduce the perceived dialectal variants. Whatever the ultimate adaptive value of dialect-- whether selective breeding or group cohesion--we can hardly doubt its biological status nor the need for the specialized sensorimotor processes that it entails.

Finally, we should not shrink from viewing man's capacities for speech and language as both central and without biological parallel. We would not have come to understand how the barn owl tracks its prey from study of its peripheral auditory input alone. Nor would we expect to advance our knowledge of, say, echolocation in the bat solely by studying the auditory neural responses to bat sonar signals of chin-chillas. We can, of course, learn much of interest about the common properties of different mammalian auditory systems that may guide us in our study of speech. But, in the end, we must recognize that speech is peculiar to man. The purpose of Darwin's great work was not, after all, to demonstrate that all animals are the same, but to explain why they are not.

ACKNOWLEDGMENTS

The arguments developed in this paper rest squarely on the work of others, mostly of my colleagues at Haskins Laboratories. I thank them all, but absolve them from responsibility for the conclusions. I am particularly grateful to Alvin Liberman, Ignatius Mattingly and Bruno Repp for invigorating discussions. Writing of the paper was supported in part by Grant NICHD 01994 to Haskins Laboratories.

REFERENCES

1. Bailey, P.J. and Summerfield, Q. (1980) Information in speech: Obser-vations on the perception of [s] + stop clusters. J. Experimental Psychology: Human Perception and Performance, 6, 536.

2. Best, C.T., Morrongiello, B. and Robson, R. (1981) Perceptual equi-valence of acoustic cues in speech and nonspeech perception. Per-ception and Psychophysics, 29, 191.

3. Blumstein, S.E., Cooper, W.E., Zurif, E.B. and Caramazza, A. (1977) The perception and production of voice onset time in aphasia. Neuropsychologia, 15, 371.

4. Bullock, T.H. (1982) Where do we go from here: need for cross-taxa comparisons. Paper read at NRP Associates Symposium on Ethological approaches to behavioral and neural plasticity, Boston, March 14-17.

5. Eimas, P. (1975) Auditory and phonetic coding of the cues for speech: Discrimination of the [r-l] distinction by young infants. Perception and Psychophysics, 18, 341.

6. Fant, C.G.M. (1962) Descriptive analysis of the acoustic aspects of speech Logos, 5, 3.

7. Fitch, H.L., Halwes, T., Erickson, D.M. and Liberman, A.M. (1980) Perceptual equivalence of two acoustic cues for stop consonant manner. Perception and Psychophysics, 27, 343.

8. Konishi, M. (1973) How the owl tracks its prey. American Scientist, 61, 414.

9. Levy, J. (1974) Psychobiological implications of bilateral symmetry. In Dimond, S.J. and Beaumont, J.G. (eds.) Hemispheric function in the human brain. Elek, London, pp.121-183.

10. Liberman, A.M. (1970) The grammars of speech and language. Cognitive Psychology, 1, 301.

11. Liberman, A.M., Cooper, F.S., Shankweiler, D.P. and Studdert-Kennedy, M. (1967) Perception of the speech code. Psychological Review, 74, 341.

12. Liberman, A.M., Isenberg, D. and Rakerd, B. (1981) Duplex perception of cues for stop consonants: Evidence for a phonetic mode. Perception and Psychophysics, 30, 133.

13. Liberman, A.M. and Studdert-Kennedy, M. Phonetic perception. In Held, R., Leibowitz, H. and Teuber, H.-L. (eds.) Handbook of Sensory Physiology. Vol. 8: Perception, Springer Verlag, New York, pp. 143-178.

14. MacKain, K.S., Best, C.T. and Strange, W. (1981) Categorical perception of English [r] and [l] by Japanese bilinguals. Psycholinguistics, 2, 369.

15. Mann, V.A., Madden, J., Russell, J.M. and Liberman, A.M. (1981) Further investigation into the influence of preceding liquids on stop consonant perception. J. Acoustical Society of America, 69, 591.

16. McGurk, H. and MacDonald, J. (1976) Hearing lips and seeing voices. Nature, 264, 746.

17. Milner, B. (1974) Hemispheric specialization: scope and limits. In Schmitt, F.O. and Worden, F.G. (eds.) The Neurosciences: Third study program. M.I.T. Press, Cambridge, pp. 75-89.

18. Milner, B., Branch, C. and Rasmussen, T. (1964) Observations on cerebral dominance. In DeReuck, V.S. and O'Connor, M. (eds.) Disorders of Language (Ciba Foundation Symposium). J. and A. Churchill, London, pp. 200-214.

19. Miyawaki, K., Strange, W., Verbrugge, R., Liberman, A.M., Jenkins, J. J. and Fujimura, O. (1975) An effect of linguistic experience: The discrimination of [r] and [l] by native speakers of Japanese and English. Perception and Psychophysics, 19, 331.

20. Rand, T.C. (1974) Dichotic release from masking for speech. J. Acoustical Society of America, 55, 678.

21. Remez, R.E., Rubin, P.E., Pisoni, D.B. and Carrell, T.D. (1981) Speech perception without traditional speech cues. Science, 212, 947.

22. Repp, B.H., Liberman, A.M., Eccardt, T. and Pesetsky, D. (1978). Perceptual integration of acoustic cues for stop, fricative and affricate manner. J. Experimental Psychology: Human Perception and Performance, 4, 621.

23. Riedel, K. (1982) Durational factors in the phonetic perception of aphasics. Unpublished doctoral dissertation, City University of New York.

24. Roberts, M. and Summerfield, Q. (1981) Audiovisual presentation demonstrates that selective adaptation in speech perception is purely auditory. Perception and Psychophysics, 30, 309.

25. Studdert-Kennedy, M. (1974) The Perception of Speech. In Sebeok, T. A. (ed.) Current Trends in Linguistics, Vol. 12. Mouton, The Hague, pp. 2349-2485.

26. Studdert-Kennedy, M. and Shankweiler, D.P. (1970) Hemispheric Specialization for Speech Perception. J. Acoustical Society of America, 48, 579.

27. Summerfield, Q. (1979) Use of visual information for phonetic perception. Phonetica, 36, 314.

28. von Uexküll, J. (1957) A stroll through the worlds of animals and men. Reprinted in Schiller, C.H. (ed.) Instinctive Behavior. International Universities Press, New York, pp. 5-80.

29. Werker, J.F. (1982) The development of cross-language speech perception: the effect of age, experience and context on perceptual organization. Unpublished doctoral dissertation, University of British Columbia, Vancouver, B.C.

30. Werker, J.F., Gilbert, J.H.V., Humphrey, K. and Tees, R.C. (1981) Developmental aspects of cross-language speech perception. Child Development, 52, 349.

31. Zaidel, E. (1976) Language, dichotic listening and the disconnected hemispheres. In Walter, D.O., Rogers, L. and Finzi-Fried, J.M. (eds.) Conference on Human Brain Function. Brain Information Service/BRI Publications Office, UCLA, Los Angeles.

32. Zaidel, E. (1978) Lexical organization in the right hemisphere. In Buser, P.A. and Rougent Buser, A. (eds.) Cerebral correlates of conscious experience. Elsevier/North-Holland, Amsterdam, pp. 177-197.

© 1982 Elsevier Biomedical Press
*The Representation of Speech in the Peripheral
Auditory System*, R. Carlson and B. Granström eds.

REPRESENTATION OF COMPLEX SOUNDS AT COCHLEAR NERVE AND COCHLEAR NUCLEUS
LEVELS

E. F. EVANS

Department of Communication & Neuroscience, University of Keele, Staffs.,
ST5 5BG, U.K.

INTRODUCTION

In the last 10-20 years, stimuli more complex than steady tones and clicks
have been increasingly employed in physiological experiments, in order to try
to determine the neural representation of the signals used in psychophysical
and speech studies. These stimuli range from amplitude and frequency-modulated
tones (reviewed in 8, 12, 39; see also 27), multicomponent tone complexes
(14, 16), noise signals having comb-filtered ('ripple-noise') spectra (summarized in 8, 12, 13), animal vocalizations (e.g. summarized in 3, 7) to speech
stimuli themselves (e.g. 26, 29, 30, 32, 33, 41, 51, 54, 60, 61).

The objective of this brief review is to outline some of the salient properties of neurones at the cochlear nerve and nucleus levels in response to
complex sounds, which properties can throw light on the question of the representation of speech sounds. It will largely exclude speech sounds, which will
be dealt with specifically elsewhere in this volume by Sachs and Delgutte.

COCHLEAR NERVE LEVEL: SHORT-TERM SPECTRAL ANALYSIS OF COMPLEX SOUNDS

The cochlear nerve considered as a bank of filters. Each of the 30,000
fibres in the mammalian cochlear nerve can be considered, to a first approximation, to act as a narrow band filter. Each fibre has a preferred, centre
frequency (the characteristic frequency, CF) reflecting its origin along the
cochlear partition. Stimulus energy falling within the triangular response
area bounded by the frequency threshold ('tuning') curve (FTC; see continuous
curve 'tone threshold' in Fig. 1A) will evoke an acceleration of the mean rate
of impulse activity of the fibre above its resting discharge of 0-120 spikes/s.
The cut-offs and the bandwidths of the FTC depends upon the fibre's characteristic frequency. For fibres with CF above about 2kHz, the FTC is asymmetrical
and the cut-offs steep, particularly on the high frequency side, approaching
(in the cat and guinea pig) 500 dB/oct. For lower CFs, the curves are more
symmetrical and the cut-offs become progressively less steep, from 50-100
dB/oct at 1kHz to about 10-20 dB/oct at 0.2kHz (8). The effective bandwidths
of the cochlear fibre filters for broad-band signals are approximately their
half-power bandwidths (21). They range from about 100 Hz for fibres with CFs

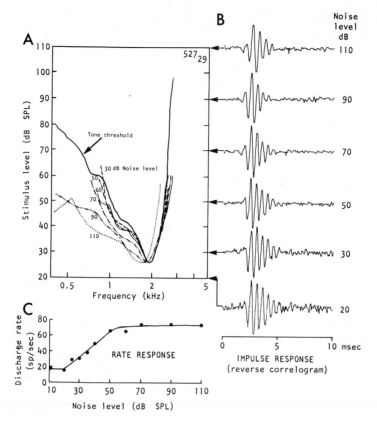

Fig. 1. Filtering characteristics of a cochlear fibre, derived by reverse correlation at different noise stimulus levels.
A: Frequency threshold ('tuning') curve (continuous line) with pure tone stimulation for comparison. Interrupted lines: Fourier transforms of the impulse responses (B) obtained by reverse correlation of the spike discharges with the broad-band noise stimulus. C: Discharge rate versus stimulus level function for the responses in A, B, showing the restricted dynamic range (30-40 dB) typical of the majority of cochlear fibres. (From 9)

up to about 1kHz, and 10% of the CF thereafter (Fig. 4; 21). Although there is systematic variation in these values from individual to individual (see the differences between cats in Fig. 4), they are representative of measurements of filtering employing pure tone, broad-band and comb-filtered noise stimuli (21), within limits to be described later.

This remarkably sharp filtering is also reflected in the temporal patterning of the discharges for frequencies up to about 4-5kHz (Figs. 1, 3). In Fig. 1, the results of <u>reverse correlation</u> analysis with a noise stimulus (technique of 6) are shown for a fibre in the cat's cochlear nerve having a CF of 2kHz and

the FTC shown by the continuous curve in Fig. 1A (9). The reverse correlation
analysis yields the impulse response of the cochlear filter, shown in Fig. 1B
for various levels of the wideband noise stimulus. The Fourier transforms of
the impulse responses are shown for comparison with the pure tone FTC. Several
points may be noted. First, the correlation analysis indicates that the
filtering represented by the pure tone FTC is reflected in the frequencies
dominating the temporal patterns of discharge, on which the analysis depends.
In other words, the discharge pattern tends to follow preferentially frequencies within the effective bandwidth of the fibre. Secondly, the impulse response is more like that of a multiple pole band-pass than a resonant filter,
reflecting the U (rather than V) shape of the FTC tip. Thus, the cochlear filter appears to have effected an optimal compromise between spectral and
temporal resolution, the latter being of the order of 5ms for fibres with CFs
in the region of 1kHz. Thirdly, the bandwidth of the cochlear filter increases
and the low-frequency cut-off decreases with stimulus level, particularly above
30-40 dB above threshold. This does not happen in all fibres, at least in the
cat (rodents appear to be more susceptible to level effects: 25, 38), and in
any case, the effective bandwidths increase by a factor of only 1.1-2.5 at the
highest noise levels (100-110 dB SPL), again in the cat. The small but systematic shift in the CF with level is CF dependent: for fibres with CF above about
1kHz, it shifts downwards by about 10%, and for those below 1kHz, it shifts
upwards (9).

The properties are also reflected in the temporal pattern of activity of
cochlear fibres to stimuli having multiple frequency components (Figs. 2, 3)
(14, 16). The fibre in Fig. 2 is being stimulated with a 10 harmonic (equal
amplitude) complex centred on its CF (1.4kHz), the fundamental frequency being
200 Hz. The degree to which the temporal patterns of discharges synchronize
with each harmonic ('phase-locking') is plotted as the 'vector strength' (vd.
4, 22) against the signal level. These vector strengths are plotted against
frequency in Fig. 3, on a logarithmic scale so that comparison may be made with
the pure tone FTC. Again, at stimulus levels near threshold, the frequency
weighting of the vector strengths reflects the FTC. At higher stimulus levels,
similar changes in selectivity are reflected in the vector strengths as
described in the case of reverse correlation (16).

To a first approximation therefore, cochlear nerve fibres act for broad-band
and multicomponent stimuli as if they were linear filters having the filter
characteristics described by their pure tone FTC. Given a fibre's CF, its
properties in response to complex sounds can therefore be reasonably well

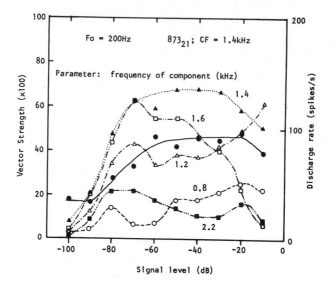

Fig. 2. Mean discharge rate and phase-locking indices of activity for a single cat cochlear fibre of CF = 1.4kHz, against the level of a ten-component harmonic complex centred on its FTC. Continuous line: mean discharge rate in response to 3 presentations each of 10s duration of the 10-component harmonic complex. Interrupted lines: vector strengths of phase-locked responses to the given individual harmonic components. OdB = 106 dB SPL. (From 16)

predicted, and simulated by simple electronic analogues (11, 15, 34). In other words, it is those frequencies that fall within the effective bandwidth of the fibre's filter, that tend to dominate its mean discharge rate, and the temporal pattern of the discharges. As has been indicated above, this is true for the latter over a very wide dynamic range of intensity.

In the case of mean discharge rate, however, the above approximation breaks down above levels of about 40 dB above threshold. Fig. 1C shows how the level of the stimulus can be signalled in the mean discharge rate of the fibre only over a range of about 30-40 dB, before it saturates. The continuous line in Fig. 2 shows a similarly limited dynamic range for mean discharge rate for another cochlear fibre. At stimulus levels above saturation then, cochlear fibres cannot manifest their frequency selectivity in their discharge rate properties, although as indicated in Figs. 1 and 3 for those with CFs below about 3-5 kHz (the limit of 'phase locking') they can do so in the degree of synchrony of their temporal discharge patterns with the stimulus.

Cochlear fibre responses to complex stimuli, particularly two component stimuli also deviate from the above first approximation description, in respect of

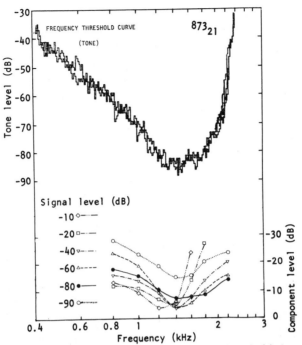

Fig. 3. Mean discharge rate threshold (Frequency Threshold Curve) of the single cochlear fibre of Fig. 2, compared with the vector strengths of its phase-locked response to individual harmonics of a ten harmonic tone complex at different stimulus levels. Vector strengths plotted on a log power scale for comparison. 0dB = 106 dB SPL. (From 16)

certain cochlear non-linearities responsible for intermodulation distortion and 'lateral suppression' effects. Of the former, the $2f_1-f_2$ cubic distortion product is the most important (e.g. 24), although its presence is evident only in carefully contrived stimulus conditions. The latter non-linear effect, termed two-tone suppression or inhibition (e.g. 53; although it is not limited to two tones, nor is neural inhibition) means that the excitation generated by a stimulus at one frequency (e.g. at the CF) can be suppressed by that at another, particularly lower, frequency. This suppression is reflected in both the mean discharge rate response and in the degree of synchrony exhibited by the temporal discharge patterns. Thus, in the fibre of Fig. 3, the synchrony to harmonic frequencies at and above the CF (e.g. 1.6kHz) becomes progressively more suppressed with stimulus level, reflecting the increasing dominance of the frequency components below the CF. This phenomenon has been termed 'synchrony suppression' (50). For speech stimuli, these lateral suppression effects mean that the lower frequency, higher energy first formant will have suppressing effects on the rate and synchrony of the responses to the higher formants (60). It should be emphasised, however, that these effects are not strong features of the responses of the majority of cochlear fibres having spontaneous discharge rates above about 20 sp/s. The effects are strongest in the smaller subpopulation of the fibres with the lowest spontaneous discharge rates (54).

Physiological and psychophysical filtering

The above measurements of physiological cochlear filtering are relevant also because they are consistent with measurements of human frequency selectivity obtained by psychophysical methods. Thus, the physiological effective band-widths (obtained in cats, see data points in Fig. 4) approximate to the values of the human 'critical bands' (dashed line in Fig. 4), becoming smaller than the latter for frequencies above 1kHz (21; see 10 for review). The shapes and cut-off slopes of the cochlear fibre FTCs are consistent with those obtained by tone-on-tone masking techniques yielding the so-called 'psychoacoustic tuning curves' (e.g. 58, 62). It is not possible to reconcile entirely the filter bandwidths derived from all the different psychoacoustic (e.g. 28, 40) and animal behavioural (e.g. 45, 46) techniques of measurement in order to compare them with the physiological effective bandwidths. Taken together, they suggest that a value of about 10% (i.e. about $^1/6$ octave) would be more appropriate for the effective bandwidth of the ear's peripheral filter bank than the value of $^1/3$ octave commonly employed in modelling the 'front-end' of the auditory system, and representing the larger critical band value obtained in simultaneous masking.

This limited frequency resolution imparts important constraints on the first stage of the processing of complex stimuli by the auditory system. It sets limits on the closeness of individual frequency components that can be resolved; and conversely, it determines which components of a complex sound will interact so that the gross and fine temporal structure of the discharge patterns reflect the amplitude envelope and periodic structure of the filtered stimulus complex (see 12, 14; 27). Animals having poorer frequency selectivity than cats and man, for example chinchillas, cannot distinguish vowels having closely spaced formants (e.g. /ae/ from /a/: 38). In impairment of hearing due to pathological conditions of the cochlea, where deterioration in frequency selectivity is predicted from the physiology (e.g. 21) and has been confirmed psychoacoustic-ally (e.g. 48, 56, 58), impairment of intelligibility for the back vowels has been observed (e.g. 43). Here, the separation of the first two formants is

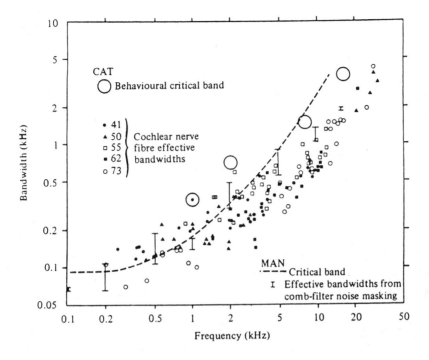

Fig. 4. Comparison of neural and psychophysical effective filter bandwidths. Each small symbol represents the effective bandwidth of an individual
cochlear nerve fibre filter plotted against its characteristic frequency.
Individual cats are identified by different symbols. Dashed line represents
the 'critical band' of human hearing, one estimate of the bandwidth of human
auditory filters determined psychophysically. Human effective bandwidths
determined by comb-filtered noise masking are also included. Open circles:
behavioural measurements of 'critical band' in the cat (data from 45).
(From 17).

likely to be too small compared with the increased   peripheral filter bandwidth (see 13, and for review). Similar, but smaller, deterioration in frequency selectivity for sound complexes occurs at high sound levels (particularly
70 dB SPL and above), as measured physiologically (Figs 1 and 3 above; see 9,
25, 38) and psychophysically (47).

This limited peripheral frequency resolution means that it is doubtful
whether the harmonic structure of speech sounds could be sufficiently resolved
to be of value for extracting the voice fundamental frequency on the basis of
pattern recognition pitch extraction mechanisms (such as reviewed by 5, 23, 59).
On the other hand, for the same reason, interaction of harmonics within the
effective bandwidths of the cochlear fibre filters would produce significant
modulation of discharge at the frequency of the fundamental, corresponding to
the amplitude envelope of the filtered signal.

Representation of the frequency spectrum: place or time?

Neglecting the effects of lateral suppression and the generation of responses to combination tones, the profile of changes in mean discharge rate across the tonotopically organized cochlear fibre array yields a spectrographic-like representation of signals having resolvable frequency components with energy below some 40-60 dB SPL. This has been demonstrated to be the case for the representation of the first 3 formants in certain steady-state vowels (e.g. 61). This is the classical 'place' theory of the neural representation of signals. For higher sound levels, however, such as those often encountered in practice, the discharge rates of the majority of cochlear fibres are, in cat experiments at least, saturated (Fig. 5), and are consequently unable to signal thereby the spectral distribution of energy in a complex sound. This has been well demonstrated for speech sounds (e.g. 61) and even is the case for single component stimuli (35; but see 16). This is the dynamic range problem, which is the greatest obstacle to a straight-forward acceptance of classical 'place' coding theory (see 12, 16 for reviews).

A number of possible solutions to this dynamic range problem have been proposed. Firstly, not all cochlear fibres have a dynamic range limited, in terms of mean discharge rate, to some 40 dB. The existence of fibres with dynamic ranges in excess of 60 dB has been reported (42, 52). In our material, however, these fibres are a small minority (Fig. 5; 44): only 9% of the total population had dynamic ranges in excess of 60 dB, and 5% in excess of 70 dB. These are an interesting minority: their spontaneous activity is low (20, 55) and their thresholds tend to be higher than the majority of fibres (e.g. 36). In principle, therefore, and in practice to an extent (see 61), this minority of fibres could serve to represent, in a 'place' distribution of changes in mean discharge rate, the speech formants. It is difficult to see, however, how this small number of fibres could adequately convey spectral information at high stimulus levels, and a larger and probably different population serve the same purpose at lower stimulus levels, without a substantial change in speech quality becoming noticeable.

A second, more parsimonious solution, is that because the fine-time structure of the discharge patterns of cochlear fibres reflect their filtering (for frequencies up to 4-5kHz) for all sound levels regardless of saturation of the mean discharge rate, this could be utilized to extract the 'place' of synchronized activity in the cochlear fibre array. If the higher levels of the auditory system could in fact extract this information, it would be a very robust 'place' representation of the spectra of complex sounds such as speech,

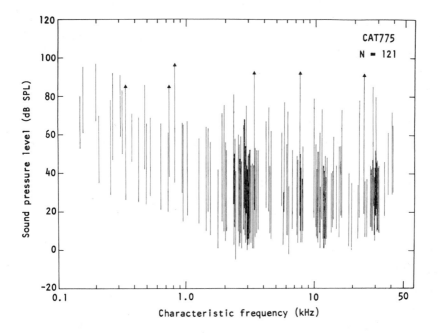

Fig. 5. Dynamic ranges of mean discharge rate for 121 cochlear fibres in one cat cochlear nerve. Each vertical line represents the dynamic range of a single cochlear fibre plotted at its characteristic frequency. The extent of the line indicates the range of levels of 100 ms tones at the characteristic frequency between threshold (lower limit of line) and saturation of the mean discharge rate (upper limit). Arrows indicate fibres not saturated at the highest sound levels employed. (From 44)

valid across a very wide dynamic range, as has been beautifully demonstrated (60) for a steady-state vowel, in terms of a 'localized synchronized' measure.

It should be noted that unless the higher levels of the auditory system are able to perform the equivalent of the physiologist's period histogram i.e. to determine the degree of synchronization of a cochlear fibre's discharges to the period of the stimulus frequency corresponding to its 'place' in the tono-topic cochlear nerve array, then this 'localized synchronized' measure may not be strictly valid. However, because the filtering of a cochlear fibre is still represented in the fine-time structure of its discharges pattern even above saturation of its mean discharge rate (Figs. 1 and 3 above), then a mechanism capable of performing some form of autocorrelation on a fibre's discharge pattern could in principle extract the information without having to have precise 'knowledge' of the stimulus period corresponding to the fibre's 'place'.

Effects of adaptation, middle ear and the efferent system.

A number of problems confound comparisons of the above sort between physiological and psychophysical data. The first is that physiological experiments conducted with complex stimuli such as speech, typically use continuous stimuli of long duration: of the order of tens of seconds. It can be shown that these stimuli introduce adaptation effects such that the peripheral dynamic range is substantially reduced compared with shorter duration stimuli (e.g. 10-100ms; 14). While this does not solve the dynamic range problem (for the results of Fig. 5 were obtained with 100 ms duration stimuli), the question needs to be raised when extrapolations to running speech are made from stimulation with isolated speech sounds: which are the more appropriate to use - short-duration or long-duration stimuli?

A second form of long-term adaptive effect acts in the opposite direction: the presence of background wideband noise of duration longer than 10s can 'bias' the dynamic range of cochlear fibres towards higher sound levels (7). This effect presumably reflects some sort of AGC type mechanism rather than that of lateral suppression, the effects of which are apparent immediately.

The third is that comparisons are inevitably being made between the behaviour of neurones in the anaesthetized cat and the psychophysics of the awake human ear. Such factors as the activity of the middle ear muscles, and of the efferent nervous system, are rendered inactive by the anaesthesia used in physiological experiments, and may conceivably play a more crucial role than is apparent at present in extending the dynamic range of the peripheral auditory system. Certainly, in patients lacking middle-ear protective mechanisms, deterioration in speech intelligibility has been reported to occur at levels above about 80 dB SPL (2).

COCHLEAR NUCLEUS LEVEL: ENHANCEMENT OF SPECTRAL AND TEMPORAL CONTRASTS

The cochlear fibre array projects, in a strict tonotopic manner, to several subdivisions of the cochlear nucleus. Each subdivision appears to represent the first stage of a number of apparently parallel processing sub-systems or pathways. In each division the 'place' representation of frequency is preserved, but each pathway reflects different types of neural processing (18, 31, 49; see 8 for review).

The most obvious difference between neural response properties at the cochlear nucleus and cochlear nerve levels, is the presence of lateral

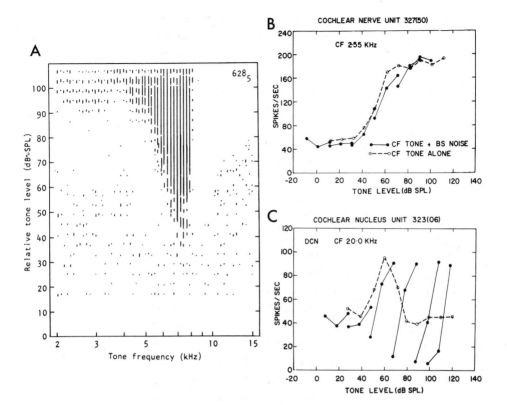

Fig. 6. Enhancement of spectral contrast by lateral inhibition at the
cochlear nucleus.
A: Excitatory and inhibitory response areas of neurone in dorsal cochlear
nucleus of cat. Randomized frequency response analysis, the length of each
vertical line representing the number of spike discharges evoked by a 60 ms
tone burst, the frequency and intensity of which is denoted by the centre of
the line. Note large blank upper and lower frequency sidebands of inhibition
of the spontaneous discharges on each side of the central excitatory response
area. (From 12).
B, C: Response of cochlear nerve fibre and dorsal cochlear nucleus to tone
signals in band-stop noise. The open circles joined by dashed lines indicate
the mean discharge rate of the unit to gated tones alone, of 500 ms duration,
at the CF. Triplets of solid circles joined by continuous lines indicate
response to the tone burst signal in the presence of continuous band-stopnois
noise (stop bandwidth: 3 x CF/5) determined at three tone levels (-10, 0,
+ 10 dB) relative to each masker level. The masker level, which is constant for
each triplet, corresponds to 4 dB below the level indicated by the middle point
of each triplet when measured within a bandwidth of CF/5 (i.e. approximately
human critical band). (After 19).

inhibition (Fig. 6A). This is particularly strong in the dorsal cochlear
nucleus, and is neurally mediated, in contrast to lateral suppression at the
cochlear nerve level. Inhibition at the cochlear nucleus level serves to
enhance the spectral and temporal contrasts of the responses to stimuli.

Enhancement of spectral contrast

Lateral inhibition (Fig. 6A) means that in addition to receiving excitatory
inputs from cochlear nerve afferents, cochlear nucleus cells receive inhibit-
atory inputs from cochlear fibres having neighbouring CFs. Signal components
having frequencies adjacent to the CF are able to inhibit the spontaneous
activity (as seen in Fig. 6A) and also the driven activity of the cochlear
nucleus neurone. This inhibition is very powerful (compared with lateral
suppression at the cochlear nerve level). It serves to enhance the contrast
between more active and less-active regions of the neural array representing
in the 'place' of activity, the distribution of spectral energy in a complex
stimulus, as originally suggested by Allanson & Whitfield (1). This has been
demonstrated in connection with bandstop noise masking (19; Palmer & Evans,
in Press) and with the representation of comb-filtered noise stimuli (9).
The former experiments illustrate the effect most clearly (Fig. 6C). At the
cochlear nerve level (Fig. 6B), the presence of simultaneously present high-
and low-pass (i.e. band-stop) masking noise has little effect on the change in
discharge rate with increase in stimulus level in response to a tone. At the
level of the dorsal cochlear nucleus especially, if the bandstop maskers
coincide with the side-bands of lateral inhibition (as in 6A), the inhibition
serves to 'bias' the activity of the cell well below saturation of its
discharge rate. This has the effect that, providing the surrounding maskers
are comparable in level to the signal, changes in signal level can be reflected
in changes in cell discharge rate over a substantial dynamic range, approaching
100 dB, without signs of deterioration in contrast even at the highest levels
(Fig. 6C). This 'biassing' effect is analogous to that operating in the
retina (57).

Similar effects are found with multicomponent stimuli, e.g. comb-filtered
noise (9).

What is not yet clear is how these cells receive their information on the
level of the signal components: whether it is from the small percentage of
cochlear nerve fibres not completely saturated at high stimulus levels, or
whether the fine time structure of the cochlear nerve discharges is decoded
somehow at this level (see 12 for review).

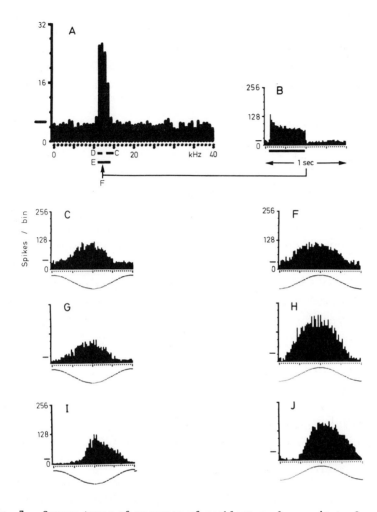

Fig. 7. Common types of response of cochlear nucleus unit to frequency and amplitude modulated tones. All analyses at 20 dB above threshold. A: Frequency response histogram of response to 100 msec tones as a function of frequency. B: Post-stimulus time histogram at CF. C, G, I: Modulation histograms of averaged firing density in response to sinusoidal frequency modulation over band of frequencies indicated by bar C under A. Waveform of modulation indicated under modulation histogram. Modulation rate: 1, 10, 40 c/s in C, G, I respectively. F, H, J: Amplitude modulation (depth 80%) at CF(F) at modulation rates of 1, 10 and 40 c/s respectively. At the higher rates of modulation (H, J) note depression of "tails" of distributions below spontaneous level (indicated by bars against ordinates). Data collected for about 30 sec in each analysis. (From 8).

Temporal contrast enhancement

Following excitation of a cochlear nerve fibre, there is a short period of depression of spontaneous activity and reduced excitability. At the cochlear nucleus level, the effects are enhanced by the inhibition, presumably neurally mediated. This means that, for amplitude modulated signals, for example (Fig. 7 F, H, J) the contrast between the responses to the peaks and valleys of the modulation becomes enhanced at the higher rates of modulation. Thus, in Fig. 7J, the 'tails' of the distributions are reduced below the level of spontaneous activity (indicated by the horizontal bars against the ordinate).

Similarly, and probably for the same reason, the responses to frequency-modulated signals are enhanced (Fig. & C, G, I). Under these conditions, the frequency region of excitation becomes more sharply defined and narrower. This has been described in detail by Moller, (39).

REFERENCES

1. Allanson, J.T. and Whitfield, I.C. (1956) in: Cherry, C. (Ed.), 3rd London Symposium on Information Theory, Butterworths, London, pp. 269-284.

2. Borg, E. and Zakrisson, J.-E. (1973) J. Acoust. Soc. Am., 54, 525-527.

3. Bullock, T.H. (Ed.) (1977) Recognition of Complex Acoustic Signals, Dahlem Konferenzen, Berlin.

4. Buunen, T.J.F. and Rhode, W.S. (1978) J. Acoust. Soc. Am., 64, 772-781.

5. De Boer, E. (1976) in: Keidel, W.D. and Neff, W.D. (Eds.), Handbook of Sensory Physiology, Vol. 5/3, Springer-Verlag, Berlin, pp. 479-583.

6. De Boer, E. and Kuyper, P. (1968) IEEE Trans. Biomed. Eng. BME-15, 169-179.

7. Evans, E.F. in: Schmitt, F.O. and Worden, F.G. (Eds.), The Neurosciences: Third Study Program, M.I.T. Press, pp. 131-145.

8. Evans, E.F. (1975) in: Keidel, W.D. and Neff, W.D. (Eds.), Handbook of Sensory Physiology, Vol. 5/2, Springer-Verlag, Heidelberg, pp. 1-108.

9. Evans, E.F. (1977a) in: Evans, E.F. and Wilson, J.P. (Eds.), Psychophysics and Physiology of Hearing, Academic Press, London, p. 347.

10. Evans, E.F. (1977b) Proc. 9th Internat. Cong. on Acoustics, Vol of Invited Review Lectures, Spanish Acoustical Society, Madrid, pp. 55-65.

11. Evans, E.F. (1977c) in: Bullock, T.H. (Ed.), Recognition of Complex Acoustical Signals, Dahlem Konferenzen, Berlin, pp. 145-159.

12. Evans, E.F. (1978a) Audiol., 17, 369-420.

13. Evans, E.F. (1978b) in: Ludvigsen, C. and Barfod, J. (Eds.), Sensorineural Hearing Impairment and Hearing Aids, Scand. Audiol. Suppl., 6, pp. 9-44.

14. Evans, E.F. (1980a) in: van der Brink, G. and Bilsen, F. (Eds.), International Symposium on Psychophysical, Physiological and Behavioural Studies in Hearing, Delft University Press, 1980.

15. Evans, E.F. (1980b) J. Physiol., 298, 6-7P.

16. Evans, E.F. (1981) in: Syka, J. and Aitken, L. (Eds.), Neuronal Mechanisms of Hearing, Plenum Press, New York, pp. 69-85.

17. Evans, E.F. (1982) in: Barlow, H.B. and Mollon, J.D. (Eds.), The Senses, Cambridge University Press, Cambridge, pp. 307-331.

18. Evans, E.F. and Nelson, P.G. (1973) Exp. Brain Res., 17, 428-442.

19. Evans, E.F. and Palmer, A.R. (1975) J. Physiol., 252, 60-62P.

20. Evans, E.F. and Palmer, A.R. (1980) Exp. Brain Res., 40, 115-118.

21. Evans, E.F. and Wilson, J.P. (1973) in: moller, A.R. (Ed.), Basic Mechanisms in Hearing, Academic Press, New York, pp. 519-551.

22. Goldberg, J.M. and Brown, P.B. (1969) J. Neurophysiol., 32, 613-636.

23. Goldstein, J.L. (1978) Audiol., 17, 421-445.

24. Goldstein, J.L. and Kiang, N.Y.S. (1968) Proc. IEEE, 56, 981-992.

25. Harrison, R.V. and Evans, E.F. (1982) Hearing Research, 6, 303-314.

26. Hashimoto, T., Kayayama, Y., Murata, K. and Taniguchi, I. (1975) Japanese Journal of Physiology, 25, 633.

27. Javel, E. (1980) J. Acoust. Soc. Am., 68, 133-146.

28. Johnson-Davies, D. and Patterson, R.D. (1979) J. Acoust. Soc. Am., 65, 765-770.

29. Kiang, N.Y.S. (1975) in: Tower, D.B. (Ed.) The Nervous System, Vol. 3, Human Communication and its Disorders, Raven Press, New, York, pp. 81-96.

30. Kiang, N.Y.S. (1979) J. Acoust. Soc. Am., 68, 830-835.

31. Kiang, N.Y.S., Morest, D.K., Godfrey, D.A., Guinan, J.J., and Kane, E.C. (1973) in: Moller, A.R. (Ed.), Basic Mechanisms in Hearing, Academic Press, New York, pp. 455-475.

32. Kiang, N.Y.S. and Moxon, E.C. (1972) Annals of Otology, 81, 714-730.

33. Kiang, N.Y.S. and Moxon, E.C. (1974) J. Acoust. Soc. Am., 55, 620-630.

34. Kiang, N.Y.S., Eddington, D.K. and Delgutte, B. (1979) Acta Otolaryngol., 87, 204-219.

35. Kim, D.O. and Molnar, C.E. (1979) J. Neurophysiol., 42, 16-30.

36. Liberman, M.C. (1978) J. Acoust. Soc. Am., 63, 442-455.

37. Miller, J.D. (1977) in: Bullock, T.H. (Ed.), Recognition of Complex Acoustic Signals, Dahlem Konferenzen, Berlin.

38. Moller, A.R. (1977) J. Acoust. Soc. Am., 62, 135-142.

39. Moller, A.R. (1978) Audiol., 17, 446-468.

40. Moore, B.C.J. (1978) J. Acoust. Soc. Am., 63, 524-532.

41. Moore, T.J. and Cashin, J.L. (1974) J. Acoust. Soc. Am., 56, 1565-1576.

42. Nomoto, M., Suga, N. and Katsuki, Y. (1964) J. Neurophysiol., 27, 768-787.

43. Owens, E., Talbott, C.B. and Schubert, E.D. (1968) J. Speech and Hearing Res., 11, 648-655.

44. Palmer, A.R. and Evans, E.F. (1979) Exp. Brain Res., Suppl. II, 19-26.

45. Pickles, J.O. (1975) Acta Otolaryngol., 80, 245-254.

46. Pickles, J.O. (1979) J. Acoust. Soc. Am., 66, 1725-1732.

47. Pick, G.F. (1980) J. Acoust. Soc. Am., 68, 1085-1095.

48. Pick, G.F., Evans, E.F. and Wilson, J.P. (1977) in: Evans, E.F. and Wilson, J.P. (Eds.), Psychophysics and Physiology of Hearing, Academic Press, London, pp. 273-281.

49. Rose, J.E., Galambos, R. and Hughes, J.R. (1959) Johns Hopkins Hosp. Bull., 104, 211-251.

50. Rose, J.E., Kitzes, L.M., Gibson, M.M. and Hind, J.E. (1974) J. Neurophysiol 34, 685-699.

51. Rupert, A.L., Caspary, D.M. and Moushegian, G. (1977) Annals of Otology, 86, 37-48.

52. Sachs, M.B. and Abbas, P.J. (1974) J. Acoust. Soc. Am., 56, 1835-1847.

53. Sachs, M.B., and Kiang, N.Y.S. (1968) J. Acoust. Soc. Am., 43, 1120-1128.

54. Sachs, M.B., and Young, E.D. (1979) J. Acoust. Soc. Am., 66, 470-479.

55. Schalk, T.B. and Sachs, M.B. (1980) J. Acoust. Soc. Am., 67, 903-913.

56. Schorn, K., Wurzer, H., Zollner, M. and Zwicker, E. (1977) Lar. Rhinol. Otol., 56, 121-127.

57. Werblin, F. (1972) Ann. N.Y. Acad. Sci., 193, 75-85.

58. Wightman, F., McGee, T. and Kramer, M. in: Evans, E.F. and Wilson, J.P. (Eds.), Psychophysics and Physiology of Hearing, Academic Press, London, pp. 295-306.

59. Wilson, J.P. (1974) in: Schmitt, F.O. and Worden, F.G. (Eds.), The Neurosciences: Third Study Program, M.I.T. Press, Cambridge, pp. 147-153.

60. Young, E.D. and Sachs, M.B. (1979) J. Acoust. Soc. Am., 66, 1381-1403.

61. Young, E.D. and Sachs, M.B. (1981) in: Myers, T., Laver, J. and Anderson, J. (Eds.), The Cognitive Representation of Speech, Elsevier, Amsterdam, pp. 75-92.

62. Zwicker, E. (1974) in: Zwicker, E. and Terhardt, E. (Eds.), Facts and Models Hearing, Springer-Verlag, Heidelberg, pp. 132-140.

© 1982 Elsevier Biomedical Press
The Representation of Speech in the Peripheral
Auditory System, R. Carlson and B. Granström eds.

NEUROPHYSIOLOGICAL BASIS FOR PERCEPTION OF COMPLEX SOUNDS

AAGE R. MØLLER

Division of Physiological Acoustics, Department of Otolaryngology, University of
Pittsburgh School of Medicine, Pittsburgh, Pennsylvania 15213 (U.S.A.)

INTRODUCTION

The sounds that reach the ear are subjected to a series of complex processings
before the information reaches the cerebral cortex, where we assume that the
information in the discharge patterns of millions of neurons forms our perception
of sound. Our present understanding of the signal processing that takes place in
the auditory nervous system is based upon the results of experiments in which the
discharge patterns of single nerve fibers and nerve cells were recorded. This
information was then related to the physical characteristics of different types of
sounds. Due to technical difficulties and to the increasing complexity of neural
organization as one moves closer to the cerebral cortex, such studies usually focus
on the activity in peripheral nuclei such as the cochlear nucleus rather than on the
functions of the central nuclei.

Temporal and Spectral Analysis in the Cochlea

The first major step in processing the signals of the sounds that reach the ear
takes place in the ear. This first step mostly involves separation of sounds
according to their spectra; the coding of different spectral components takes
place in different groups of auditory nerve fibers.

Recordings of the discharge patterns of single nerve fibers of the auditory
nerve in response to simple sounds such as tonebursts and clicks (1-5) have,
together with measurements of the vibration of the basilar membrane (6-10),
provided us with a basic understanding of the function of the auditory peripheral
analyzer. These studies emphasize the role of the ear as a spectrum analyzer, but
recordings of the discharge patterns of single nerve fibers also show that the
temporal pattern of a sound indeed is coded in the discharge pattern. Numerous
investigations on cochlear mechanics have yielded results that supported the
general conception of the ear as a spectrum analyzer, although these results were
quantitatively different from those obtained by recording from single nerve
fibers. In particular, in regard to the acuity of the spectral analysis performed,
the mechanical tuning of the basilar membrane has been found to be much broader
than the neural tuning seen in single nerve fibers. One study on the vibration of

the basilar membrane (10) showed that the basilar membrane vibrates in a nonlinear way, the result of which is that the acuity of frequency selectivity decreases with increasing sound intensity.

Various hypotheses which explain how neural sharpening of the broad tuning of the basilar membrane is effected have been proposed (5). Indirect measurements of the spectral acuity of the tuning of the cochlea based on the response of neurons in the cochlear nucleus to click pairs, however, showed that neural tuning is instantaneous, thus making it unlikely that the narrow tuning of auditory nerve fibers is a result of neural sharpening involving neural delay (11). Intracellular recordings from inner hair cells showed that they possess frequency selectivity similar to that evidenced by primary auditory nerve fibers, confirming the belief that the frequency selectivity of the auditory nerve fibers already exists at the level of the hair cells, and most likely is mechanical in origin. Recently, hypotheses have been presented (12) which speculate that mechanical processes in the cochlea are responsible for sharpening of the broad spectral tuning of the basilar membrane.

Using more complex sounds as stimuli in neurophysiological experiments on the frequency selectivity of the cochlea supported the finding that the cochlea is a spectrum analyzer. One of these techniques uses random noise as stimuli and the noise that precedes every discharge is averaged (13-15). The averages of the stimulus that precedes every discharge, also called reverse correlograms, had the shape of damped oscillations when they were obtained as a result of recording from single auditory nerve fibers in cats. These results were taken to indicate that the system under test had a bandpass characteristic. The Fourier transform of these reverse correlograms had a bandpass characteristic, the shape of which was similar to the frequency tuning curves of the fibers that were tested (15,16). The reverse correlation method, as well as the method described below, are all based on the fact that the first-order cross-correlation between the input and the output of a system is an estimate of the first-order Wiener kernel (17) which, in a linear system, corresponds to the impulse response function of the system.

Later studies showed that complex sounds are coded in the discharge patterns of single auditory nerve fibers in such a way that the peripheral spectrum analyzer appears to be nonlinear: the spectral selectivity is greater at lower sound intensities than it is at higher sound intensities and the center frequency of the tuning shifts downwards in frequency with increasing sound intensity (18-20). In these studies pseudorandom noise was used as the stimulus, and a period histogram of the discharges over one noise period is cross-correlated with one period of pseudorandom noise (21-24).

Examples of results obtained in experiments in an anesthetized rat using noise of different intensities as the stimulus are shown in Figure 1. It may be seen that the damped oscillation has a much longer duration when the stimulus sound is of a lower intensity than it does when the stimulus sound is of higher intensity. At 20 to 30 dB above threshold six to seven waves can be discerned, whereas at 70 to 80 dB above threshold only two or three waves can be discerned in these cross-correlograms.

UNIT 260.5

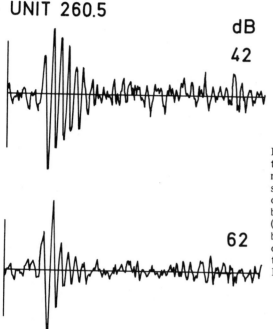

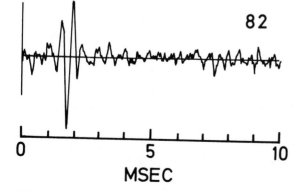

Fig. 1. Cross-correlograms of the response of a typical nerve fiber in a rat when stimulated with pseudorandom noise at intensities between 42 and 82 dB SPL (measured in 1/3-octave bands). The amplitude of the correlograms is normalized to the same maximal value . From Møller, 1977 (18).

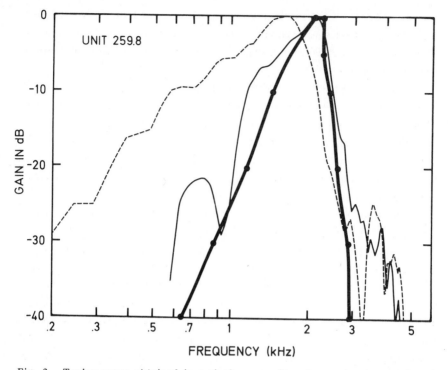

Fig. 2. Tuning curve obtained in a single nerve fiber in a rat using tonebursts (heavy line) and the transfer function of the same nerve fiber obtained using pseudorandom noise as the stimulus at 15 dB above threshold (solid line) and 70 dB above threshold (dashed line). From Møller, 1978 (19).

In a linear system the Fourier transforms of such cross-correlograms are identical to the frequency transfer function of the system obtained using sinusoidal excitation (21-25). Fourier transforms of cross-correlograms, such as those seen in Figure 1, are presented in Figure 2 for different stimulus intensities together with the frequency tuning curve (heavy line) obtained from the same single auditory nerve fiber in the conventional way by using pure tones to determine the threshold. From Figure 2 it is evident that the responses to pseudorandom noise near threshold are similar to the tuning curve of the fibers measured in response to pure tones, whereas the results that were obtained using pseudorandom noise of higher intensity show a broader tuning and the center frequency is shifted downwards in frequency. The finding that the bandwidth of the auditory spectrum analyzer changes with sound intensity is supported by the results obtained by Rhode (10) when he measured vibration of the basilar membrane, and the results of recording neurophysiologically from several hundred nerve fibers in the same animal in response to the same few tonal stimuli (26). In all of these studies a similar decrease in the spectral acuity occurred with increasing sound intensity.

There is thus strong experimental evidence that indicates that the peripheral auditory analyzer acts as a spectrum analyzer not only when pure tones are used as stimuli but also when more complex sounds are used. However, there is at least one fundamental difference between the auditory spectrum analyzer and the commonly used man-made spectrum analyzer, namely the peculiar nonlinearity of the auditory analyzer that results in changes in both the bandwidth and the center frequency with changes in stimlus sound intensity.

There is yet another difference between the spectral analysis performed by the cochlear frequency analyzer and that performed with bandpass filters using lumped components (27). This difference consists of a change in the instantaneous frequency as a function of time of the damped oscillation of the cross-correlograms obtained from recording from single nerve fibers when the ear is stimulated with pseudorandom noise. This change is seen when the instantaneous frequency of the oscillation of cross-correlograms, such as those displayed in Figure 1, is plotted as a function of time (27). This is illustrated in Figure 3 which shows cross-correlograms obtained at three different sound intensities. It is seen that the frequency of the oscillation increases with time to about the same degree in the three correlograms shown. The increase is more than 50 percent. Bandpass filters made of lumped components have a damped oscillation which has the same frequency throughout its entire course. That the frequency of the damped oscillation of the cross-correlograms obtained from the auditory system changes in frequency is most likely due to the fact that the cochlear analyzer has distributed components according to the transmission line properties of the basilar membrane (27); this frequency modulation is not likely to be related to the nonlinearity described above.

It should be noted that when correlation techniques were used to evaluate spectral selectivity of the peripheral auditory system, the results concern the phase-locked responses of single nerve auditory fibers. The results are therefore only valid for stimulus frequencies below 5 to 6 kHz because phase-locking of neural discharges to the waveform of the stimulus sound does not occur at higher frequencies. Due to lack of experimental data, we know much less about the nature of the spectrum analysis performed in the auditory system at frequencies that are higher than 6 kHz.

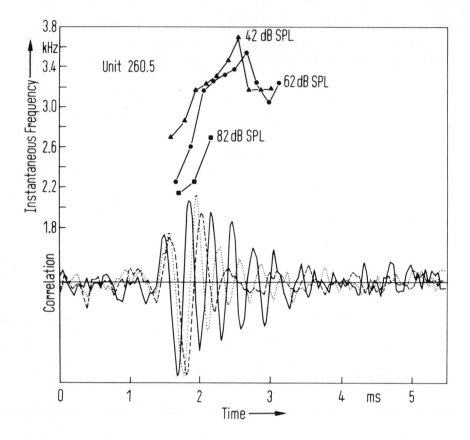

Fig. 3. Cross-correlograms (lower curves) obtained from the response of a single nerve fiber in a rat at different intensities: solid line, 42 dB; dotted line, 62 dB; dashed line, 82 dB. The upper curves show the instantaneous frequency of oscillation as a function of time. The sound level is in dB SPL measured in 1/3-octave bands of the noise. From Møller and Nilsson, 1979 (27).

What Information is Coded in the Discharge Patterns of Auditory Nerve Fibers?

On the basis of our present knowledge about the function of the auditory periphery, it may be possible to make some prediction as to what information is carried in the discharge patterns of single auditory nerve fibers for a few typical sounds, such as pure tones, click sounds, and broadband noise. As was described in the preceding section of this paper, it is well known that a pure tone may be represented in the discharge pattern of single auditory nerve fibers in two ways: namely, by which groups of nerve fibers are activated (place principle) and by phase-locking of the discharges in a particular nerve fiber (temporal principle). At intensities well above threshold, phase-locking is presumed to occur in many nerve fibers simultaneously, and the discharges in response to a steady tone will be phase-locked to the same frequency but the phase relationship between the tone and the discharges will vary in a systematic way among nerve fibers due to the time it takes for the traveling wave to move along the basilar membrane. The fibers that terminate on the most basally located hair cells of the group of nerve fibers that are activated by the tone will be phase-locked to the tone with the smallest phase difference relative to the tone, while those fibers terminating on more apically located hair cells, which become excited with a delay, will have larger phase differences relative to the tone due to the longer time it takes the stimulus to reach these hair cells.

A loud click will activate a large number of fibers and since the basilar membrane responds with a damped oscillation, the frequency of which is equal to the center frequency of the individual fibers, all the fibers that respond to frequencies below 5 to 6 kHz will be phase-locked to this damped oscilation frequency. Unlike the case for pure tones, the frequencies to which the fibers are phase-locked do not provide any information about the stimulus (except its arrival time and whether or not it has exceeded threshold). Rather, this oscillation provides the more central parts of the auditory system with information about the center frequency of the individual fibers. Transient sounds may thus remind the central auditory nervous system about the center frequency of individual nerve fibers. In this way transient sounds may play a role in the ontogenetic development of the auditory nervous system by providing the developing nervous system with information about where the different nerve fibers terminate on the basilar membrane.

Broadband noise will likewise activate a large number of nerve fibers. Discharges of all nerve fibers that respond to the noise will phase-lock to a bandpass-filtered version of the noise. The filter function is that of the basilar membrane at the point where the particular fiber terminates. White noise passed through a bandpass filter can be likened to a sinusoid, the amplitude of which is modulated by a random signal. The frequency of the sinusoid is equal to the center frequency of the bandpass filter, and the bandwidth of the noise is a function of the width of the filter function of the basilar membrane. It is interesting that the frequency of this sinusoid for a certain fiber is different for different sound intensities (see Figure 3).

Phase-locking of the discharges of individual nerve fibers when stimulated by broadband noise thus also provides information about which frequency the individual fibers are tuned to. Naturally the degree of activation of various nerve fibers provides information about the spectral distribution of the noise (place principle).

The above-presented hypotheses are only applicable to the frequency range over which the discharges of individual nerve fibers are phase-locked to the waveform of the sound (or rather to the waveform of the vibration of the basilar membrane). Because frequencies higher than 5 to 6 kHz do not seem to give rise to a phase-locked response in any fiber, it seems as if information about the frequency can only be conveyed to higher centers by the place principle. It is not only fibers that are tuned to low frequencies that can phase-lock. High-frequency fibers can also phase-lock to the low-frequency components when the sound intensity is high enough.

Physiological Basis for Pitch Perception

In the preceding sections we have dealt with the coding of different types of information in the discharge patterns of single auditory nerve fibers. It is generally assumed that information about the time pattern of a sound coded in the time pattern of neural discharges must be extracted in the periphery of the auditory nervous system since precise time-locking is gradually lost as the sound is relayed over neurons of the ascending auditory pathway.

It has been hypothesized that the delay of excitation along the basilar membrane due to the relatively slow propagation of the traveling wave, together with some form of auto- or cross-correlation analysis performed in the cochlea or the auditory nervous system, would be a possible mechanism for extracting periodicity information from sounds (28-31).

It has been recognized that the ascending auditory nervous system is well able to extract interaural time delays from sounds heard binaurally. It has been suggested that the delays that result from the relatively slow propagation of the traveling wave along the basilar membrane are utilized in neural analysis that is similar to cross-correlating the output of hair cells at different locations along the basilar membrane. However, it has been difficult to prove such a hypothesis, as well as to formulate more detailed hypotheses, due to the lack of experimental information. One severe experimental limitation is related to the fact that it was not previously possible to manipulate the delays of the traveling wave along the basilar membrane experimentally. The recent development of cochlear implants has made it possible to stimulate several points on the basilar membrane independently, thus making it possible to vary the time delay between stimulation at different locations. The results of such experiments have led to the development of a hypothesis which describes how neurons in the medial nucleus of the superior olivary complex compare the phase-locked discharge trains originating at separate locations on the basilar membrane (32). The type of analysis which is thought to take place is similar to nonlinear cross-correlation analysis of the information from different points along the basilar membrane. Loeb et al. (32) found from computer simulation of such a process that input from locations at the basilar membrane with a spacing of 0.3 to 0.4 wavelength was optimal for recovering the spectral information of a sound.

Coding of Changes in Spectrum and Amplitude in the Ascending Auditory Pathway

Cochlear Nucleus. When recording from neurons in the cochlear nucleus in response to pure tones, frequency selectivity is the most characteristic feature of the response. Frequency threshold curves of cochlear nucleus units are rather similar to those of primary auditory nerve fibers. Except for the fact that frequency threshold curves of cochlear nucleus cells are generally somewhat broader at their tip compared to those of primary auditory nerve fibers (33), only a few cells have frequency threshold curves that differ significantly from those of the auditory nerve fibers. Those can have a variety of shapes and have more than one peak.

Whereas all cochlear nerve fibers respond to tonebursts in about the same way, as judged from peristimulus time (PST) histograms, neurons in the cochlear nucleus respond to tonebursts with PST histograms of a variety of different shapes, and a classification of neurons has been derived on the basis of such histograms (34). Among other differences between cochlear nucleus units and primary auditory neurons is that many neurons of the cochlear nucleus respond poorly or not at all to broadband noise (35).

When the responses to sounds with changing frequency and intensity are obtained, a number of characteristics of the auditory system emerge that could not be predicted on the basis of knowledge about the response to tonebursts or click sounds. Thus, we find that most neurons of the cochlear nucleus respond to tones, the frequencies of which change, in a way that depends on the rate of change in frequency (36-38). Thus, when the response pattern to tones with rapidly varying frequency is compared to the response patterns to tones of slowly varying frequency, the distribution of nerve impulses as a function of frequency of the stimulus tones is much narrower for the tone with rapidly varying frequency than it is to a tone of slowly varying frequency (22,39,40). Histograms of the response to tones with slowly varying frequency well above threshold have a rather broad peak at the frequency to which the neuron is tuned, whereas the histogram of the response to tones with rapidly varying frequency has a peak that becomes narrower and increases in height as the rate of change in frequency is increased up to a certain value. There is for each neuron a specific rate of change in frequency where the histogram of the responses has its maximal height. Faster or slower changes in frequency result in a broadening of the histogram with a decrease in its height. The peaks in the histograms of the responses to descending frequency are often slightly higher than those in histograms recorded in response to increasing frequency, and the peaks representing the responses to decreasing frequency attain their maximal height at a slightly slower change in frequency than do the peaks recorded in response to increasing frequency (39). The maximal height of the peaks in the histograms occurs at different rates of change in frequency for different units, and the amount of increase in height from a slowly varying frequency to a tone, the frequency of which varies at the rate where the peaks have their maximal value, also varies from one nerve cell to another (38-40). Some neurons show very little frequency selectivity in response to tones with slowly varying frequencies, and some show only inhibition when presented with tones of slowly varying frequencies. In addition, when the frequency is varied above a certain rate these neurons show frequency selectivity, and in very much the same way as do neurons which display frequency selectivity to tones with slowly varying frequencies (39).

The responses of neurons of the cochlear nucleus to bandpass-filtered noise have certain interesting characteristics. The responses of many nerve cells in the cochlear nucleus to noise decrease as the bandwidth of the noise is increased, and many cells do not respond at all when the bandwidth is larger than a certain value (35). However, when the center frequency of bandpass-filtered noise is varied at a certain rate, all neurons studied respond with a great degree of frequency selectivity to the noise (38,41). Even those neurons which did not respond to the noise when its center frequency was held constant respond vigorously when the center frequency is varied at a certain rate. That is illustrated in Figure 4, which compares histograms of the responses to tones, the frequencies of which were varied at different rates with histograms of the response to bands of noise, the frequencies of which were varied in a similar fashion.

The relative increase in the height of the peaks in the histograms of the responses to bandpass-filtered noise that takes place when the rate of change in the center frequency of the noise is increased is larger for wider bands of noise than for narrower bands of noise and for tones (41). The reason for that is that the response of these neurons is smaller to broadband noise than it is to narrowband noise or to tones when the center frequency is varied at a slow rate, but the response to noise with rapidly varying center frequency is about the same.

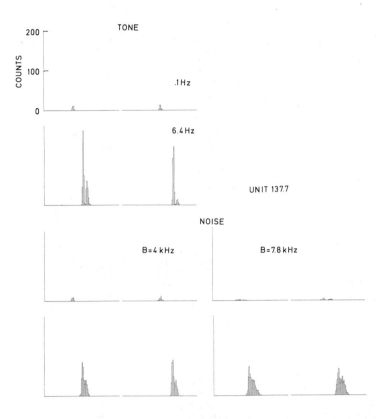

Fig. 4. Histograms of the responses to stimulation with tones (upper graphs) and to stimulation with bands of noise (lower graphs) of a neuron in the cochlear nucleus that does not respond to broadband noise. The frequencies of the tones and the center frequency of the bandpass-filtered noise was varied trapezoidally up and down repetitively. The repetition rate of the modulation was varied to obtain different rates of frequency change (indicated on the different histograms). Results obtained with two different bandwidths of the noise (4 and 7.8 kHz) are shown. From Møller, 1978 (49).

Another indication that neurons in the cochlear nucleus respond selectively to changes in the properties of a complex sound comes from studies of the responses of single neurons in the cochlear nucleus to sounds that are amplitude modulated. These studies have shown that when sinusoidally modulated tones or noise are used as stimuli, the discharge rate of these neurons is modulated at the modulation frequency of the sound to a degree that varies with the modulation depth and the modulation frequency of the sound (21,33,36,42-44).

Typical results of recording to sinusoidally modulated tones in the rat are shown in Figure 5, where period histograms of the recorded neural responses to amplitude-modulated tones time-locked to the modulation waveform are presented. The different histograms were obtained at different modulation frequencies (indicated on the histograms) and the graph in the middle shows the relative amplitude of the modulation of the different histograms plotted as a function of the modulation frequency. This latter is known as the modulation transfer function.

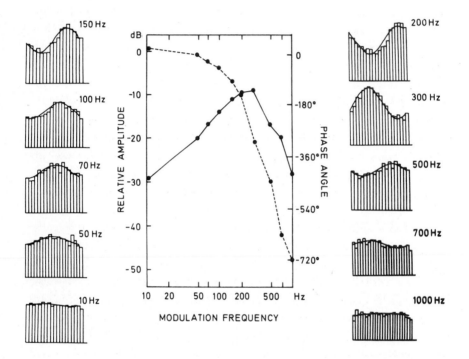

Fig. 5. Period histograms of the response of a neuron in the cochlear nucleus of a rat to amplitude-modulated tones. The different histograms represent different modulation frequencies. The graph in the middle shows the relative modulation of the histograms as a function of the modulation frequency (solid line) and the phase angle between the modulation of the sound and the modulation of the histogram (dashed line). From Møller, 1972 (36).

Most neurons in the cochlear nucleus are most sensitive to modulation in the range of modulation frequencies of 50 to 200 Hz. In that range, a modulation of 1 to 2 dB will in many cases result in as much as 50% modulation of the discharge rate. This modulation of the discharge rate is, in many neurons, nearly constant over an intensity range of as much as 50 dB, despite the fact that the mean discharge rate in most units has reached its saturation level at a much lower intensity (42). It thus seems possible for these units to reproduce fast changes in the intensity of a sound despite the fact that they have a nearly constant discharge rate over a large intensity range for steady-state sounds.

The reproduction of amplitude modulation of tones or noise has also been studied using pseudorandom noise as a modulation signal (21,45,46). In such experiments period histograms of discharges, locked to the periodicity of the pseudorandom noise, are cross-correlated with one period of the pseudorandom noise. The resulting cross-correlograms are estimates of the impulse response function of the system with regard to amplitude changes (17). Consequently, the Fourier transforms of these cross-correlograms yield estimates of the modulation transfer function. Modulation transfer functions obtained using noise modulation have been shown to be similar to those obtained using sinusoidal modulation (21). The shape of these modulation functions varies between units, but generally two different types can be discerned: one which is nearly a lowpass function and remains so over a large range of stimulus intensities, and the other also having the shape of a lowpass function at sound intensities just above threshold, but changing to a bandpass function for all higher intensities. These latter units thus seem to be tuned to a certain modulation frequency which varies from unit to unit, but does not seem to have any relationship to the characteristic frequency of the units (46).

In experiments in which two tones were presented simultaneously, one at the unit's center frequency and one at a higher frequency at which the unit's response to the tone at center frequency is decreased as a result of inhibition, it was shown that the presence of such an unmodulated inhibitory tone increased the sensitivity to modulation of the tone at the unit's center frequency (43). It thus seems as if the sensitivity to modulation may be even higher in the case of complex sounds containing many spectral components.

Inferior colliculus. Recent studies of the firing pattern of neurons in the inferior colliculus, using amplitude-modulated tones and noise (47) and tones with rapidly changing frequency (48), have shown that neurons in this nucleus, like those in the cochlear nucleus, respond better to sounds which change in frequency and amplitude than they do to steady-state sounds.

There is, however, a fundamental difference between the response pattern of neurons in the cochlear nucleus and that of neurons in the inferior colliculus when both are stimulated by amplitude-modulated tones. The neurons of the inferior colliculus respond best to modulation frequencies of 20-50 Hz and seldom respond to modulation frequencies above 100 Hz, while the neurons in the cochlear nucleus respond best to modulation frequencies of 50-200 Hz. Figure 6 shows the modulation transfer function of a typical neuron in the inferior colliculus of a rat. It has a shape that is similar to that shown for the cochlear nucleus (Figure 5), but the peak occurs at a lower modulation frequency.

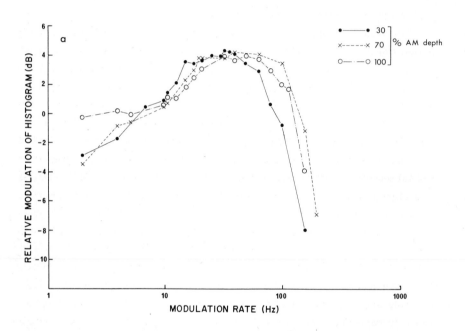

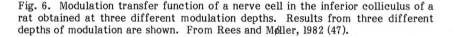

Fig. 6. Modulation transfer function of a nerve cell in the inferior colliculus of a rat obtained at three different modulation depths. Results from three different depths of modulation are shown. From Rees and Møller, 1982 (47).

The response of neurons in the inferior colliculus to changes in the frequencies of tones is also different from what is seen in the cochlear nucleus. The neurons in the inferior colliculus have a much more diversified pattern of response, and they often respond only when the frequency changes in one direction (48).

Although we do not have as much information about coding of time-varying sounds in the inferior colliculus as we do about coding in the cochlear nucleus, it is obvious from the results of experiments discussed above that the acoustic information undergoes a further transformation between the cochlear nucleus and

57

the inferior colliculus, and yet another transformation in the inferior colliculus itself. It is somewhat puzzling that neurons in the cochlear nucleus seem to prefer relatively high modulation frequencies, whereas neurons in the inferior colliculus respond best to much lower modulation frequencies. One unanswered question is how the information about high modulation frequencies which characterizes the response patterns of cochlear nucleus neurons is transmitted to more central nuclei.

Implication for Coding of Natural Sounds

The results of the experiments described above show that the response patterns of neurons in the cochlear nucleus and the inferior colliculus are highly dependent on the rate with which the frequency or spectrum changes. This has relevance to the study of how natural sounds such as speech sounds are coded. The fact that neurons in both the cochlear nucleus and in the nucleus of the inferior colliculus are activated much more by sounds with spectra which change than by sounds with steady or slowly varying frequencies is probably just one of the many important facts that we need to know about the neural processing of natural sounds that takes place in the ascending auditory pathway. Such selective activation of neurons enhances features of the sounds which carry information of relevance to the animal.

Speech sounds are characterized by more or less rapid changes in spectrum, and it may very well be that the responses of nerve cells in the cochlear nucleus involve the selection of sounds with changing spectrum and suppression of sounds that have constant or slowly varying spectra. Vowel sounds in many ways resemble amplitude-modulated tones in which the modulation frequency is the voice fundamental frequency and the carrier frequencies are the formant frequencies. The fundamental frequency of voiced speech sounds covers the same frequency range as that over which the neurons in the cochlear nucleus enhance the modulation frequencies of amplitude-modulated tones.

REFERENCES

1. Tasaki, I. (1954) Nerve impulses in individual auditory nerve fibers of guinea pig. J. Neurophysiol. 17, 97-122.

2. Katsuki, Y., Sumi, T., Vehiyama, H., and Watanabe, T. (1958) Electric responses of auditory neurons in cat to sound stimulation. J. Neurophysiol. 21, 569-588.

3. Kiang, N.Y.S., Watanabe, T., Thomas, E.C., and Clark, L.F. (1965) Discharge Patterns of Single Fibers in the Cat's Auditory Nerve. MIT Press, Cambridge.

4. Evans, E.F. (1972) The frequency response and other properties of single fibers in the guinea-pig cochlear nerve. J. Physiol. 226, 263-287.

5. Evans, E.F. (1975) Cochlear nerve and cochlear nucleus. in: Keidel, W.D. and Neff, W.D. (Eds.), Handbook of Sensory Physiology Vol. 5, Pt. 2, Auditory Systems, Springer-Verlag, New York, pp. 1-108.

6. Bekesy, G. von. (1942) Uber die Schwingungen der Schneckentrennwand beim Praparat und Ohren model. Akust. Zeits 7, 173-186.

7. Bekesy, G. von. (1949) The vibration of the cochlear partition in anatomical preparations and in models of the inner ear. J. Acoust. Soc. Am. 21, 233-245.

8. Johnstone, B.M. and Boyle, A.J.F. (1967) Basilar membrane vibration examined with the Mossbauer technique. Science (New York) 158, 389-390.

9. Johnstone, B.M., Taylor, K.J., and Boyle, A.J.F. (1970) Mechanics of the guinea pig cochlea. J. Acoust. Soc. Am. 47, 504-509.

10. Rhode, W.S. (1971) Observations of the vibration of the basilar membrane in squirrel monkeys using Mossbauer technique. J. Acoust. Soc. Am. 49, 1218-1231.

11. Møller, A.R. (1970) Studies of the damped oscillatory response of the auditory frequency analyzer. Acta Physiol. Scand. 78, 299-314.

12. Zwislocki, J.J. and Kletski, E.J. (1980) Micromechanics in the theory of cochlear mechanics. Hear. Res. 2, 505-512.

13. de Boer, E. (1967) Correlation studies applied to the frequency resolution of the cochlea. J. Aud. Res. 7, 209-217.

14. de Boer, E. (1968) Reverse correlation. I. A heuristic introduction to the techniques of triggered correlation with application to the analysis of compound systems. Proc. kon. Nedrl. Akad. Wet. 71, 472-486.

15. de Boer, E. (1969) Reverse correlation. II. Initiation of nerve impulses in the inner ear. Proc. kon. Nedrl. Akad. Wet. 72, 129-151.

16. Evans, E.F. (1977) Frequency selectivity at high signal levels of single units in cochlear nerve and nucleus. in: Evans, E.F. and Wilson, J.P. (Eds.), Psychophysics and Physiology of Hearing, Academic Press, New York, pp. 185-195.

17. Lee, Y.W. and Schetzen, M. (1965) Measurement of the Wiener kernels of a non-linear system by cross-correlation. Int. J. Control 2, 237-254.

18. Møller, A.R. (1977) Frequency selectivity of single auditory nerve fibers in response to broadband noise stimuli. J. Acoust. Soc. Am. 62, 135-142.

19. Møller, A.R. (1978a) Frequency selectivity of the peripheral auditory analyzer studied using broadband noise. Acta Physiol. Scand. 104, 24-32.

20. Møller, A.R. (1978b) Responses of auditory nerve fibers to noise stimuli show cochlear nonlinearities. Acta Otolaryngol. 86, 1-8.

21. Møller, A.R. (1973) Statistical evaluation of the dynamic properties of cochlear nucleus units using stimuli modulated with pseudorandom noise. Brain Res. 57, 443-456.

22. Møller, A.R. (1974a) Use of stochastic signals in evaluation of the dynamic properties of a neuronal system. Scand. J. Rehab. Med. 3, 37-44.

23. Møller, A.R. (1982) Use of pseudorandom noise in studies of the dynamic properties of the linear part of a sensory neural system. in: Shriver, B.D., Grams, R.R., Walker, T.H. and Sprague, R.H. (Eds.), Proceedings of the Fifteenth Hawaii International Conference on System Sciences, Honolulu, Hawaii, Western Periodicals Company, California, Vol. II, pp. 337-351.

24. O'Leary, D.P. and Honrubia, V. (1975) On-line identification of sensory systems using pseudorandom binary noise perturbations. Biophys. J. 15, 505-532.

25. Marmarelis, P.Z. and Marmarelis, V.Z. (1978) Analysis of Physiological Systems. Plenum Press, New York.

26. Pfeiffer, R.R. and Kim, D.O. (1975) Cochlear nerve fiber responses: Distribution along cochlear partition. J. Acoust. Soc. Am. 58, 867-869.

27. Møller, A.R. and Nilsson, H.G. (1979) Inner ear impulse response and basilar membrane modelling. Acustica 41/4, 258-262.

28. Huggins, W.H. (1952) A phase principle for complex-frequency analysis and its implications in auditory theory. J. Acoust. Soc. Am. 24, 582-589.

29. Shupljakov, V., Murray, T., and Liljencrantz, J. (1968) Phase dependent pitch sensation. Speech Transmission Laboratory, Royal Institute of Technology, Stockholm, Sweden. QPSR 4, 7-14.

30. Nieder, P. (1971) Addressed exponential delay line theory of cochlear organization. Nature (Lond.) 230, 255-257.

31. Licklider, J.C.R. (1962) Periodicity and related auditory process models. Int. Audiology 1, 11-36.

32. Loeb, G.E., White, M.W., and Merzenich, M.M. (1982) A new theory of acoustic pitch perception. (In press)

33. Møller, A.R. (1972a) Coding of sounds in lower levels of the auditory system. Quart. Rev. Biophys. 5, 59-115.

34. Pfeiffer, R.R. (1966) Classification of response patterns of spike discharges for units in the cochlear nucleus: Tone-burst stimulation. Exp. Brain Res. 1, 220-235.

35. Greenwood, D.D. and Goldberg, J.M. (1970) Responses of neurons in the cochlear nucleus to variations in noise bandwidth and to tone-noise combinations. J. Acoust. Soc. Am. 47, 1022-1040.

36. Møller, A.R. (1972b) Coding of amplitude and frequency modulated sounds in the cochlear nucleus of the rat. Acta Physiol. Scand. 86, 223-238.

37. Møller, A.R. (1974b) Coding of amplitude and frequency modulated sounds in the cochlear nucleus. Acustica 6, 292-299.

38. Møller, A.R. (1981) Coding of complex sounds in the auditory nervous system. in: Syka, J. and Aitkin, L. (Eds.), Proceedings of the Symposium on Neuronal Mechanisms of Hearing, Prague, Czechoslovakia, Plenum Press, New York, pp. 87-103.

39. Møller, A.R. (1969) Unit responses in the cochlear nucleus of the rat to sweep tones. Acta Physiol. Scand. 76, 503-512.

40. Møller, A.R. (1971) Unit responses in the rat cochlear nucleus to tones of rapidly varying frequency and amplitude. Acta Physiol. Scand. 81, 540-556.

41. Møller, A.R. (1974c) Coding of sounds with rapidly varying spectrum in the cochlear nucleus. J. Acoust. Soc. Am. 55, 631-640.

42. Møller, A.R. (1974d) Response of units in the cochlear nucleus to sinusoidally amplitude-modulated tones. Exp. Neurol. 45, 104-117.

43. Møller, A.R. (1975) Dynamic properties of excitation and inhibition in the cochlear nucleus. Acta Physiol. Scand. 93, 442-454.

44. Hirsch, H.R. and Gibson, M.M. (1976) Responses of single units in the cat cochlear nucleus to sinusoidal amplitude modulated tones and noise: Linearity and relation to speech perception. J. Neurosci. Res. 2, 337-356.

45. Møller, A.R. (1976a) Dynamic properties of excitation and two-tone inhibition in the cochlear nucleus studied using amplitude-modulated tones. Exp. Brain Res. 25, 307-321.

46. Møller, A.R. (1976b) Dynamic properties of the responses of single neurons in the cochlear nucleus of the rat. J. Physiol. (Lond.) 259, 63-82.

47. Rees, A. and Møller, A.R. (1982a) The responses of neurones in the inferior colliculus of the rat to AM and FM tones. To be published.

48. Rees, A. and Møller, A.R. (1982b) Unpublished observation.

49. Møller, A.R. (1978c) Frequency analysis in the peripheral auditory system. in: Hanske, G. and Butenandt, E. (Eds.), Kybernetik, Munchen, Oldenburg, Germany, pp. 263-287.

© 1982 Elsevier Biomedical Press
The Representation of Speech in the Peripheral
Auditory System, R. Carlson and B. Granström eds.

EXPERIMENTAL LESIONS TO COCHLEAR INNER AND OUTER HAIR CELLS

Berit Engström and Erik Borg
Department of Otolaryngology, University Hospital, S-750 14 Uppsala,
Sweden and Department of Audiology, Karolinska sjukhuset, S-104 01
Stockholm, Sweden

INTRODUCTION

The ability to understand speech generally deteriorates in proportion
to the shift that occurs in the hearing threshold in the mid frequency
range in subjects with inner ear lesions. There are, however, large individual differences between subjects with respect to their ability to
discrimnate speech, even when hearing thresholds for pure tones are the
same. Speech discrimination may differ considerably between the two ears
of one and the same subject with a bilaterally symmetric pure tone loss.
The individual differences are likely, to some extent, to be due to a
difference in the capacity of the central nervous system to handle a distorted message from the damaged inner ear. It has, however, to be assumed
that there exist other differences in the message from the damaged ear to
the brain that are not revealed by pure tone audiometry. A more sofisti-
cated identification of inner ear function than the pure tone threshold
would be of importance both in order to understand the hearing handicap
and to obtain a precise diagnosis of the cochlear lesion. Such methods
must be related to a morphological reference and therefore, require animal experimentation to a large extent. From morphological studies, it is
known that inner ear lesions are often associated with a varying proportion of loss of and damage to the outer hair cells (OHC), the inner hair
cells (IHC), the stria vascularis and the auditory nerve fibers. There
certainly also exist numerous, as yet undefined, pathological features in
the cochlea of a person with impaired hearing.

In order to improve our basic knowledge of cochlear physiology and to
facilitate the interpretation of symptoms and loss of function, it is desirable to study inner ears with selective lesions to its different cell
types. In a series of experiments in rabbits, we have been able to induce
an apparently selective destruction of OHC with kanamycin and a predomi-
nant lesion of the IHC with noise.

METHODS

Rabbits of the small chinchilla strain were used for the present experiments. Removal of the OHC was achieved by kanamycin treatment (400
mg/kg for 10 days). Lesions to the IHC-cilia was induced by short exposure to high level noise (2-7 kHz, 115 dB SPL, 15 or 30 min). The loss
of auditory sensitivity was assessed by following the shift of the threshold of the middle ear muscle reflexes in the frequency range 0.5-12 kHz
and of the auditory brain stem response (ABR, 1/3-octave filtered pulses
of full cycle sine waves), and, in some cases, behaviorally with a conditioned suppresion technique (1). After the end of the experiment, (a
few minutes up to 11 months) the rabbits were transcardially perfused
with a fixative and processed for scanning electron microscopy (2, 3).

In addition, the hair cells of eight human temporal bones were examined
in the scanning electron microscope. The cochleas of the human temporal
bones were fixed by perilymphatic perfusion with Karnowsky's solution (4)
within six hours after death.

RESULTS

Lesion of OHC. Fig. 1A shows a loss of threshold sensitivity in a
rabbit treated with kanamycin for 10 days, measured by ABR and by the
conditioned suppresion technique. There is an increase both in the behavioral threshold and the stapedius reflex threshold and there is a total loss of outer hair cells (Fig. 1B) in the basal 1.5 to 2 turns. It
has to be noted that the hearing loss slopes gradually and attains a
maximum at about 60 dB.

Lesion of IHC. The characteristic finding in all rabbits exposed to
noise was an extensive and widespread fusion and fracturation of the IHC
cilia (Fig. 3A). In large areas where the ICH:s had alterations in their
cilia, there was no hair-cell loss and the OHC appeared to be normal when
examined in SEM and/or TEM (Fig. 3B, C). In addition, in a rather narrow
range of noise doses, there was no OHC damage observed at all and at a
somewhat higher noise dose, there was an OHC loss in the 2-4 kHz range
as well as some disturbance of the OHC cilias in the apical turns. An ABR
threshold shift of 30 dB and a reflex threshold shift of 20 dB corresponding well to the extent of abnormal IHC cilia.

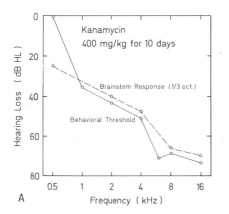 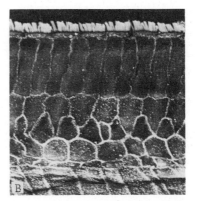

Fig. 1A. Shift of hearing 2 months after kanamycin treatment.

Fig. 1B. A scanning electronmicrograph from a rabbit 2 months after kanamycin treatment. All OHC are missing and all IHC are present.

Fig. 2A,B. Normal and pathologically altered IHC as seen in the basal turn of two old human subjects.

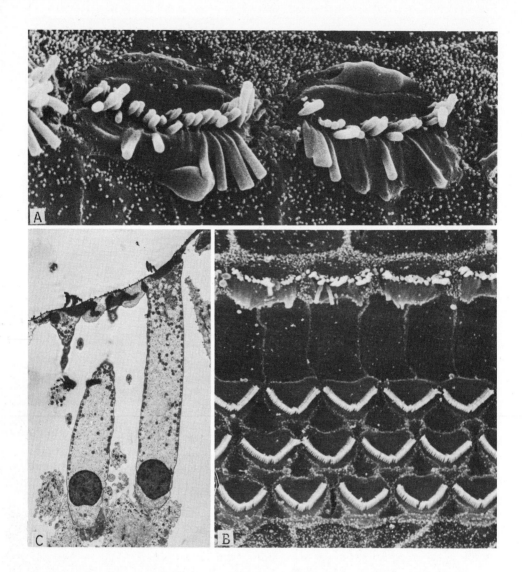

Fig. 3A. Fusion of stereocilia of two IHC from a noise exposed rabbit.

Fig. 3B. Scanning electronmicrograph of OHC and IHC from a noise exposed rabbit. The OHC appear normal while the IHC-cilia are fused, especially the long ones.

Fig. 3C. Transmission electronmicrograph of two of the OHC seen in 3B.

Human temporal bones. In order to investigate the validity of the observations in rabbits with respect to human auditory pathology, eight temporal bones were investigated with SEM. One of them had a known history of massive noise exposure. In all eight ears abnormal IHC cilia were observed and there were OHC losses of varying degrees and the ear with known noise exposure had large OHC losses as well as many IHC:s with altered cilia. Fig. 2 shows examples of abnormal cilia of IHC in one human subject.

DISCUSSION

The observations in rabbits indicate that the two quite different types of inner ear pathology both produce a shift of auditory sensitivity measured with different methods in rabbits. Of course, the morphological analysis of hair cells can never give complete information about the functional state of the cell. We have to assume that the cells where severe pathological changes are found function worse than cells without visible changes or those having only very minor changes.

It has for a very long time been known that there is often a poor correlation between the loss of hair cells and the loss of auditory sensitivity. Even if we do not consider that the abnormal hair cell cilia completely explain this discrepancy, the present observations in rabbits and human temporal bones indicate that they may explain a part of this discrepancy and, in addition, that they may explain part of the discrepancy between pure tone loss and loss of auditory function measured as the ability to discriminate speech.

REFERENCES

1. E. Borg & B. Engström. Hearing thresholds in the rabbit, a behavioral and electrophysiological study. Acta Otol (1982) (accepted).
2. E. Borg & B. Engström. Acoustic reflex after experimental lesions to inner and outer hair cells. Hearing Res 6 (1982) 25-34.
3. B. Engström & E. Borg. Lesions to cochlear inner hair cells induced by noise. Arch Otorhinolaryngol 230 (1981) 279-284.
4. J.J. Karnovsky. A formaldehyde-glutaraldehyde fixative of high osmolarity for use in electron microscopy. J Cell Biol 27 (1965) 137-138

© 1982 Elsevier Biomedical Press
The Representation of Speech in the Peripheral
Auditory System, R. Carlson and B. Granström eds.

SIGNAL ANALYSIS AS REVEALED BY AN ACOUSTIC AUTONOMIC REFLEX SYSTEM

ERIK BORG

Department of Physiology II, Karolinska Institute, Box 60 400,

S-104 01 Stockholm (Sweden)

INTRODUCTION

The physiological investigation of auditory signal processing of speech is hampered by the fact that speech is exclusively a human phenomenon. Consequently the methods of animal physiology, e.g. direct recordings from neural elements and controlled lesions, have limited applicability in direct investigation of speech signal analysis. Nevertheless, animal experiments are inevitable but have to be interpreted carefully. It has to be assumed that the validity of the results will be gradually reduced as the focus of interest moves towards the higher nervous mechanisms and cortical speech processes. In order to judge the validity of information obtained in physiological studies in animal models it is important to find ways of testing the models, i.e. conditions where identical or similar observations and experiments can be made both in man and animals. This problem can be approached by studying such unconditioned acoustic reflexes as can be observed under closely similar conditions both in humans and animals. It is thereby assumed that the reflex has basic features in common with signal processing in general, at least at peripheral level. In addition, the acoustic reflexes are interesting since they form complete sensory-motor systems and offer possibilities to study both coding and decoding aspects of auditory signal processing.

Two types of acoustic reflexes have been widely studied in humans, the stapedius reflex and the acoustic-autonomic (arousal) reflexes. The stapedius reflex relates in a fairly simple way to the variations in sound level of the speech signal (1) whereas in the autonomic reflexes a more complex signal processing takes place (e.g. 2).

The aim of the present study is to illustrate how an acoustic-autonomic reflex reacts to variations in sound level and, particularly, to show that it can reveal features of temporal and intensity resolution, properties of relevance for speech discrimination.

MATERIALS AND METHODS

The experiments were performed on albino Sprague-Dawley rats. The experimental design is schematically shown in Fig. 1. The rats were acclimatized to a wire-

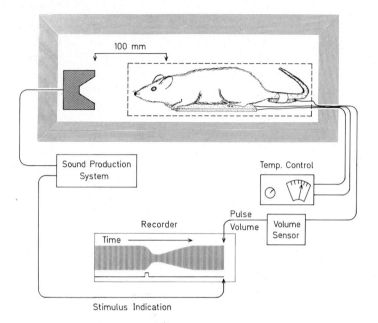

Fig. 1. Experimental set-up for study of tail artery response to sound. The rat rests on a temperature-regulated pad in a wiremesh cage. A short sound burst from the speaker, 10 cm in front of the rat´s head, elicits a vasoconstriction evident as a decline in amplitude of pulse volume recorded from the tail of the animal. (Reproduced from Borg, 1981: Acta Otolaryngol Suppl 381)

mesh tubing in which they were slightly warmed in order to induce vasodilatation in the tail (3). Temperature is a very critical factor and overheating can totally block the response. A sound signal elicited a vasoconstriction, the size of which was quantified by the duration.

The acoustic stimulus used in these series of experiments was a broadband noise with controlled duration, rise time, and amplitude. The spectrum of the noise was assessed with a Brüel & Kjaer 4135 microphone placed in the inter-aural plane of the rat and connected to a Brüel & Kjaer 2607 measuring ampli-fier: maximal level was in the frequency range 5 - 15 kHz.

The significance of several parameters of the noise stimulus have been inves-tigated, but attention will be given here to the effects of pauses in the noise, rise time, and stepwise increases of its sound level (4 - 7).

RESULTS

Pauses of different duration. A constant wide band noise at 80 dB SPL produces
a long duration vasoconstriction which, however, habituates slowly. After approximately one hour the vasoconstriction has habituated and volume pulsations
have returned to pre-stimulus amplitude despite ongoing sound. An interruption
of the noise will cause a renewed vasoconstriction. If the pause is long a small
vasoconstriction will usually be observed at the end of the sound (an off-set
response at the beginning of the pause) with a more marked reaction at the
reinsertion of the noise, but if the pause is short (less than about 1 sec),
only one vasoconstriction will be observed. Whether this single reaction is
initiated by the start or end of the pause cannot be resolved. Fig. 2 A shows
pulsations before, during, and after introduction of a 0.1 sec pause in the
ongoing sound. A decrease of pulse amplitude with a duration of nearly one
minute is observed.

Fig. 2 B shows the duration of the vasoconstriction as a function of pause
duration. It can be seen that even a pause of 5 ms results in a significant
vasoconstriction.

Pauses in 80 dB SPL noise

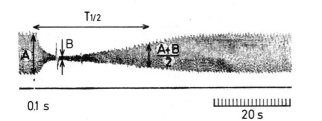

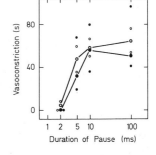

Fig. 2 A   Fig. 2 B

Fig. 2 A. Recordings of arterial pulsations obtained by a non-invasive technique from the tail of a non-anaesthetized rat. Decline of pulse amplitude is
elicited by pauses in 80 dB SPL prolonged noise. 0.1 s pause.
(Reproduced from Borg, 1978: Acta Otolaryngol 86:155-159)

B. Duration of vasoconstriction as a function of duration of pause in
prolonged 80 dB SPL noise. Experiment 2: 2 ms to 100 ms pauses. Median ± 25 % (●)
and mean ± S.E.M. (o) of all responses. Measurements on 10 rats.
(Reproduced from Borg, 1978: Acta Otolaryngol 86:155-159)

Rise time. A four second burst of noise at 80 dB SPL was used in this series of experiments and the rise and fall times were varied between 1 ms and one second. Fig. 3 shows the duration of vasoconstriction as a function of rise time. It is seen that rise time of 10 and 100 ms produced the same duration of response whereas a 1 sec rise time gave in most cases a clearly smaller response.

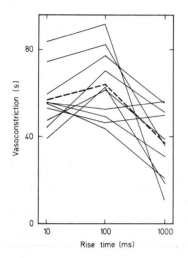

Fig. 3. Duration of vasoconstriction as a function of rise time (10, 100, and 1000 ms) of a 4 s burst of 80 dB SPL noise, Each thin continuous line represent one animal in which up to 5 determinations at each rise time were obtained. Heavy broken line shows the mean values. (Reproduced from Borg, 1978: Acta Otolaryngol 85:332-335)

Step changes of sound level. The burst of one sec duration gives rise to a vasoconstriction with approximately linearly increasing duration. It was thought that this intensity dependence might be determined by one of two factors: a sensitivity to the size of the intensity change, or a sensitivity to the attained level as such. Correspondingly, a series of studies was performed where step size and steady state level were changed independently. The vasoconstriction was allowed to habituate to an ongoing noise; thereafter a new noise level was introduced and the ensuing reaction was observed.

It was found (Fig. 4 A) that the duration of the vasoconstriction was the same for all sizes of intensity changes (from 10 to 50 dB) as long as the final level reached was the same (80 dB SPL). However, the vasoconstriction duration was larger for the 10 dB step from 70 to 80 dB SPL and it was for the 10 dB step between 30 and 40 or between 50 and 60 dB SPL (Fig. 4 B).

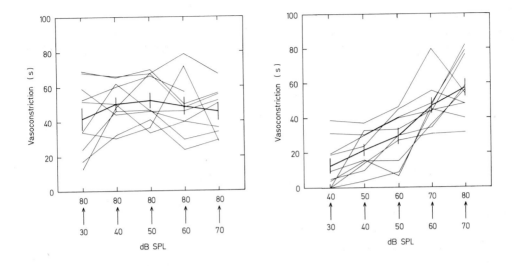

Fig. 4 A

Fig. 4 B

Fig. 4 A. Duration of vasoconstriction elicited by bursts superimposed on a variable background. The level of the background and the incremental stimulus were varied in such a way that the total level always reached 80 dB SPL (10 animals - thin lines; average - heavy line, ± S.E.).
(Reproduced from Borg, 1980: Brain Res 188:43-51)

   B. Duration of vasoconstrictions elicited by a 10 dB increase in noise level as a function of total level (10 animals - thin lines; average - heavy line, ± S.E.).
(Reproduced from Borg, 1980: Brain Res 188:43-51)

In summary, the acoustic-autonomic reflex of the vessels in the tail of the rat is differentially sensitive to several features of temporal variations in the acoustic stimulus.

DISCUSSION
The presentation of these results at this symposium has been motivated by two reasons. First of all, an acoustic-autonomic reflex system, a vasoconstriction, can be studied in humans as well as in animals, thereby establishing a link between animal experiments and human studies. Secondly, it can be assumed that some basic features of information processing are common in speech signal analyses and simpler reflex systems, particularly those of the peripheral auditory system.

In man, a similar acoustic-autonomic reflex can be recorded, e.g. as volume pulsations of the fingers. Vasoconstriction in human fingers have been found also to depend on changes on frequency and level of the stimulus sound (2). No direct comparable data are as yet available, but can in principle be easily aquired.

These results represent a pilot study of this model and the incorporated stimuli have not been specifically chosen for their relevance to the processing of speechlike sound. The particular accomplishment of this method is in exemplifying that an acoustic-autonomic reflex system can detect a variety of changes in an acoustic signal. Some observations may have relevance for the problem of the speech analyses as such, e.g. the reaction to very short pauses. There is a quantitative agreement between our present results and psychophysical determinations of the ability to detect temporal gaps.

In conclusion, the results obtained show that an acoustic-autonomic reflex system can extract different features of an acoustic stimulus. Therefore it can be suggested to be profitable to further investigate speechlike sound in acoustic-autonomic reflex systems both in animals and humans in order to test the validity of animal models for physiological analysis of speech processing.

ACKNOWLEDGEMENTS

This study was supported by grants from Swedish Work Environment Fund (74/24 and 77/49).

REFERENCES

1. Borg, E. and Zakrisson, J-E. (1973) Stapedius reflex and speech features. J Acoust Soc Am 54, 525-527.

2. Jansen, G. (1974) Studies on psychophysiological effect of noises with different significance. Soz Praeventivmed 19, 209.

3. Borg, E. (1977) Tail artery response to sound in the unanesthetized rat. Acta Physiol Scand 100, 129-138.

4. Borg, E. (1978) Peripheral vasoconstriction in the rat in response to sound. I. Dependence on stimulus duration. Acta Otolaryngol 85, 153-157.

5. Borg, E. (1978) Peripheral vasoconstriction in the rat in response to sound. II. Dependence on rate of change of sound level. Acta Otolaryngol 85, 332-335.

6. Borg, E. (1978) Peripheral vasoconstriction in the rat in response to sound. III. Dependence on pause characteristics in continuous noise. Acta Otolaryngol 86, 155-159.

7. Borg, E. (1980) Processing of intensity-correlated information in an acoustic-autonomic reflex system. Brain Res 188, 43-51.

© 1982 Elsevier Biomedical Press
The Representation of Speech in the Peripheral
Auditory System, R. Carlson and B. Granström eds.

REPRESENTATION OF AUDITORY INFORMATION BASED ON A FUNCTIONALISTIC PERSPECTIVE

JERKER RÖNNBERG AND LARS-GÖRAN NILSSON
Department of Psychology, University of Umeå, Sweden

There is a superior short-term memory performance of auditorily as opposed to
visually presented information. This empirical phenomenon, which is referred
to as the modality effect, holds across a wide variety of experimental paradigms. The theoretical interpretations offered to explain this phenomenon are
of two types.

According to one of these views there are modality-specific short-term memory stores differing in capacity (1). The capacity of the auditory store is
assumed to be larger than that of the visual store. This difference in capacity between the hypothetical modality-specific stores is assumed to be responsible for the difference in short-term memory performance.

A contrast to this "two-store" interpretation of the modality effect is the
"one-store" view, which assumes a single short-term store being acoustic-
auditory in nature and therefore this store is more apt for auditory than for
visual presentation (2). In the case of visual presentation there has to be
a translation of the items to an acoustic-auditory form. This translation is
seen as reducing the processing capacity of the short-term store.

There is a considerable amount of data supporting each of these two views.
As of yet, however, there are no data presented, which have been decisive as
to which of these two views should be preferred. It appears that the experiments designed to test these views cover separate aspects of the modality
effect with no or little overlap in common contentions to be tested.

In addition to this diverging state of affairs between the two views presented there are two more aspects of these notions which, in retrospect, seem
to warrant a theoretical reorientation for interpreting the modality effect.
In line with traditional research in the field these two views (a) focus the
explanation on the hypothetical memory entity per se, and (b) fail to take
into account a proper analysis of the stimulus or the information presented.

The approach to be proposed here differs from traditional conceptions in
the field in the sense that no particular memory entity is assumed and that
an analysis of the stimulus is always undertaken. More particularily, memory
or remembering is seen as an interaction between available cognitive capabilities and particular demands at hand in any given situation. From the point
of view of this conceptual framework there are somewhat different questions

to be approached. Since situational demands are assumed to play a crucial role in remembering, the first question to be asked is whether the auditory superiority could be reduced or even eliminated if these situational demands were arranged accordingly. The point of departure was an assumption that the modality effect might be an effect of the compatibility between the temporal nature of the presentation of the words to be remembered in this type of experiment and the temporal character of the auditory system. For the visual system, on the other hand, there is no similar compatibility since this system is spatial in nature or possibly spatio-temporal (3).

Thus, if the nature of the presentation could be changed such that the temporal order between words would not be that important, one should expect a reduction or perhaps even an elimination of the auditory superiority. This was also found to be the case in a series of such experiments (4). Actually, the method used in these experiments was to have the visual system favored to the same extent as the auditory system had been favored in the usual modality experiment. This was accomplished by having the subjects to encode the words presented according to an ortographic-structural task. When doing this the auditory supremacy was not only eliminated; there was even a visual superiority demonstrated (4). This result is possible to explain from the point of view of the theoretical notion proposed here, since a stimulus analysis carried out revealed different situational demands between a regular temporal presentation and the type of presentation employed by Nilsson (4). This difference in its turn implies, according to the theoretical notion prosed, that different sets of cognitive capabilities are used in the two situations. None of the existing theories of the modality effect could explain the visual supeiority in the experiments described.

Along the same line of thinking, Rönnberg and Ohlsson (5) demonstrated that auditorily presented TBR (to-be-remembered) items were distracted to a larger extent by an auditory distraction activity than visual TBR items were by a visual distractor of the same sort. This finding also runs counter to the two traditional conceptions of the modality effect, since it is, on logical grounds, hard to reconcile the superior auditory short-term capacity with a negative correlation to recall performance.

In the work by Nilsson and **colleagues** (5), (6), (7), (8) short-term performance has been evaluated under various conditions by means of mixed-modality lists (where auditorily and visually presented items occur in random fashion in the same list) and single-modality lists. The key difference between these two presentation methods is that predictability is low with respect to presentation modality in the former case. The basic finding from these studies is that low predictability of presentation mode, provokes a larger superiority for the auditory presentation mode whereas high predictability decreases the modality effect. Data from other paradigms investigating the modality effect can also be capured by this predictability dimension (9).

In the same vein, Rönnberg (10), (11) has further investigated the task demand of predictability for auditorily presented lists in a series of experiments. For instance, it can be demonstrated that both recency (short-term) and prerecency (long-term) portions of the serial portion curve benefit from manipulations of interitem intervals.

Recency items should, according to traditional encoding, storage and retrieval models, be unaffected by presentation rate. However, it has been clearly demonstrated in all studies that both a successive "speeding up" or "slowing down" of presentation rate can boost recall for recency items. Regarding prerecency items, traditional models predict enhanced performance with a slow presentation rate. Even in this case, it can be demonstrated that with a fast beginning of list presentation, recall for prerecency items is facilitated. Hence, it can be concluded that by presenting stimuli of a more dynamic character than more traditional static presentations, the subsequent theoretical formulations need to move from static capacity notions to a functional reorientation.

The experiments reported so far have been designed to emphasize manipulations of situational demands with the intention of making conclusions accordingly about the cognitive capabilities employed. The experiment to be reported now was carried out from a different perspective. The intention was to have subjects with supposedly different sets of cognitive capabilities available. The subjects participating in this experiment were persons with severe hearing handicaps and normally hearing subjects. Both groups of subjects were given a visual presentation of common words and were instructed to recall these immediately after the presentation of the words.

The prediction was that the hard of hearing subjects would have developed compensatory cognitive capabilities after having acquired their hearing handicap. The contention was that these capabilities would be more potent for the hearing handicap people than for the normally hearing people. The results obtained in this experiment (12) were exactly those predicted. That is, hearing handicapped subjects showed a superior short-term memory performance as compared to the performance of the normally hearing subjects. This difference in performance, indicating compensatory cognitive capabilities for hearing handicapped subjects, appeared in the recency portion of the serial position curve which is exactly where the auditory superiority appears in regular modality experiments.

Finally, the issue of peripheral versus central processing is to be discussed in terms of the model for modality effects proposed by Rönnberg and Ohlsson (5). In short, this model postulates that each automatic information processing capability (e.g. the auditory and visual systems) can be characterized by a processing distribution dimension (for a complete description of the model, see Rönnberg and Ohlsson (5)), which operates on a semantic-modality specific (central-peripheral) continuum. According to this model, processing of information can be distributed over different levels of analysis and processing occurs simultaneously at all levels in the system. However, capabilities vary with respect to their mean depth of processing, summed across tasks. The auditory system is assumed to have a more superficial mean depth on this continuum than the visual system. Further, the typical range of processing, at different levels, is larger for the visual than for the auditory system. Hence each capability can be characterized by a distribution of processing levels, and capabilities differ in terms of mean and variance for these distributions.

Independent evidence support this theorizing. Shallice (13) has cited clinical data on STM patients which support the view that the audio-verbal STM is a store that can be used for retaining superficial phonological structures, so that possible "backtracking" and reconstruction of a message becomes possible. Gardiner and Gregg (14) has shown that the "negative recency" effect obtained in final free recall only holds for auditory stimuli, but not for visual stimuli. Negative recency refers to the fact that recency items that were recalled with higher probability in immediate recall than prerecency items, drop in probability for recall to a level lower than prerecency items. The inference made is thus that these recency items are more superficially encoded and therefore less resistant to forgetting and therefore visual items are coded to a more deep semantic level. Engle (15) has demonstrated visual superiority for the first two prerecency items in a list and Engle and Mobley (16) have argued that this result indicates that auditory processing is more superficial than visual processing. Nelson, Brooks and Borden (17) have demonstrated that when visual and phonemic similarity was orthogonally combined with aural and visual presented modes, sensory interference occured with both types of similiarity for visual lists, but only for phonemic similarity with auditory lists. This result is interpreted as support for the idea that the visual system has a larger variance in its processing distribution. In conjunction with the other data cited, it is reasonable to conclude that mean and variance on the postulated continuum has psychological reality and that the auditory and visual systems differ in term of these parameters.

Given the validity of the processing distribution dimension we are now in the position to specify its interaction with task demands. One task demand of central importance to memory research is the question of short-term and long-term retention tasks. A vast amount of data demonstrate than semantic features dominate encoding and retrieval processes for long-term retention and acoustic features for short-term retention (e.g. (18)). In this context, the auditory and visual systems interact with time of test. The more superficial auditory system is beneficial to short-term retention while the visual system benefits long-term retention.

As a further specification, Rönnberg and Ohlsson (5) assume an overall capacity limit for the memory system as a whole. This overall capacity can be utilized in different ways, depending on the particular task demands. This utilization is then expressed as the extent to which extra processing in the system is allocated to different levels, i.e. processing can be allocated to a superficial level or to a semantic level. As was demonstrated by Rönnberg and Ohlsson (5), a modality specific distractor causes allocation of processing to a superficial level, hence leaving less room for a semantic analysis. Since a larger number of auditory items are held in a modality specific state, compared to visual items the auditory system will also be more susceptible to auditory distraction. This allocation process can also be magnified by using supraspan lists.

In conclusion, it can be stated that the problem of central-peripheral processing can only partially be solved by stating that the auditory system has more peripheral properties than the visual system. Compatibilities with task properties must be accounted for and further conceptualized to reach a fuller understanding of remembering and presentation modality.

REFERENCES
1. Murdock, B.B., Jr. and Walker, K.D. (1969) J. Verbal Learning and Verbal Behavior, 8, pp. 679-83.
2. Craik, F.I.M. (1969) J. Verbal Learning and Verbal Behavior, 8, pp. 658-64.
3. Kirman, J.H. (1973) Psychological Bulletin, 80, pp. 54-74.
4. Nilsson, L.-G. (1979) Scandinavian J. Psychology, 20, pp. 259-65.
5. Rönnberg, J. and Ohlsson, K. (1980) Acta Psychologica, 44, 253-67.

78

6. Ohlsson, K. and Rönnberg, J. (1982) Umeå Psychological Reports, No. 159, Department of Psychology, University of Umeå, Sweden.

7. Nilsson, L.-G., Ohlsson, K. and Rönnberg, J. (1977) in: Dornič, S. (Ed.), Attention and Performance VI, Lawrence Erlbaum Ass., Hillsdale, New Jersey, pp. 629-45.

8. Nilsson, L.-G., Ohlsson, K. and Rönnberg, J. (1980) Acta Psychologica, 44, pp. 41-50.

9. Rönnberg, J. (1980b) Conceptions of remembering as task-skill interactions. Doctoral dissertation at Uppsala University, Sweden.

10. Rönnberg, J. (1980a) Scandinavian J. Psychology, 21, pp. 83-95.

11. Rönnberg, J. (1981) Scandinavian J. Psychology, 22, pp. 189-95.

12. Rönnberg, J. (1981) Umeå Psychological Reports, No. 157, Department of Psychology, University of Umeå, Sweden.

13. Shallice, T. (1979) in: Nilsson, L.-G. (Ed.), Perspectives on memory research, Lawrence Erlbaum Ass., Hillsdale, New Jersey, pp. 257-77.

14. Gardiner, J.M. and Gregg, V.H. (1979) When auditory memory is not over-written (Manuscript). Dep. of Social Sciences and Humanities, The City University, London, England.

15. Engle, R.W. (1974) J. Experimental Psychology, 107, pp. 824-29.

16. Engle, R.W. and Mobley, L. (1976) J. Verbal Learning and Verbal Behavior, 15, 519-27.

17. Nelson, D.L., Brooks, D.H. and Borden, R.C. (1974) J. Experimental Psychology, 103, pp. 91-96.

18. Murdock, B.B., Jr. (1974) Human Memory: Theory and Data, Lawrence Erlbaum Ass., Potomac, Maryland.

© 1982 Elsevier Biomedical Press
The Representation of Speech in the Peripheral
Auditory System, R. Carlson and B. Granström eds.

AUDITORY MASKING PHENOMENA IN THE PERCEPTION OF SPEECH

MANFRED R. SCHROEDER   AND SÖNKE MEHRGARDT
 Drittes Physikalisches Institut, Universität Göttingen, Bürgerstrasse 42-44,
 D-3400 Göttingen (Federal Republic of Germany)

ABSTRACT
  New results on auditory masking in the time domain, relevant to speech
perception, are presented. These results suggest the existence of (short)
"time windows" during which the ear can perceive tones which would be below
masked threshold on the basis of frequency-domain models of masking.

SPEECH QUALITY AND MONAURAL PHASE
  In the 1950s, when I (MRS) first became interested in speech synthesis, I was
almost immediately intrigued by the problems of subjective quality of synthetic
speech. Vocoders had a reedy, electronic "accent" and I thought that the
excitation waveform, consisting of sharp pulses, was perhaps to blame. To investigate this question more deeply, I built a generator for 31 coherent harmonics of variable fundamental frequency. The phase of each harmonic could be
chosen to be either 0 or π - a total of 2^{30} = 1,073,741,824 different waveforms,
each of which appeared to have its own intrinsic timbre - their identical power
spectra notwithstanding. (I wish Seebeck, Ohm and Helmholtz had had a chance to
listen to these stimuli!)
  For all phase angles set equal to 0, one obtains a periodic cosine-pulse, as
shown in Figure 1. When used as an excitation signal for a speech syntheziser,
the result is the reedy quality already mentioned. By contrast, if one ran-
domizes the phase angles, one gets a less peaky waveform and a mellower sound
[1]. A better-than-random choice for the phase angles is given by the formula

$$\varphi_n = \pi n^2/N \quad ,$$

where n is the harmonic number and N the total number of harmonics in the flat-
spectrum stimulus [2]. A more general formula, for arbitrary spectra, is given
in Ref. 2.
  The corresponding waveform, having a three times smaller "peakfactor", is
shown in Fig. 2 (drawn to the same scale as Fig. 1).
  The great variety of timbres producible by phase manipulations alone
suggested to me that it might be possible to produce (marginally) intelligible
voiced speech from stimuli having flat (or otherwise fixed) line spectra.

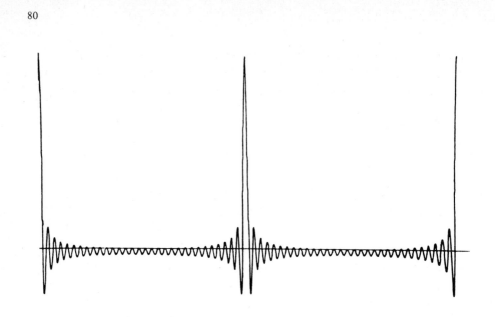

Fig. 1. Periodic waveform, consisting of 31 harmonics in zero phase, typical of excitation waveform in speech synthesizers.

Fig. 2. Waveform with same power spectrum as in Fig. 1 but phase-angles 0 or π selected to minimize the peak factor. Speech synthesizers excited with this waveform sound softer and do not need a voiced-unvoiced detector. (See Ref. 2 for phase-angle formula.)

However, this hypothesis remains as yet untested.

In playing around with my "phase organ", I discovered - by serendipity as it were - a number of noteworthy auditory phenomena. For example, if I changed the phase of only one frequency component from 0 to π, so that the phase spectrum looked like

$$0, 0, ..., 0, \pi, 0, ..., 0 \quad ,$$

I heard a tone whose pitch corresponded *nearly* (but not precisely) to the frequency whose phase had been inverted. Of course, on an oscilloscope one could *see* the inverted frequency component between the periodic spikes - but the ear cannot see and, in any case, any hair cell in the inner ear is stimulated by only a portion (a critical band) of the total spectrum.

Numerous other monaural phase percepts could be produced by the harmonic generator, such as "edge tones", when all phases up to (or beginning with) a selected component were inverted. In fact, I succeeded in producing little melodies by sheer phase manipulations ("Mary had a little lamp ...").

Some monaural phase effects can be explained by the concept of an "inner spectrum" - the spectrum available to the hair cells in the inner ear, i.e. the spectrum of the stimulus applied to the outer ear as modified by nonlinear distortion in the middle and inner ears [3]. It is known that identical external power spectra can lead to substantially different inner spectra for different phase angles. However, the results reported here are not so explainable; rather they point to the existence of short *time windows* during which the ear can perform a waveform analysis.

Time Windows

Let us consider a tone complex with a speechlike power spectrum (up to about 6 kHz), fundamental frequencies between 30 Hz and 300 Hz (submultiples of 1200 Hz) and a duration of 300 msec. The phase angles of the individual harmonics have either constant phase or "random" phase. These are our maskers. The signal is a pure tone (a sinewave) at 1200 Hz. The absolute detection threshold is determined in a 3-alternative-forced-choice (3AFC) experiment.(Duifhuis [4,5] published measurements using a different paradigm, but only on zero-phase stimuli.) Figure 3 shows the masked thresholds as a function of the fundamental frequency of the masking complex for "random" phases (●) and zero phases (o). For random phases the threshold rises with decreasing fundamental frequency as more and more masking components fall into the critical band around the signal frequency. By contrast, for the zero-phase masker, the threshold *decreases* for fundamental frequencies below 200 Hz. The discrepancy between these measurements

82

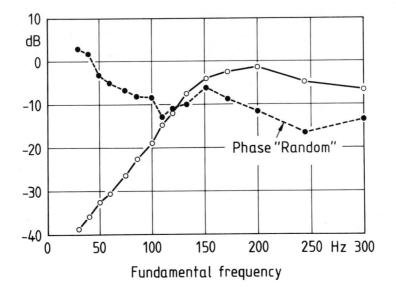

Fig. 3. Threshold of a test tone (1200 Hz), masked by a harmonic complex.
Amplitudes of harmonics according to 1/f, Phases constant (o) or "random" (●).
Fundamental frequencies are chosen to be submultiples of 1200 Hz.

and critical-band theory exceeds 40 dB (!) at 30 Hz. The reason, we believe, is
that the zero-phase masker exhibits a "silent" time interval in its waveform in
which the ear can perceive even a weak signal - just as the eye can see a single
frequency component in a zero-phase (pulse-like) background waveform.

To illustrate this point, consider Fig. 4a showing a waveform consisting of
many (31) harmonics with equal phases. In Fig. 4b the same signal is shown
with the seventh harmonic doubled in amplitude; it is clearly visible (and
audible).

By contrast, Fig. 5a shows a waveform with the same power spectrum as the
signal in Fig. 4a but "random" phases. If the seventh harmonic of *this* waveform
is now doubled, see Fig. 4b, it is not visible (and not audible).

Of course, the receptor (hair) cells in the inner ear are not supplied with
the full-band waveform, but rather only with bandfiltered versions (critical
bands around their "best frequencies"). However, what we said about full bands
is still true for critical bands: they, too, can exhibit time windows - albeit

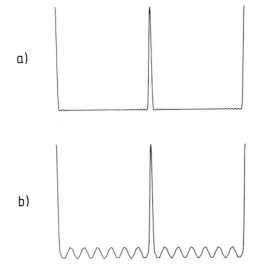

Fig. 4. a) Waveform consisting of 31 harmonics with Hamming-weighted amplitudes and zero phases.

b) Same signal as a), but amplitude of seventh harmonic doubled. The added sinusoidal component can easily be seen (and heard).

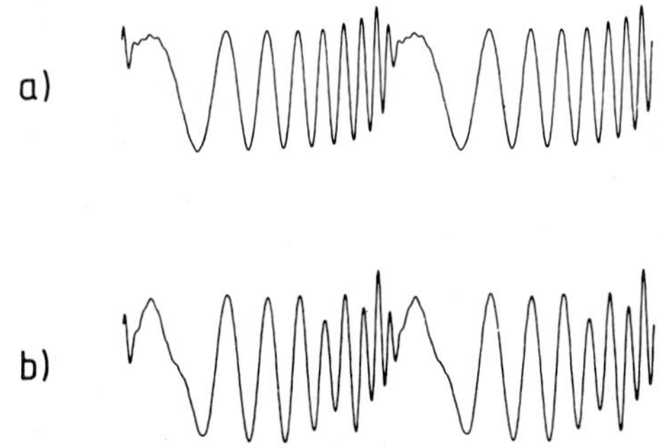

a)

b)

Fig. 5. Waveforms of signals with same power spectra as in Fig. 4, but with "random" phases. The added component in b) is not readily visible (and cannot be heard).

usually not as well defined. Figure 6 illustrates this important point, showing waveforms one third-octave (roughly a critical band) wide. In Fig. 6a, for a fundamental frequency of 80 Hz, there are short "pauses" between successive pulses. For a fundamental frequency of 40 Hz, Fig. 6b, the pause is more than twice as long and it seems reasonable that a pure tone of, say 1200 or 1500 Hz is more easily detectable at 40 Hz fundamental than at 80 Hz. (In fact, cf. Fig. 3, the threshold at 40 Hz is more than 12 dB lower than at 80 Hz.)

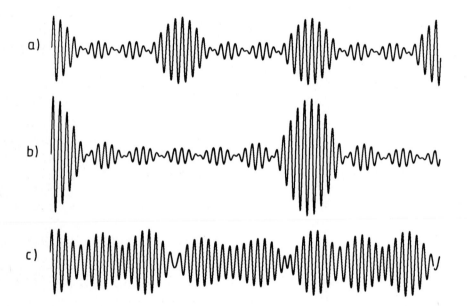

Fig. 6. Third-octave filtered complex of harmonics with equal amplitudes. Bandpass centered at 1500 Hz.
a) Fundamental frequency 80 Hz, zero phase
b) Fundamental frequency 40 Hz, zero phase
c) Fundamental frequency 40 Hz, "random" phase.

By contrast, if the harmonics falling into the critical band have "random" phase angles, Fig. 6c, the waveform has no pause, i.e., there is no "time window" for a tone to be detected. And, indeed, cf. Fig. 3, the detection threshold (●) is 37 dB higher than for the constant-phase masker (o).

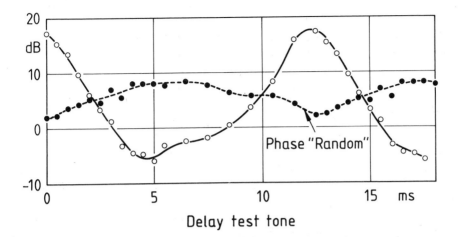

Fig. 7. Threshold of a test tone burst (1200 Hz, 5 msec) as function of the test tone delay. Masker as described in Fig. 3, fundamental frequency 80 Hz. Phases of harmonics are constant (o) or random (●).

The time-window phenomena in masked thresholds is further illustrated by Fig. 7 showing the masked threshold of a short test-tone burst (1600 Hz, 5 ms) as a function of its position within the fundamental period (12.5 ms) of the masker. For the constant-phase masker, the threshold fluctuates by 23 dB. By contrast, for the random-phase masker, which exhibits no time window (see Fig. 6c), the threshold remains within a 6-dB range.

Another impressive demonstration of the time-window effect is illustrated in Fig. 8. The signal is a 800-Hz tone and the masker a highpass-filtered harmonic complex. When the masker spectrum begins at the harmonic coinciding with the test-tone, the masked threshold is a maximum (-8 dB). As expected, with increasing cut-off frequency of the masker, i.e. fewer masker harmonics, the threshold drops precipitously (to -28 dB) when the lowest-order harmonic is the 24th harmonic.

But, surprisingly, as more masking harmonics are added *below* the test-tone frequency, the threshold *also* drops - in fact, it drops to -33 dB when the lowest-order harmonic of the masker is the first harmonic (i.e., for the full-band masker). Thus, the masked threshold is *lowered* by 25 dB as the masker level is *increased* by more than 15 dB.

The reason for this astounding effect is, of course, again that the addition of more and more lower harmonics (at constant phase!) produces a "cleaner" time window in which the test tone can be detected.

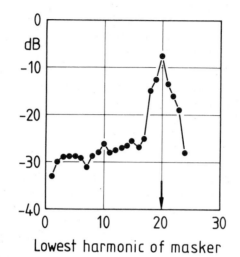

Fig. 8. Threshold of an 800-Hz tone masked by a highpass harmonic complex as function of the cut-off frequency. Fundamental frequency 40 Hz, harmonics have constant phases. The arrow marks the position of the test tone.

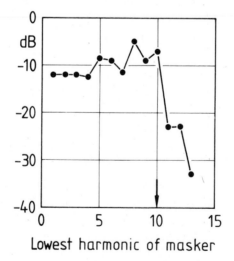

Fig. 9. Same as Fig. 8, but with "random" phases of the masking harmonics.

How important it is that the added lower harmonics have constant phase, is
illustrated by Fig. 9 in which the phase angles of the masker are random: for
the random-phase masker the threshold stays near -10 dB, instead of dropping
by 25 dB as in Fig. 8.

CONCLUSION

Results of masking experiments are described that are not consistent with the
predictions of critical-band masking theory. Rather, these results suggest the
existence of short time windows for periodic, constant-phase maskers during
which the ear can perform a waveform analysis.

As a result of this postulated detection mechanism, the masked thresholds for
constant (or smooth) phase maskers lie up to 40 dB (cf. Fig. 3) below those for
random phase maskers (for which no such time window exists). Since speech signals have more nearly constant or smooth phases (rather than random phases),
the results reported here are believed to be relevant to the perception of
speech signals - both natural and synthetic.

REFERENCES

1. Schroeder, M.R. (1959) New Results Concerning Monaural Phase Sensitivity,
   J. Acoust. Soc. Amer. 31, 1579(A).

2. Schroeder, M.R. (1970) Synthesis of Low-Peak-Factor Signals and Binary
   Sequences With Low Autocorrelation, IEEE Transactions on Information Theory,
   Vol. IT-16, No. 1, January 1970.

3. Schroeder, M.R. (1975) Models of Hearing, IEEE Proc., Vol. 63, No. 9, 1975.

4. Duifhuis, H. (1970) Audibility of high harmonics in a periodic pulse,
   J. Acoust. Soc. Amer. 48, 888.

5. Duifhuis, H. (1971) Audibility of high harmonics in a periodic pulse.
   II. Time Effect, J. Acoust. Soc. Amer. 49, 1155.

6. Mehrgardt, S. (1982) Kanteneffekte der Mithörschwelle bei Hochpaß- und
   Tiefpaß-Maskierern aus harmonischen Tonkomplexen. To be published in:
   Fortschritte der Akustik - FASE/DAGA '82.

7. Mehrgardt, S. (1982) Zur Mithörschwelle bei Maskierern aus harmonischen
   Tonkomplexen: Zeiteffekte. To be published in: Fortschritte der Akustik -
   FASE/DAGA '82.

© 1982 Elsevier Biomedical Press
The Representation of Speech in the Peripheral
Auditory System, R. Carlson and B. Granström eds.

HOW DOES THE PERIPHERAL AUDITORY SYSTEM REPRESENT FORMANT TRANSITIONS?
A PSYCHOPHYSICAL APPROACH

FRANCISCO LACERDA[1] and HENRIQUE ONOFRE MOREIRA[2]
[1]Centro de Linguistica da Universidade de Lisboa (INIC), Av.5 Out., 85-6,
1000 Lisboa(Portugal) and [2]Centro de Analise e Processamento de Sinais,
Complexo Interdisciplinar (INIC), Av.Rovisco Pais, 1000 Lisboa (Portugal)

INTRODUCTION

As it is well known from psychoacoustic experiments using stationary stimuli, lateral suppression occurs if two tones of adequate frequencies and intensities are presented simultaneously to the auditory system. Another well known psychoacoustic phenomenon is the forward masking effect which means that, after having stimulated a given frequency channel of the auditory system, the excitation level does not immediately drop to zero when the physical stimulus is turned off.

If the auditory system is taken as a bank of filters and scanned by a frequency sweep, then, due to the forward masking effect, the output of each scanned filter will show some residual excitation after having been excited by the sweep stimulus. Assuming that the sweep rate is fast enough to reach a channel´s suppression area before its residual excitation fades out, it can be expected that lateral suppression will act on the residual excitation still present in previuosly stimulated channels.

This paper reports a psychoacoustic experiment designed to study the experimental question of a possible interaction between the residual excitation produced by the sweep in the scanned channels and its subsequent suppression as the sweep moves onwards in the frequency domain. In other words, the hypothesis to be examined states that:

The residual excitation evoked by the sweep in a given frequency channel can be reduced if the sweep excites the suppression area of that channel before the forward masking effect fades out.

If this hypothesis is true, the interaction should be observed above a certain critical sweep rate. For low sweep rates the effect of the excitation of the suppression areas should not be observed because the residual excitation fades long before "suppression" can take place. However, if the sweep rate is high enough a sharpening effect can be expected in the auditory representation of the sweeps. This sharpening can hopefully be related to the auditory-nerve fiber or cochlear nucleus responses to sweep tones of high sweep rates where it was found that the higher the sweep rate, the higher and more localized the discharge pattern (1,2).

From a speech perception point of view this kind of sharpening effect can probably be observed in the auditory representation of formant transitions at relatively high speech rates. A second formant transition like the one in "we", where F_2 sweeps from about .6kHz to 2.2kHz in a time interval of about 100ms, is likely to be fast enough (16kHz/s) for the interaction to be observed. Carrying the speculation a little further, the hypothesis can be used to explain the effect of perceptual extrapolation (3,4,5) observed in vowel identification experiments. The perceptual overshoot effect can be enhanced if suppression acts on all the residual excitation evoked by the transition except on that of its final region.

METHODS

A psychoacoustic adjustment technique was used to measure the masking patterns generated by frequency sweeps. The stimuli, simulating single formant transitions, were generated in an analog manner by a sinusoidal sweep frequency generator.

All the sweeps used in this experiment had a standard duration of 100ms and a standard intensity of 60dBspl. Therefore, from now on, the complete specification of these sweeps will be made by simply reporting the onset and offset frequencies along with the shape of the sweep function (either linear or exponential).

To obtain the masking pattern evoked by the formant transition, the masking thresholds, L_T, of a 20ms probe tone were measured for a number of different probe locations. A probe location was defined by the coordinates (T_D,F_p) of its center of gravity (see fig.1), where T_D is the time delay measured from the sweep onset to the midpoint of the probe and F_p is the frequency of the pure tone from which the probe was drawn. The masking thresholds, L_T, were a function of the probe location and were obtained by an adjustment procedure. To minimize biasing effects the maximum level of the probe tone was varied randomly by the experimenter, between consecutive observations. The subjects were forced, by this means, to adjust the potentiometer with different number of turns in order to achieve the same perceptual effect.

The sweep tones were presented in pairs. The first element was a reference sweep, (no probe tone) and the second element, presented 0.5s afterwards, was the same sweep together with the probe tone. A 4s break separated consecutive sweep pairs. Each experimental session took about 20minutes, after which the subjects were allowed to rest for about half an hour.

The subjects for these experiments were requested to listen to just the probe tone in a preliminary session. The detection threshold of the probe tone was then determined and in two cases the subjects did not participate in the formal experiments because their detection thresholds were too high. For all the other subjects the detection thresholds were within a 5dB range across subjects. After this first selection procedure the subjects were trained to detect the probe masked by the sweep. The training period

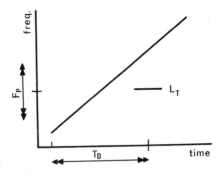

Fig.1- Coordinate system for probe location. L_T is a probe level, measured along a third axis.

lasted until they could produce reliable results (errors of no more than 5dB). If the candidates did not improve the consistency of their results, they were asked not to participate in the formal test.

As a result of this procedure, six subjects were selected and participated in the experiment.

Experimental conditions

Only three typical experimental conditions will be reported in this paper:

SWEEP	ONSET	OFFSET
Linear	0.4kHz	2.0kHz
Linear	1.8kHz	0.2kHz
Exp.(+)	0.2kHz	2.0kHz

RESULTS

Figures 2 through 4 show the masking thresholds (refered to 20uPa) of the probe tone for a number of selected frequency channels and experimental conditions. A lot of additional data points were obtained but they simply confirm the patterns shown here and were therefore not plotted.

Figure 2 shows the probe thresholds versus time that were obtained for the linear rising sweep, from .4kHz to 2.0kHz, having a sweep rate of 16kHz/s. The data points correspond to the 1.0kHz channel.

It should be noted the "dip" obtained for the 50ms delay. This kind of pattern can be taken as an indication that lateral suppression is acting upon the residual excitation evoked by the sweep when it excited the 1kHz channel.

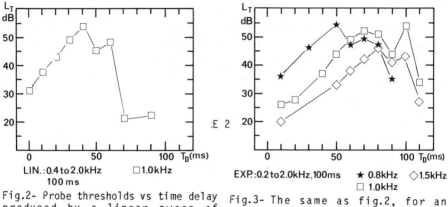

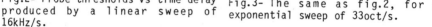

Fig.2- Probe thresholds vs time delay produced by a linear sweep of 16kHz/s.

Fig.3- The same as fig.2, for an exponential sweep of 33oct/s.

If the hypothesis is true then a similar pattern should be observed for the other rising sweep, because the suppression area "follows" the exponential sweep in much the same way that it does for the linear rising one.

In fact this is what can be seen in figure 3. The data points are shown for three frequency channels and in all the channels a dip can be seen after the main peak. The differences in the time location of the maxima reflect the non-stationary nature of the stimulus. The lower frequency channels are hit before the higher ones because the stimulus is a positive exponential sweep. It should also be noted that the time delays between the maxima and the dips are in accordance with the predicted stimulation and suppression areas.

For the downward frequency sweep (fig.4) a different masking threshold pattern can be expected due to the assymetry of the (stationary) lateral suppression areas. According to the stationary suppression condition, a higher level of stimulation must be necessary in order to observe lateral suppression in a downwards sweep. This is what can be seen in figure 4. It shows the masking thresholds for the same channels that were displayed in fig. 3. It should be noted that now there are no dips in the masking threshold displays.

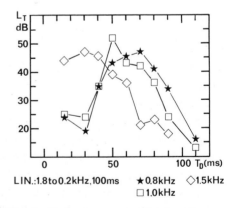

Fig.4- The same as fig.2, for a linear sweep of -16kHz/s.

DISCUSSION

The results obtained for these experimental conditions seem to support the initial hypothesis of an interaction between residual excitation and lateral suppression, which was formulated on the basis of data for stionary stimuli. They are also in agreement with physiological (6) and psychophysical (7) studies indicating that suppression cannot be taken as a simple attenuation of the masker´s excitation level. This is demonstrated by figures 2 and 3 which show that forward masking recovers from suppression as the sweep leaves the estimated channel´s suppression area.

With regard to temporal aspects the present results agree with those obtained for stationary stimuli (8). For a stationary condition a suppressor is effective in reducing forward masking excitation if it is present during the last 30 or 40ms of the masker. The studied dynamic conditions can be seen as sequences of stationary situations for which the short duration suppressor would be effective.

An interesting aspect of these results with sweep tones is that the probe does not seem to have been suppressed, although it was presented simultaneously with the sweep in most of the situations. This is difficult to explain because the suppressor should not be able to discriminate between the residual excitation in the channel and that produced by the probe tone. If this would be the case, no suppression should be observed because the amount of suppression of the forward masking excitation should equal the amount of suppression of the probe tone. However, the "stationarity" of the probe tone and its duration may be enough to put most of the probe´s energy out of the suppression area and therefore make suppression visible.

CONCLUSIONS

From a psychoacoustic point of view, this experiment indicates that dynamic stimuli can be treated as a sequence of short stationary states since the steady state conditions for lateral suppression seem to hold for time-varying stimuli (suppressed band between .8 and .9 of the "instantaneous" sweep frequency).

These results also indicate that the auditory representation of formant transitions may be supported by a sharpening effect due to lateral suppression in the case of high transition rates. This sharpening should be more effective for upward transitions than for falling transitions (of the same intensity level) due to the assymetry of the lateral suppression areas.

The sharpening effect observed psychoacoustically is also compatible with neurophysiological results (1,2) and must occur above a critical transition rate.

The hypothesis of a perceptual overshoot serving as a compensation for articulatory undershoot does not seem to be totaly supported by the present results. The forward masking is probably not sufficiently reduced to unbalance the auditory representation towards the final sweep frequency.

ACKNOWLEDGEMENTS

Our thanks go to all the victims who spent appreciable amounts of time in the anechoic chamber listening to the exotic sounds that we used in this experiment.

REFERENCES

1. Sinex,D.G. and Geisler,C.D.(1981) Auditory-nerve fiber responses to frequency-modulated tones, Hearing Research,4,127-148.

2. Møller,A.R.(1974) Coding of sounds with rapidly varying spectrum in the cochlear nucleus, J. Acoust. Soc. Am.,55,631-640.

3. Lindblom,B. and Studdert-Kennedy,M.(1967) On the role of formant transitions in vowel recognition, J. Acoust. Soc. Am.,42,830-843.

4. Stevens,K. and House,A.(1972) Speech perception, in:Tobias(Ed.),Foundations of Modern Auditory Theory,Vol.II,Academic Press, New York,pp.1-62.

5. Holmgren,K.(1979) Formant frequency target vs. rate of change in vowel identification, PERILUS, Experiments in Speech Perception, University of Stockholm, pp.84-91.

6. Harris,D.M. and Dallos,P.(1979) Forward masking of auditory-nerve fibers responses, J. Neurophysiology,42,1083-1107.

7. Moore,B.C.(1980) Mechanism and frequency distribution of two-tone suppression in forward masking, J. Acoust. Soc. Am.,68,814-824.

8. Weber,D.L. and Green,D.M.(1978) Temporal factors and suppression effects in backward and forward masking, J. Acoust. Soc. Am.,64,1392-1399.

© 1982 Elsevier Biomedical Press
The Representation of Speech in the Peripheral
Auditory System, R. Carlson and B. Granström eds.

ARGUMENTS AGAINST FORMANTS IN THE AUDITORY REPRESENTATION OF SPEECH

ANTHONY BLADON
Phonetics Laboratory, University of Oxford, 41 Wellington Square,
Oxford, OX1 2JF (U.K.)

Many authorities have endorsed the role of formants in the auditory representation of speech, often hypothesizing a peak estimation algorithm. Recent influential examples include Chistovich et al. (1979), Klatt (1979) and Carlson & Granström (1979). Indeed, given the fundamental nature of the acoustic formant, whether regarded as a resonance frequency in vocal tract acoustic theory (Fant (1960), Stevens & House (1961) etc.) or as an energy peak in the spectral envelope (Joos (1948) etc.), it would be natural to expect the formant to be a candidate as a hypothetical perceptual parameter also. Despite this, the concept of an auditory 'formant' is open to criticism on at least three major counts, labelled here as reduction, determinacy and perceptual adequacy.

In passing, a further issue can be briefly reviewed, and dismissed. It is this. It has been claimed that a formant-based view gains strength from recent psychoacoustic and physiological findings which have identified mechanisms - such as lateral suppression (Houtgast 1974) and the temporal response pattern of auditory nerve fibres (Young & Sachs 1979) - capable of retaining or enhancing frequency-peak information in vowel-like stimuli. However, suppose we advocate (as will be the case) not a formant-based view but an approach to auditory representations which reflect gross spectral shape. In that event, any mechanism whose putative effect is to enhance spectral peaks against a saturating background will inevitably also reinstate the spectral shape. Such evidence, then, supports both theories, and does not discriminate between them: accordingly it will be considered no further.

THE REDUCTION OBJECTION

To propose that the auditory system tracks formants is to invite criticism on methodological grounds. The data reduction process implied by auditory formant extraction would involve discarding information in a non-trivial way while our knowledge about the selective utilization of auditory features is still far from com-

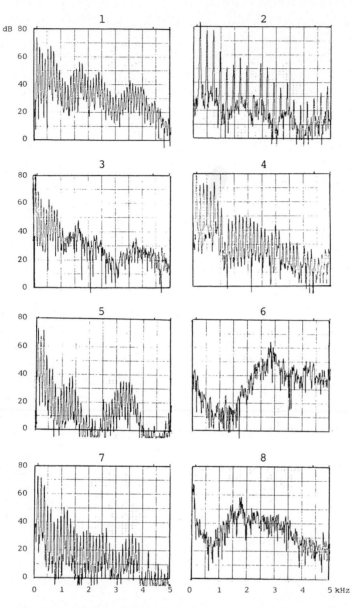

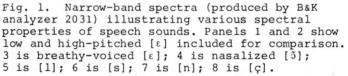

Fig. 1. Narrow-band spectra (produced by B&K analyzer 2031) illustrating various spectral properties of speech sounds. Panels 1 and 2 show low and high-pitched [ε] included for comparison. 3 is breathy-voiced [ε]; 4 is nasalized [ɔ̃]; 5 is [l]; 6 is [s]; 7 is [n]; 8 is [ç].

plete. No doubt this loss would be minimized for the speech stimuli which are best investigated to date, namely vowels. But this narrow perspective should not be allowed to precondition our methodology, because evidence abounds that the discarded information would contain much that is auditorily relevant. For example, Fig. 1 displays some familiar speech sound spectra chosen as reminders that the importance of the frequency location of formants is not paramount. The damping of formants as illustrated in panels 4 (a nasalized vowel [ɔ̃]) and 7 (a nasal consonant [n]) is known to be important to the perception of nasality (Hecker 1962). In panel 5 the lateral [l] is seen to be distinguished from a true vowel mainly by its deep spectral trough or antiformant centred at about 2200 Hz, while in panels 6 [s] and 8 [ç] each of the fricatives has a low frequency antiformant of broader bandwidth, distinguished by their frequency location. Another example of the importance of a spectral component other than formant frequency is given in panel 3 which illustrates a breathy-voiced vowel [ɛ̤] which could be contrastive in many languages; the exceptionally high amplitude of the fundamental in relation to other low harmonics is characteristic of such spectra and has been shown (Bickley 1982) to be the major cue to the perception of breathy vowel quality. Lastly, the now well known studies of stop consonant bursts (Blumstein & Stevens 1980, Kewley-Port 1982) have demonstrated that identification of place features is successfully achievable from templates of spectral tilt and other aspects of gross spectral shape.

What this evidence collectively suggests, then, is that a methodologically justified approach to representing the auditory quality of speech sounds should regard with caution the highly reductive concept of a formant. Instead it might proceed more parsimoniously by attempting to characterize the auditory spectrum shape as a whole.

THE DETERMINACY OBJECTION

Imagine that, believing the reduction argument to be insufficient, we revert to the assumption of the formant as a perceptual parameter. Then there surfaces immediately the problem of the indeterminacy of the formant. It is a familiar but inadequately emphasized fact that formants, in the sense of underlying poles in the complex frequency domain, are notoriously elusive in any physical representation of the speech wave. One new example must suffice: a low back

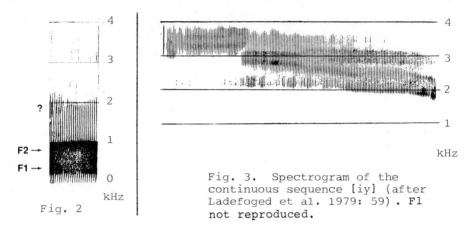

Fig. 2

Fig. 3. Spectrogram of the
continuous sequence [iy] (after
Ladefoged et al. 1979: 59). Fl
not reproduced.

vowel of the [ɑ] type shown in Fig. 2 will frequently reveal
acoustic energy distributed widely over a range of frequencies,
making peak picking impossible by most current techniques. The
same problem would be encountered in the nasalized vowel of Fig. 1
panel 4. The physical phenomenon of the formant, then, is not
fully determinable by our instruments. Indeed, to the extent that
these stimuli are of a kind believed to be best suited to formant
determination - they were vowels, spoken with a 'good' voice source
and with minimal channel noise - it must be concluded that the
prognosis for formant detection algorithms is markedly worse than
these comments indicate.

Next, even where physical formants are determinable, there may
be a poor correlation with the hypothetical auditory 'formant'-like
percept. Consider the spectrogram in Fig. 3 of a vowel sequence
[iy] produced with a gradual and continuous increase in lip-rounding.
Although the perceptual change is continuous also, the apparent
physical formants do not shift gradually throughout. The effects
of discontinuity, split and merger in F2, F3 and F4 will be well
known to many experienced spectrogram readers. But it is not easy
to see how the theory can map from this behaviour onto a continuous
auditory 'formant'.

In a comparable but more complex fashion, problems of auditory
'formant' determination arise at even moderately high fundamental
frequencies. Fig. 4 illustrates how Fl frequency, measured spect-
rographically, shifts as a function of changing F0, in RP English
words spoken in sentences at a conversational pitch range. Controls

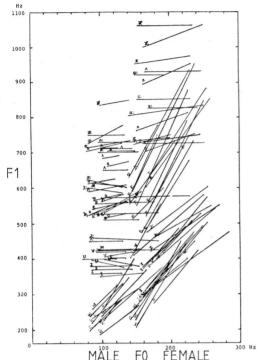

Fig. 4. Ten RP speakers, 5 male left,
5 female right; each producing eleven
vowels once on a falling F0, the limits
of which are shown as connected by a line.

ensured that these shifting F1's are perceived not as diphthongized but as static vowel qualities. Now, these data show that the nature of the F0-dependence of the acoustic F1 cannot be modelled in the ways previous studies have suggested. There is not the simple linear relationship which was claimed by Fujisaki & Kawashima (1978). Nor is perceived vowel quality a function of a constant F1-F0 distance on a Bark scale, as was argued by Traunmüller (1981). Rather the data suggest what might be termed a harmonic efficiency criterion, by which only if the harmonic spacing is sufficiently narrow in relation to the F1 frequency (say F1 > 3.5 x F0) will the physical spectrum peak be unperturbed and static: otherwise the peak will undergo a substantial shift in frequency, following the nearest harmonic.

In concluding this section it emerges quite clearly that, except in some ideal instances, a measured acoustic formant may differ in rather complex ways from a hypothetical auditory 'formant' percept.

THE PERCEPTUAL ADEQUACY OBJECTION

So far we have outlined some methodological, practical and theoretical reasons for doubting the viability of a formant-based theory of the auditory representation of speech sounds. A potentially still stronger case is made by the empirical evidence next presented in support of a spectrum-shape processor model and at the expense of a formant extractor.

The evidence is from experimentally-derived listener judgements of vowel distance. Let us consider how to model the performance of the listener's on-line 'distance metric' in a particular example where it is comparing an incoming token of RP English [i] with two stored templates for [e] and [æ]. A first hypothesis might be that the [i-e] distance would be assessed as roughly half that of [i- æ]. This notion would follow, for example, from the phonetician's expectations about articulatory vowel space, as evidenced by x-rays of tongue positions in vowels, as well as by conventional vowel diagrams. Significantly, the same hypothesis would also follow from our knowledge of acoustic formant frequencies for those vowels.

However, there is strong reason to believe that normal untrained listeners, comparing incoming vowels, do not behave like this. At the very least, they have no prior knowledge of 'how back' or 'how high' a given vowel is. Instead they apparently behave, in judging vowel qualities, according roughly to a "ceiling effect" reported by Lonchamp (1980) and modelled in a preliminary way by Terbeek and Harshman (1972) who had noted it in their experimental subjects too. The effect was such that vowels whose articulatory targets or formant frequencies are rather far apart are underestimated perceptually. If these claims regarding the perceptual nonlinearity of vowel distance are valid, a proper model of the auditory representation of vowels should predict the perceptual behaviour.

New experiments (detailed in Bladon 1981, experiments 8 and 9) have confirmed the dramatic nonlinearities in listener judgements of vowel distance. Fig. 5 shows the results, for 20 vowel pairs of RP English. On the ordinate, judged auditory distance between a symbolized pair of vowels increases towards the value 1. It is clear that larger vowel distances such as [i- æ] are judged to be far from equal to twice the [i-e] distance. The ear emphatically does not behave in an additive way, whereby a vowel distance might equal the sum of its component distances.

At the same time, Fig. 5 also shows that a spectrum-shape auditory model (described in Bladon & Lindblom 1981) predicts as $D_{A,X}$ these rather dramatic nonlinearities very well ($r = 0.91$).

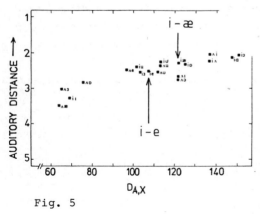

Fig. 5

This is a striking result. It was further confirmed on the similarly nonlinear judgement data of Hanson (1967).

The theoretical implications of these results are important; the more so because a distance metric based on the frequency spacing of formants cannot predict the nonlinear behaviours. This can be demonstrated in a simplified manner by Figure 6, from which on the left it is apparent that the area differences for [i-ę] and for [i-ɑ] are not greatly different. Given a conception of vowel quality perception by spectral shape, the nonlinear behaviour by listeners is therefore to be expected. By contrast, a formant frequency basis for the distance metric would perforce predict that the [i-ę] distance would be very much the smaller (since the F1's, like the F2's, are closer together). In sum, an approach to vowel distance based upon formant frequency differences cannot express the apparent fact that, once a peak in the auditory spectrum increases in frequency enough to escape from the skirts of another peak, the integrated spectral shape differences do not change much any longer; hence the formant based approach is inadequate to model the experimental demonstration that judged vowel quality differences do not subsequently increase very much. Rather, it seems, properties of the spectral gestalt and of auditory masking control the percept, and the most effective tool for modelling these ought to be a properly defined auditory-spectrum shape measure.

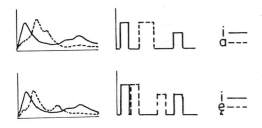

Fig. 6   Auditory spectra (left) and stylized versions of the same (right), showing that area differences between spectra for the [i-ɑ] and [i-ę] pairs are not greatly different.

ACKNOWLEDGEMENTS

This work was supported in part by the U.K. Science and Engineering Research Council (grant no. B/03894) and by the Royal Society in a Scientific Investigations Grant.

REFERENCES

Bickley, C. (1982) MIT Working Papers in Speech Communication, 1, 73-83.

Bladon, A. (1981) Acoustic and Auditory Modelling of Vowel Perception, Report to S.E.R.C.

Bladon, A. and Lindblom, B. (1981) J. Acoust. Soc. Am., 69, 1414-22.

Blumstein, S.E. and Stevens, K.N. (1980) J. Acoust. Soc. Am., 67, 648-662.

Carlson, R. and Granström, B. (1979) RIT Stockholm STL-QPSR 3-4 /1979, 84-104.

Chistovich, L.A., Sheikin, R.L. and Lublinskaja, V.V. (1979) in: Lindblom, B. and Ohman, S. (Eds.), Frontiers of Speech Communication Research, Academic, London, pp. 143-158.

Fant, G. (1960) Acoustic Theory of Speech Production, Mouton, The Hague.

Fujisaki, H. and Kawashima, T. (1968) IEEE Trans. Audio Electroac., AU-16, 73-77.

Hanson, G. (1967) Dimensions in Speech Sound Perception, Ericsson Technics, Stockholm.

Hecker, M.H.L. (1962) J. Acoust. Soc. Am., 34, 179-188.

Houtgast, T. (1974) Acustica, 31, 320-324.

Joos, M. (1948) Acoustic Phonetics (Language Monograph 23).

Kewley-Port, D. (1982) J. Acoust. Soc. Am., 71, S103.

Klatt, D. (1979) J. Acoust. Soc. Am., 66, S86.

Ladefoged, P., Wright, J. and Linker, W. (1979) UCLA Working Papers in Phonetics, 45, 53-59.

Lonchamp, F. (1981) J. Acoust. Soc. Am., 69, S94.

Stevens, K.N. and House, A.S. (1961) J. Sp. Hrg. Res., 4, 303-320.

Terbeek, D. and Harshman, R. (1972) UCLA Working Papers in Phonetics 22, 13-29.

Traunmüller, H. (1981) J. Acoust. Soc. Am., 69, 1465-1475.

Young, E.D. and Sachs, M.B. (1979) J. Acoust. Soc. Am., 65, 1381-1403.

© 1982 Elsevier Biomedical Press
The Representation of Speech in the Peripheral
Auditory System, R. Carlson and B. Granström eds.

PERCEPTION OF TIMBRE: EVIDENCE FOR SPECTRAL RESOLUTION BANDWIDTH DIFFERENT FROM CRITICAL BAND?

HARTMUT TRAUNMÜLLER

Albert Målares väg 3G, S - 183 45 Täby, Sweden.

INTRODUCTION

A hypothesis drawn up by Chiba and Kajiyama (1) and by Potter and Steinberg (2) says that within limits, a certain spatial pattern of stimulation along the basilar membrane may be identified as a given sound regardless of position along the membrane. Fig. 1 shows some identifications of one-formant vowels (3). As for the relative position of the formant F vs. the fundamental f_0, these data support the hypothesis as long as $f_0 < 350$ Hz. If $f_0 > 350$ Hz, the distance between the first two partials is apparently too large to allow the ear to extract F. Instead, the second partial is interpreted as the first formant. This is not at all surprising, considering the peripheral frequency selectivity of the ear. Rather, it raises the question why this does not happen already at a lower f_0. After all, with a resolution bandwidth of 1 Bark, corresponding to the critical band, a clearly pronounced dip between the first two partials is to be expected already at a smaller separation between them. The actually observed results could be explained on the basis of an effective bandwidth close to 3 Bark.

In some experiments by Chistovich et al. (4), (5), subjects had to match vowel-like two-formant sounds with one-formant sounds by adjusting the frequency position of a formant. The results showed that the single formant was placed in the middle between the formants of the two-formant stimulus as long as their tonality distance Δz remained below a critical value Δz_c of 3.0 to 3.5 Bark. The preferred position of the single formant could be moved continuously between the two

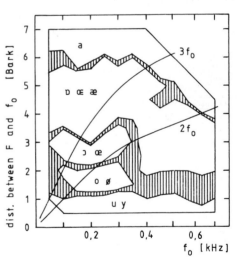

Figure 1. Identifications of one-formant vowels by Austrian subjects with Bavarian dialect. Phonemes with same degree of openness (or "vowel height") collapsed. Dashed areas: Boundary regions with low conformity between subjects. First three partials also shown.

formants by variation of their relative levels. If Δz was increased above Δz_c, this was not feasible any more, and the single formant was placed close to either one of the two formants. Qualitatively, even these results are to be expected, but Δz_c is too large to be explained by the physical bandwidth of the formants increased by 1 Bark.

Further evidence for an effective bandwidth larger than 1 Bark was obtained by Benedini (6), investigating the timbre differences between complex tones consisting of four, five, or six of the first six harmonics of 100 Hz. In a model simulation, presupposing gaussian shaped spreading of each partial, Benedini arrived at $\sigma = 1$ Bark, equivalent to a bandwidth of roughly 2 Bark.[1]

The results of these different experiments might be explained by one and the same, and possibly quite peripheral feature of the auditory system. The present experiments were intended to further illuminate this possibility.

METHOD

In order to avoid perceptual non-uniformities, such as phoneme boundary effects, speech-unlike two-formant noises were chosen to be matched with simple tones. The method of pair comparison was used. Each pair consisted of a two-formant noise followed by a tone equal in frequency, either to one of the formants, or to their tonality mean. The subjects had to rate the similarity between noise and tone on a five-degree scale identical with that used in Swedish schools to rate the achievements of students. Initially, 12 pairs of stimuli were presented for the purpose of "calibration". The mean frequency in these was either 1.0 or 2.5 kHz, while it was invariably 1.6 kHz in all the following two-formant stimuli.

In a second experiment (Exp. 2), the noises and tones of Exp. 1 were replaced by buzz-excited two-formant and one-formant sounds.

Stimuli

The stimuli were generated by computer simulation of electrical circuits. In generating the n-formant sounds, the filters of Tables 1 and 2 were fed with white noise or with pulses (duration 25 μs, rep. freq. 100 Hz). Sampling frequency was 40 kHz throughout. The formant bandwidths were chosen as close to $B = 0.05 F + 50$ Hz, as consistent with the requirement of equal formant intensity (without ear-correction). The maxima of the different frequency-envelopes, shown in fig. 2, were equalized. Fig. 3 shows the temporal shape of the stimuli. Each pair was repeated three times consecutively. The levels of the simple tones and one-formant sounds were all kept such that their loudness was half that of the loudest two-formant sound. The stimuli were recorded on tape

in randomized order, though not allowing immediate repetition of the same two-
formant sound, and organized into groups of eight, with pauses of 12 s in
between. Each stimulus combination occurred twice.

TABLE 1: Circuit specification

	filter type	order	limit. freq.		bandwidth
1	inverted low pass	1st	500 Hz		
2	low pass	1st	100 Hz		
3	inverted low pass	2nd	3200 Hz		1750 Hz
4	low pass	2nd	3000 Hz		6000 Hz
5	high pass	2nd	F1	(Table 2)	B1
6	low pass	2nd	F2	(Table 2)	B2
7	low pass, 3 dB/octave		below 100 Hz		

Filters 1 and 2 not essential in present context. Filters 3 and 4 compensate
for frequency response of ear. Filter 7 (in hard ware) not used for tones. All
filters coupled in series.

TABLE 2: Formant data

Δz (Bark)	0	1	2	3	4	5	6
F2 (Hz)	1600	1720	1850	2000	2150	2320	2500
F1 (Hz)	1600	1480	1370	1270	1170	1080	1000
B2 (Hz)	130	138	147	157	167	179	191
B1 (Hz)	130	122	115	108	102	96	92

Frequency to tonality conversion acc. to (7). In one-formant sounds of Exp. 2,
F2 = F1 and B2 = B1 (values from this table).

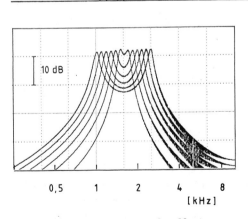

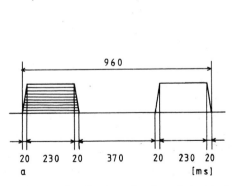

Figure 2. Envelopes of all two-
formant sounds of Exp. 1. Sweep
frequency tracings generated via
filters 1, 2, 5, and 6 of table 1.

Figure 3. Temporal structure and
organization of stimuli. a) Single
pair. b) (above) Repetitions of same
pair. Dashed: Two-formant sound.

Procedure

The stimuli were presented binaurally via headphones, Sennheiser HD 414, to a heterogenous group of altogether 24 subjects without essential hearing loss. A frequency response correction circuit, dimensioned with the aid of an artificial head with microphones at the ear-canal entrances, was used. The subjects were asked to rate the similarity between noise and tone, neglecting differences in loudness. No further explanation about the kind of similarity to listen for was given. The participants in Exp. 2, however, were explicitly asked to rate the similarity in timbre. The subjects gave their responses by written numbers from 1 to 5 for worst to best agreement. The stimuli were presented at roughly 65 dB SPL.

A preliminary analysis of the results obtained from the first seven subjects (Exp. 1a) showed, unexpectedly, that most subjects apparently ignored F2. Subsequently, the stimuli were presented via a high pass filter of first order, with a limiting frequency of 4400 Hz to the next group of subjects (Exp. 1b). The level of F2 was then up to 7 dB higher than that of F1.

RESULTS

The degree of consistency, with which the subjects performed their task, varied widely. The mean difference between the first and the second rating of the same pairs varied individually between 0.56 and 1.44 in 22 subjects, while it was as low as 0.28 in two subjects. Four subjects showed a response pattern deviating systematically from that of the majority. The mean ratings by the majority are shown in fig. 4 for each experiment. No major differences in response pattern were obtained between these experiments. The majority and minority results pooled over all three experiments are also shown in fig. 4. The response patterns were less uniform among the minority, as compared with the majority.

The essential findings can be summarized as follows:
1) Most subjects largely ignored F2, in particular when it was far from F1 (Δz > 3 Bark). Their ratings were quite highly correlated with the closeness in tonality of F1 to the matched tone or single formant. Spearman's ordinal correlation coefficient r_s was 0.77, 0.95, 0.90, 0.88, 0.08, and 0.98 for the data shown in figs. 4a, b, c, d, e, and f (cf. fig. 5), respectively.
2) The perceptual saliency of F1 was much higher than that of F2, even when F1 was attenuated.
3) Subjects appeared to use the same criteria whether matching simple tones or one-formant sounds to two-formant stimuli. Because of the unequal saliency

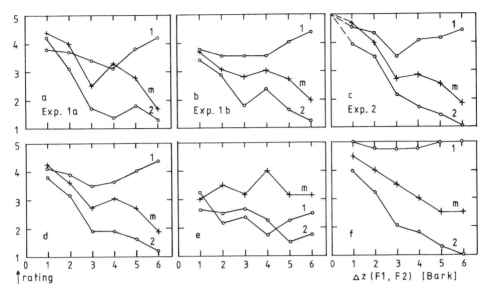

Figures 4a, -b, -c: Mean ratings of 5 of 7, 8 of 9, and 7 of 8 subjects in Exps. 1a, 1b, and 2, respectively. Figures 4d, -e: Pooled results of majority (20 subjects) and minority (4 subjects). Figure 4f: Results of two distinctly most consistent subjects. "1", "2", and "m": Tone or single formant at frequency of F1, F2, or 1.6 kHz, respectively.

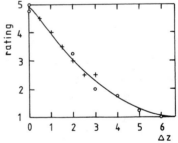

Figure 5. Plot of ratings by two most consistent subjects (Exps. 1b and 2) vs. tonality distance Δz between F1 and matched tone or single formant (see also fig. 4f). Line drawn by sight.

of F1 and F2, no particular value of Δz_c could be obtained from the majority of subjects.

4) The results of a minority of subjects can be understood presupposing a very large effective bandwidth ($\Delta z_c > 6$ Bark) and roughly equal perceptual saliency of F1 and F2.

DISCUSSION

The results are strikingly different from those obtained by Chistovich and Lublinskaya (5) with stimuli similar to those in Exp 2. In their experiment, contrary to the present findings, a preference of matches with F2 was found.

when Δz > 3 Bark. Equilibrium was obtained when F2 was 10 dB less intense than F1. The differences may be due to the procedure, or the task of the subjects. In (5) the subjects were aware of the two formants whose levels were systematically varied, and they were listening for vowel quality. The features of spectral integration effective in timbre perception might be both context dependent and purpose specific (speech specific in speech perception). In any case, non-peripheral processes must be invoked to explain these differences and those between the majority and minority in the present experiments.

ACKNOWLEDGEMENT
   This work was carried out at the phonetics laboratory, Institutionen för lingvistik, Stockholms Universitet.

FOOTNOTE
1) A more detailed analysis of these results reveals, however, that the effective bandwidth B varied proportionally with frequency in this experiment (Traunmüller, to appear).

REFERENCES
1. Chiba, T. and Kajiyama, M. (1941) The Vowel - Its Nature and Structure, Tokyo-Kaiseikan Publ. Comp., Tokyo, pp. 174-226.
2. Potter, R.K. and Steinberg, J.C. (1950) J. Acoust. Soc. Am. 22, 807-820.
3. Traunmüller, H. (1981) J. Acoust. Soc. Am. 69, 1465-1475.
4. Chistovich, L.A., Sheikin, R.L., and Lublinskaya, V.V. (1979) in: Lindblom, B. and Öhman, S. (Eds.) Frontiers of Speech Communication Research, Academic Press, London, pp. 143-157.
5. Chistovich, L.A. and Lublinskaya, V.V. (1979) Hearing Res. 1, 185-195.
6. Benedini, K. (1978) Psychoakustische Messung der Klangfarben-Ähnlichkeit harmonischer Klänge und Beschreibung der Zusammenhänge zwischen Amplitudenspektrum und Klangfarbe durch ein Modell, Dissertation, Technische Universität München.
7. Zwicker, E. and Feldtkeller, R. (1967) Das Ohr als Nachrichtenempfänger, 2nd ed., S. Hirzel Verlag, Stuttgart, p. 74.

© 1982 Elsevier Biomedical Press
The Representation of Speech in the Peripheral
Auditory System, R. Carlson and B. Granström eds.

TOWARDS AN AUDITORY SPECTROGRAPH

ROLF CARLSON AND BJÖRN GRANSTRÖM
Department of Speech Communication and Music Acoustics, KTH
S-100 44 Stockholm, Sweden

INTRODUCTION

In the forties, the sound spectrograph was developed. It has since then had an outstanding value for speech research. With the help of this new tool, linguists could visually study speech sounds in a three-dimensional pattern with frequency, amplitude, and time as parameters. New designs and new brands have appeared but the method has been kept more or less the same. Special classes are now given to students, teaching them the art of reading the print of the voice.

Is the spectrogram an optimal representation of speech sounds? In our paper we will discuss some of the limitations and suggest some modifications. We do not claim that the ideas are new or unique, but it is our strong feeling that alternative representations have to be explored in order to illuminate the transmission of the linguistic code between a speaker and a listener. The auditory system plays an important role in this process. Very little of the present knowledge about the auditory system is included in the spectrograph machine.

ANALYSIS IN THE FREQUENCY DOMAIN

In figure 1, a pure sinusoid is used as a test stimulus to illustrate some alternative representations in the amplitude/frequency domain. The sound spectrograph normally makes a bandpass analysis with a constant bandwith (e.g., 300 Hz) and a linear frequency scale (figure 1-b). This is certainly not the kind of analysis suggested by psychoacoustic research (1). If we use a Bark scale and a bandwith of one Bark, we will have a more relevant representation (figure 1-c). A psychoacoustic masking filter rather than a sharp bandpass filter has been used in figure 1-d (2). Since the test stimulus is a sinusoid, the actual shape of the masking curve is shown in the figure. Equal loudness curves (phon curves) are added in this figure, and a simple

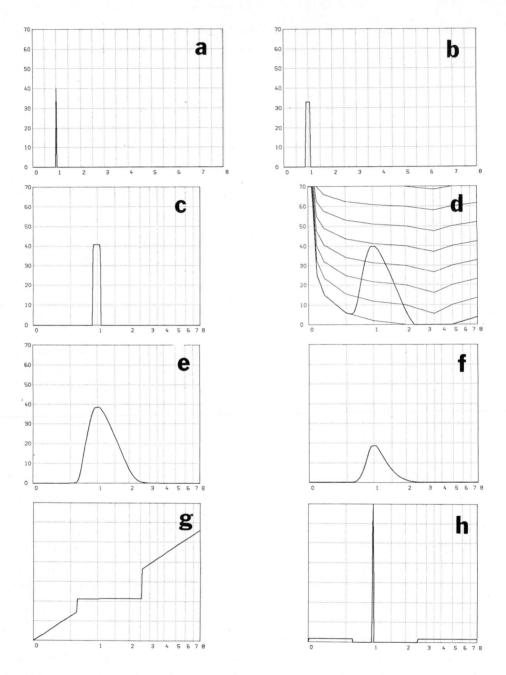

Fig.1 A sinusoid of 1 kHz in the different
       representations explained in the text.

transformation using these curves gives a phon/Bark plot (figure 1-e). Finally, we have incorporated a sone/Bark representation which often is claimed to give a good description of the percept (figure 1-f).

In figure 1-g, a new model (DOMIN) is introduced. It is based on our earlier work on vowel perception (3,4) and explores the possibility of temporal analysis in the auditory system (5). The model uses the masking filter introduced in figure 1-d to find which frequency dominates each point along the "basilar membrane." The dominant frequency is plotted along the y-axes while the x-axes still correspond to the Bark scale. It may be seen that the sinusoid generates a step in the curve, and that the width of the step correspond to the degree of dominance. If the stimulus consists of a number of resonances or cut-off frequencies, they will all generate a step in the curve. The size of the step will be dependent on the amount of masking or dominance.

Figure 1-h presents the same information in histogram form, i.e., the number of points along the Bark scale dominated by a certain frequency are plotted as a function of that frequency. Intuitively this could be regarded as the number of neurons that respond to the same dominant frequency.

ALTERNATIVE SPECTROGRAMS

Some of the above-mentioned analysis methods have been used to generate spectrograms. In figure 2, a computer generated spectrogram may be seen at the top (figure 2-a). In the mid spectrogram (figure 2-b), an analysis like the one explained in figure 1-e has been used. (i.e., a phon/Bark analysis.) We argue that this visual representation has a much closer relation to the sound that we perceive. Note the reduced emphasis on the fricative and the position of the very important second formant in the middle of the spectrogram. The perceptually prominent lowest formant is also visually enhanced.

Figure 2-c has the histogram representation added to the phon/Bark analysis. The formants are emphasized and the resonances during the occlusion of /b/ may be observed. Since the analysis bandwidth is frequency-dependent and narrow at low frequencies, the first harmonics are well marked, while they disappear at higher frequencies in favor of formants. The intonation

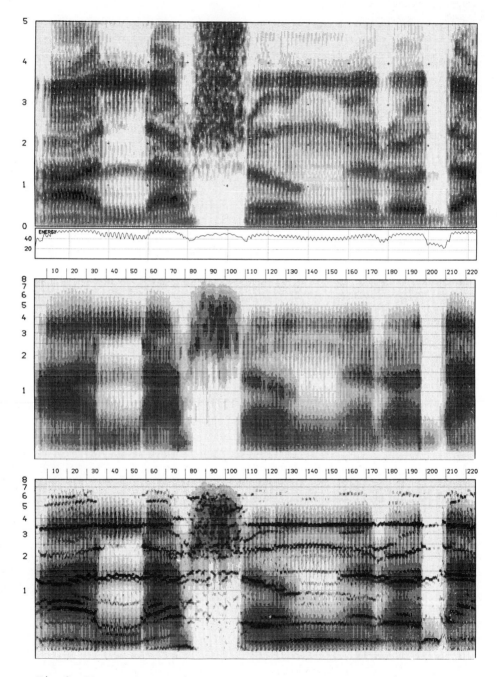

Fig.2   Three alternative spectrograms of the sentence
/ ala ɦʊŋər ɔ da ·····/. See text for details.

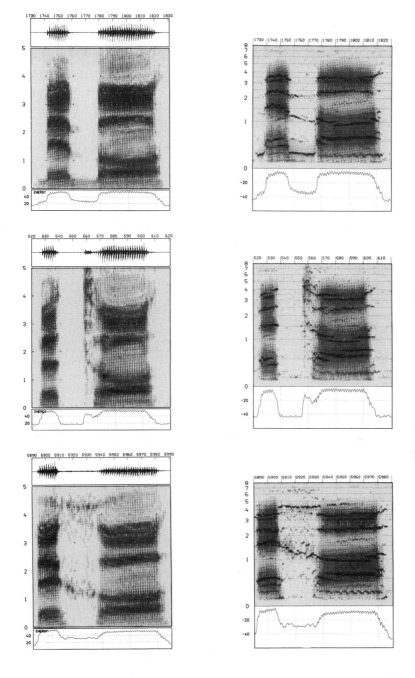

Fig.3   Spectrograms illustrating different manner and place of articulation. Standard spectrogram on the left. Phon/Bark with superimposed dominant frequency on the right.

and the formant pattern could be studied in the same representation. Another interesting effect that may be studied is the prominent cut-off effect at around 3.5 kHz. It could be hypthesized that this could be used in perception for vocal tract length normalization.

Figure 3 gives a systematic illustration of three manners of articulation. Once again, the articulatory movements during the /b/-occlusion could be studied (figure 3-a).

The auditory models behind the spectrograms presented in this paper are static even if the time is used as a parameter. No temporal masking effects have been taken into account. This kind of effects are obvious candidates for future developments of an auditory spectrograph.

FINAL REMARKS

Our purpose in this paper has been to present some alternative methods to generate spectrograms that are more closely related to psychoacoustics and speech perception. The spectrogram is, even in its modified form, only a quasi three-dimensional representation and is necessarily a crude approximation to the the multidimensional active process called speech perception.

REFERENCES

1. ZWICKER, E. & FELDTKELLER, R. (1967) Das Ohr als Nachrichtenempfänger, S. Hirtzel Verlag, Stuttgart.

2. SCHROEDER, M.R., ATAL, B.S., & HALL, J.L. (1979) Objective Measure of Certain Speech Signal Degradation Based on Masking, in: Lindblom, B. & Öhman, S. (Eds.), Frontiers of speech communication Research, Academic Press, London, pp. 217-229

3. CARLSON, R. FANT, G., & GRANSTRÖM, B. (1975) Two Formant Models, Pitch and Vowel Perception , in: Fant, G. & Tatham, M. A. A. (Eds.), Auditory Analysis and Perception of Speech, Academic Press, London , pp. 55-82

4. CARLSON, R. & GRANSTRÖM, B. (1979) Model Predictions of Vowel Dissimilarity, STL-QPSR 3-4/1979, pp. 84-104

5. SACHS, M.B. & YOUNG, E.D. (1980) Effects of Nonlinearities on Speech Encoding in the Auditory Nerve, J.Acoust.Soc.Am. 68, pp. 858-875

ENCODING OF SPEECH FEATURES IN THE AUDITORY NERVE

MURRAY B. SACHS, ERIC D. YOUNG AND MICHAEL I. MILLER

Department of Biomedical Engineering, The Johns Hopkins University School of
Medicine, Baltimore, Maryland 21205 (U.S.A.)

INTRODUCTION

The processing of any speech feature by the central nervous system is limited
by the representation of that feature in the patterns of activity it evokes in
the auditory nerve. Recent studies have explored the representation of vowels
and stop consonants in auditory-nerve fibers (1,2,3,4,28). In this paper we
will review our studies with an emphasis on how a number of speech features
might be represented in the auditory nerve. We begin with a brief review of
the two representations we have explored: the rate-place and temporal-place
representations.

According to what we have called
the rate-place representation of
speech, peaks in the acoustic
spectrum (e.g., formant peaks) of
the speech sound would result in
peaks in discharge rate in the
population of auditory-nerve fibers
at places along the basilar membrane where characteristic frequencies correspond with the formant
frequencies. An example of this
scheme for vowels is shown in Fig.
1. At the top we show the spectrum
of a synthesized steady-state vowel
/ɛ/ whose first three formant frequencies are 512, 1792 and 2432 Hz.
The center plot shows tuning curves
from three auditory-nerve fibers in
one cat. The characteristic frequencies (CFs) of these fibers are
near the formant frequencies of
the vowel. Because the vowel has
more energy in the vicinity of

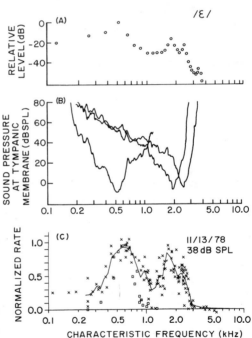

Fig. 1. A: Amplitude spectrum of /ɛ/.
B: Tuning curves from three auditory-
nerve fibers. C: Normalized rate versus
characteristic frequency for units studied
on 11/13/78 with /ɛ/ at 38 dB SPL as stimulus. (From Sachs and Young, Ref. 10)

their CFs, these units should begin to respond to the vowel at lower sound
levels than units with CFs between the formants and should respond at higher
discharge rates, at least at moderate vowel levels. The bottom plot shows a
rate-place profile for a population of auditory-nerve fibers recorded in one
cat when the /ε/ was presented at 38 dB SPL. Discharge rate is normalized in
this figure so that each fiber's rate increase to the vowel is plotted as a
fraction of its maximal rate increase for CF tones. There is some evidence
that auditory-nerve fibers with very low spontaneous rates form a separate
population (5,6). For this reason data from fibers with spontaneous rates less
than 1/sec are plotted with open square symbols and data from higher spontaneous units are plotted with Xs. The solid line is a windowed average of the
data points for the high spontaneous population. In this case, this rate profile shows peaks at CFs corresponding to the first three vowel formants, as
required by the rate-place scheme.

The basis of the temporal-place representation is the ability of auditory-
nerve fibers to respond to stimuli in a way which is temporally locked to the
stimulus waveform. The instantaneous rate (or probability of discharge) of
auditory-nerve fibers responding to stimuli with frequencies below about 6 kHz
is modulated by a rectified version of the stimulus waveform, as modified by
cochlear filtering and nonlinearities (7,8,9). Thus if an auditory-nerve
fiber is responding to a 1 kHz tone, there will be alternate 0.5 msec periods
of increased and decreased probability of discharge which will be phase-locked
to the stimulus; as a consequence, the fiber will tend to discharge at intervals of about 1 msec and multiples of 1 msec (since the fiber will not fire on
every cycle of the stimulus). Considerable information about the stimulus
spectrum can be derived from the temporal structure of auditory-nerve fiber
discharge. The existence of this information can be demonstrated by several
means: *post-stimulus time (PST) histograms* which estimate discharge probability or instantaneous rate as a function of time relative to stimulus onset;
period histograms which estimate probability of discharge as a function of
time through one cycle of a periodic stimulus and can be thought of as PST
histograms folded at the period of the stimulus; and *inter-spike interval
histograms*. Examples of period histograms of responses of four auditory-nerve
fibers to the vowel /ε/ are shown in the left column of Fig. 2. The waveform
of one cycle of the vowel is shown at the top of the column. The CFs of the
fibers are shown in the center column and the magnitudes of the Fourier transforms of the period histograms are shown in the right column. The spectrum of
this vowel is shown in Fig. 1; because it is periodic, it contains energy only

at the harmonics of its fundamental frequency (128 Hz). The Fourier transform abscissae in Fig. 2 are labelled in terms of harmonics of 128 Hz. Notice that the first formant frequency is harmonic 4, the second is harmonic 14 and the third is harmonic 19.

We have previously discussed the nature of the temporal responses to vowels in great detail (2,10) and will only briefly summarize these results here. Responses phase-locked to formant frequencies are particularly strong in the population of auditory-nerve fibers. The examples shown in Fig. 2 were chosen to illustrate this point. The top unit had a CF (0.46 kHz) near the first for-

mant frequency (0.512 kHz) and, as indicated by the Fourier transform of its period histograms, its temporal response is dominated by an 0.512 kHz component (fourth harmonic of the fundamental frequency). Peaks in the Fourier transform at harmonics 8, 12 and 16 are presumed rectifier distortion products (2) and should be thought of as part of the response to the 4th harmonic and not as separate responses to the 8th, 12th or 16th harmonics. The middle two units have CFs near the second formant (1.792 kHz) and their responses are dominated by the second formant (harmonic 14), although some response to the first formant is also seen. The CF of the bottom unit is near the third formant (2.432 kHz); its response shows a strong third formant component (harmonic 19) as well as first and second formant components. All units shown have significant distortion product components.

The fact that the formant harmonics dominate the patterns of

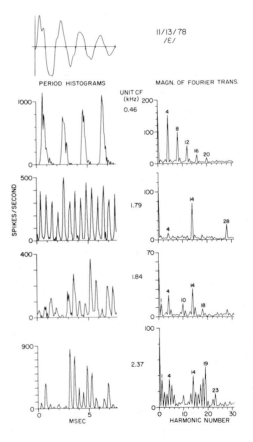

Fig. 2. Period histograms and their Fourier transforms for responses of four fibers to /ɛ/. One cycle of /ɛ/ shown at top. (From Young and Sachs, Ref. 29)

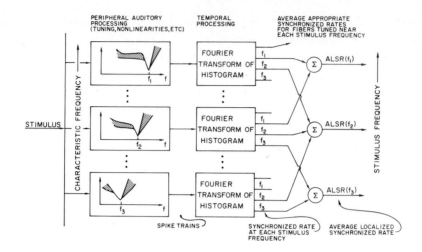

Fig. 3. Schematic representation of the construction of the average localized synchronized rate (ALSR) temporal profile.

temporal response of auditory-nerve fibers suggests that a good idea of the spectrum of a speech stimulus could be gained by comparing the amount of tempo-ral response at various harmonics of the stimulus. Figure 3 illustrates sch-matically how we have extracted a measure of the stimulus spectrum from the temporal responses of populations of auditory-nerve fibers. Fibers are ordered within the population according to characteristic frequency, i.e., according to position on the basilar membrane. Characteristic frequency is represented vertically in Fig. 3. The responses of each fiber are determined by the fil-tering properties and nonlinearities of the cochlea (first column of boxes). For each fiber a histogram (period, interval or PST) and its discrete Fourier transform are computed (second column of boxes). The result for each unit is the amplitude of its temporal response as a function of stimulus frequency (equal to the Fourier transform magnitudes). The response of the population of fibers to each stimulus frequency is then obtained by averaging the re-sponses to that frequency of all fibers whose CFs are within a range of one half or one quarter octave of that stimulus frequency. We have called the re-sulting measure average localized synchronized rate (ALSR). ALSR(f) is the *average* of the responses of fibers whose CFs are *localized* to the vicinity of frequency f; *synchronized rate* is the amplitude of a fiber's Fourier transform at frequency f in units of spikes/second. The ALSR measure gives a temporal-place representation because it reflects both place (CF) in the population and temporal response (synchronized rate).

Figure 4 shows ALSR plots for the vowel /ɛ/ presented at seven stimulus levels. The spectrum of this vowel has been compensated for effects of the external and middle ear of human beings (see Ref. 29). The points at the first three formant frequencies (harmonics 4, 14 and 19) have been plotted with filled circles. Notice that the ALSR is always largest at the first formant.

At lower sound levels the profile of the ALSR is a good reflection of the spectrum of the /ɛ/ (Fig. 1), with local maxima at the first three formant frequencies. The only serious deviation is the slightly elevated response at the second harmonic of the first formant (harmonic 8). At higher levels the first three formants continue to stand out, although the second and third formant peaks are slightly reduced at the highest level used. Responses to the second and third harmonics of the first formant (8th and 12th harmonics) grow considerably at higher levels until they are larger than the second formant response at the highest level. Except for these two distortion products related to the first formant, however, all response components between the first and second formants are suppressed at higher levels.

The lines drawn through some of the points in Fig. 4 are meant to show the extent to which the ALSR resembles the stimulus spectrum if presumed distortion components are ignored. The lines are drawn through all the points except

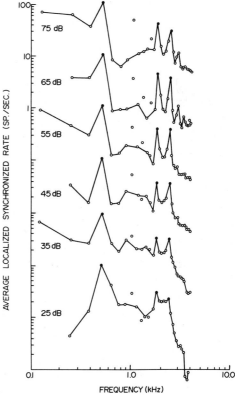

Fig. 4. Average localized synchronized rate (ALSR) for /ɛ/ presented at 7 levels. The vowel spectrum has been compensated for human external and middle ear characteristics. (From Young and Sachs, Ref. 28)

120

those at the second and third harmonics of the first two formants and
the first sum and difference tone of
the first two formants. The similarity of these plots to the spectrum of
the stimulus (Fig. 1) is clear.

Encoding of Vowels

   Let us turn now to the question of
how certain features of vowels can be
encoded in the rate-place and temporal-place representations. Figure 5
shows the spectra of three synthesized
vowels which we have considered in
our studies. The vowels /I/ and /ɛ/
are both "front" vowels (11,12) and
thus have a concentration of energy
in the vicinity of the second and
third formants. The "back" vowel /a/
has a low second formant and thus
lacks the high frequency peak seen in
the other two. The very low first
formant of /I/ and high first formant
of /a/ reflect the fact that these
are "high" and "low" vowels respect-

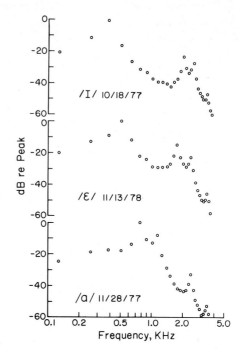

Fig. 5. Spectra of three vowels
considered in this paper.

ively. The resulting spectrum is "compact" for /a/ and "diffuse" for /I/. All
three vowels are characterized by spectra with energy only at the pitch frequency (128 Hz) and its harmonics.

   These vowel features could be represented in the auditory-nerve by any faithful reproduction of the formant structure of the vowel. Figure 6 shows that
at stimulus levels below about 50 dB SPL the rate-place profiles provide a good
representation for formant frequencies. Here we show normalized rate plotted
versus CF for three levels of /I/ and /a/. Average curves only are shown.
(Data for /ɛ/ are similar to those for /I/.) For both /I/ and /a/ there are
peaks in the rate profiles in the vicinity of the first two formant frequencies. Figure 7 shows that as sound level is increased, these formant-related
peaks disappear from the rate profiles. This disappearance of formant peaks
can be explained in terms of auditory-nerve nonlinearities (rate saturation
(13,14) and two-tone suppression (15,16)).

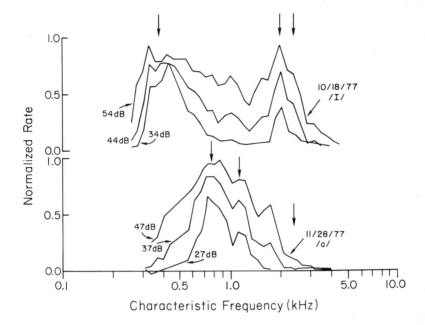

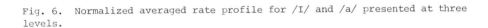

Fig. 6. Normalized averaged rate profile for /I/ and /a/ presented at three levels.

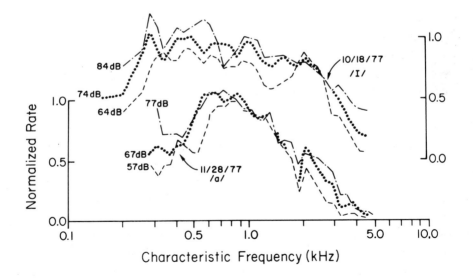

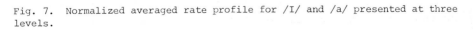

Fig. 7. Normalized averaged rate profile for /I/ and /a/ presented at three levels.

The average rate profiles shown in Figs. 6 and 7 do not include data from fibers with spontaneous rates less than one per second. These low spontaneous rate fibers have higher thresholds (5) and wider dynamic ranges (17) than the higher spontaneous rate fibers from which the rate profiles were computed. Thus, formant-related peaks are observed in rate profiles for the low spontaneous population at levels higher than those at which the high spontaneous group has saturated. This point is demonstrated by the data in Fig. 8. At 78 dB SPL, there are no peaks in the rate profiles for high spontaneous rate fibers in this population (1). Although the data are sparse in Fig. 8, there are clearly formant-related peaks in these profiles at 78 dB SPL. These low spon-

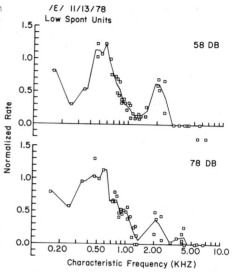

Fig. 8. Normalized average rate profiles for fibers with spontaneous rates less than one per second (From Sachs and Young, Ref. 1)

taneous fibers form less than 15% of the population (5,6); nevertheless it is possible that they could extend the range of levels over which formant-related peaks are observed in rate profiles by 20 dB or more. Notice, however, that the second formant peak for these low spontaneous fibers is considerably reduced at 78 dB SPL, presumably because of suppression by first formant energy (1). It is likely that another 20 dB increase in level would completely abolish this peak (1).

Thus, rate profiles for vowels appear to be quite unstable with regard to stimulus level; maintenance of formant peaks at high levels, if possible, seems to depend on the low spontaneous rate fibers as a separate population. The temporal-place profiles (ALSR) on the other hand are quite stable with stimulus level. Figure 9 shows ALSR for the vowels /I/, /ε/, and /a/ whose spectra are shown in Fig. 5. In these plots presumed distortion products have been removed according to an algorithm previously published (2). Each set of three plots shows data from one vowel at three sound levels, with the plots superimposed for comparison. The average response to the first formant grows or stays constant as level increases for all three vowels. The response to the second

formant may grow monotonically
(for /I/) with level or may be
suppressed somewhat at the highest
level (for /a/ and /ε/). However,
responses to stimulus components
between the first and second formants are always suppressed at the
highest level. This suppression
is sufficient to maintain a local
maximum at the second formant frequency even at the highest levels
used. Notice, that in all three
cases, the response to components
between the first and second formants is lowest at the highest
stimulus level. Because of this
synchrony suppression, a precise
representation of first and second
formant frequencies is maintained
in the temporal-place representation. The third formant is suppressed at the highest levels
shown in Fig. 9. However, we have
shown that if effects of the human
external ear are accounted for,
then at least for /ε/, a clear
third formant peak remains in the
ALSR at the highest levels used
(75 dB SPL; see Fig. 4).

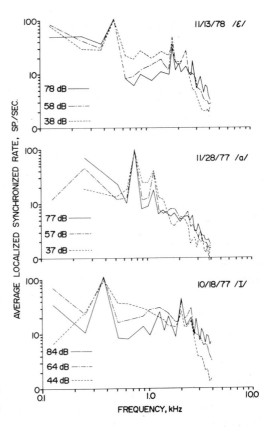

Fig. 9. Average localized synchronized
rate plots for /ε/, /a/ and /I/ presented
at three levels. (From Young and Sachs,
Ref. 2)

It is, of course, not necessary for the formant frequencies of the vowel to
result in well-defined peaks in rate- or temporal-place profiles in order that
important vowel features are preserved. Consider again the plots in Fig. 7
which compare rate-place profiles at high stimulus levels for /I/ and /a/. It
is clear that even at the highest levels used the patterns for /I/ and /a/
would be easily discriminated. As pointed out above, /I/ is a high-front vowel
and is characterized by a low first and high second formant, resulting in a
diffuse spectrum with high and low frequency energy. The rate-place profile
is similarly diffusely spread over the characteristic frequency scale. The

vowel /a/ is a low-back vowel with low second and high first formants and a correspondingly compact spectrum. The rate-place profiles for /a/ are clearly much more compact than those for /I/. This diffuse-compact difference in rate profiles is based on the gross shapes of the profiles and does not depend on formant-related peaks. The gross shapes of the profiles are stable at high stimulus levels. In particular, normalized rate appears to have saturated or is growing only slowly at CFs at and above the second formant frequency. Recall that the normalized rate measure is such that a value of one corresponds to a fiber's saturation rate for CF tones. At frequencies above the second formant for /a/ the rate profiles saturate at normalized rates considerably less than one. That is, at high stimulus levels responses of these fibers to the vowel saturate at rates less than their maximum rates to tones. It is this suppressed saturation which keeps the rate profile for /a/ from spreading to higher CFs and thus keeps it compact. Rate profiles for /ε/ (1) are intermediate between those for /I/ and /a/. Specifically, they fall less sharply at high CFs than do profiles for /a/ but more sharply than those for /I/. This difference in behavior no doubt results from the fact that the energy which is doing the suppressing (first formant energy) is more remote from the frequency region above the second formant in those vowels with shallower slopes. These gross spectral features are clearly also preserved in the temporal-place profiles of Fig. 9 where greater detail of the vowel spectra is preserved.

Encoding of Consonants

Temporal-place profiles provide a stable representation of vowel formant frequencies and any vowel features which depend on formant frequencies. On the other hand, rate-place profiles for most auditory-nerve fibers are unstable with level and a clear representation of formant frequencies at levels above 60 dB SPL is only seen in the small population of low spontaneous rate units. There are a number of reasons to question whether similar results would be obtained for consonants. The temporal profiles (ALSR) shown in Figs. 4 and 9 were derived from period histograms for perfectly periodic stimuli. It is natural to question whether a temporal representation can be used to encode the spectrum of an aperiodic signal whose spectrum varies with time. We have previously shown that the spectra of synthetic whispered vowels, produced by exciting a model of the vocal tract with noise, are well represented by a temporal-place mechanism. Such stimuli are totally aperiodic; in this case, temporal response profiles were generated from Fourier transforms of interval histograms rather than period histograms.

Stop consonants are not only aperiodic but also have time-varying spectra. Figure 10 illustrates that a temporal-place mechanism can represent the time-varying spectra of these consonants. The top plot shows the spectrum of a 20 msec segment of a synthesized syllable /da/. This segment occurred 20 msec after stimulus onset, during the formant transition of the stop. The spectral envelope shows peaks at about 0.6, 1.4, and 2.5 kHz corresponding to the average first, second and third formant frequencies during this time interval. The rapid fluctuations in the spectrum are related to the fundamental frequency of excitation (pitch) which in this case is 120 Hz (21). Responses to stop consonants were analyzed by computing PST histograms for windowed spike trains (3). ALSR plots were constructed from Fourier transforms of these histograms according to the procedure shown in Fig. 3. The bottom plot in Fig. 10 shows the ALSR constructed from PST histograms computed over the 20-40 msec interval corresponding to the spectrum at top. Because the histogram was 20 msec long, the resolution of the Fourier transform is 50 Hz; hence, ALSR points are plotted at 50 Hz increments. The resemblance of the ALSR to the stimulus spectrum is striking. There are peaks in the ALSR at the formant frequencies. In fact, formant frequencies taken directly as local peaks in such ALSR plots faithfully follow the first three formant frequencies throughout the transition and steady-state vowel segment (3). The rapid spectral fluctuations of the stimulus are also reproduced in the ALSR; we shall return to this point in our discussion of pitch below.

Figure 11 shows a comparison of ALSR plots for the syllables /da/ and /ba/. The top plots are spectra

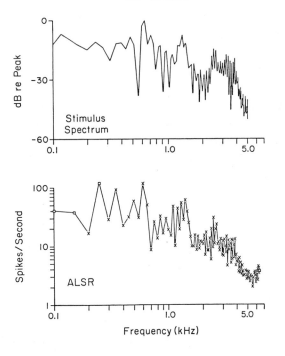

Fig. 10. Spectrum and ALSR plot for 20 msec segment of /da/, computed from PST histograms.

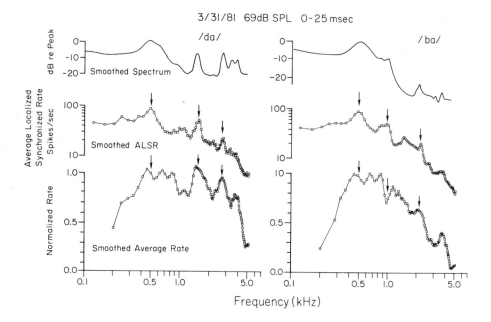

Fig. 11. Spectrum, ALSR and normalized rate profiles for the first 25 msec of /da/ and /ba/. All plots have been smoothed with a three-point triangular weighting function. Arrows point to first three formants (average value for the time interval).

computed over the first 25 msec of the two syllables. In order to emphasize the formant structure of these spectra, the raw spectra were smoothed with a three-point triangular weighting function. The second row shows the ALSR plots computed from PST histograms over the corresponding 25 msec segments. For these 25 msec PST histograms, ALSR resolution is 40 Hz. These ALSR plots have also been smoothed with the same triangular weighting function. The arrows point to the first three formant frequencies taken from the corresponding spectra. The second and third formants for /da/ are higher than those for /ba/ at this time during the stimulus. The ALSR plots clearly reflect this differ- ence. Notice that the second formant for /ba/ is better differentiated in the ALSR than in the spectrum.

   Thus, it appears that a temporal-place mechanism can provide a good represen- tation of stop consonant spectra. We have also found that a rate-place repre- sentation does a better job with stop consonants than with steady-state vowels.

Smith and his associates (22) have shown that the dynamic range of auditory-nerve fiber rate response is considerably larger when rate is measured over short (5 msec) intervals near stimulus onset than when measured over longer intervals. They have suggested that this increased dynamic range could be important in representing speech stimuli. For example, it could increase the range of stimulus levels over which a rate-place profile could represent the spectra of a stop consonant at the onset of a syllable. The bottom plots of Fig. 11 are consistent with this suggestion. These show normalized average rate plotted versus frequency for the first 25 msec of /da/ and /ba/. These plots were constructed slightly differently from those in Figs. 6, 7, and 8. As in the ALSR plots above, points are at multiples of 40 Hz. At each of these frequencies normalized rate is averaged across all units whose CFs are within 0.125 octaves of the frequency; this value is plotted versus frequency. The computation is thus just the same as the ALSR computation diagrammed in Fig. 3, except the measure is normalized rate rather than synchronized rate. The resulting rate-place profile for /da/ shows a broad peak near the first formant and well-differentiated peaks at formants two, three and one in the vicinity of the fourth and fifth formants. The rate profile for /ba/, which has closely spaced first and second formants, does not show a second formant peak. There is a small third formant peak and a clearer peak in the region of the fifth formant. For these stimuli at the same level (steady-state vowel level of 69 dB SPL) the rate profiles for the steady-state vowel segment are very similar to those for /a/ shown in Fig. 7; that is, there are no clearly differentiated formant peaks (23).

As was the case for vowels, formant peaks in these profiles are not necessary to the preservation of consonant features. Stevens and Blumstein (24), for example, have suggested that cues to place of articulation for stops might be found in the general shape of the onset (first 25 msec) spectrum of the stop. In their scheme, the onset spectrum of /da/ is characterized as rising at high frequencies, whereas that for /ba/ is either flat or falling at high frequencies. The Stevens and Blumstein characterization is based on spectra which have been given a high frequency preemphasis, which neither the spectra nor neural profiles of Fig. 11 have. Nonetheless, this difference in high frequency behavior is clearly evident in both the ALSR and average rate plots. Both the ALSR and rate profile for /ba/ fall off more rapidly above the first formant frequency than do those for /da/. Note that the stop consonants we have used thus far have not included the noise burst seen at release (24). The effect of this burst is to increase the high frequency differences between /ba/ and /da/.

Encoding of Pitch

The final feature of the speech stimuli we wish to consider is fundamental frequency or pitch. The issue of what aspects of a complex sound determine its pitch is one of the oldest in auditory theory (25). We wish here to examine how the fundamental frequency is reflected in the temporal- and rate-place representations we have discussed above. Of course, the responses of auditory-nerve fibers, phase locked to a periodic or almost periodic stimulus, will be periodic at the fundamental frequency. The pitch could thus be extracted from the instantaneous rate of a small number of fibers. That is, pitch extraction could work directly in the time domain. Goldstein (26) has argued that pitch extraction is based on recognition of periodic spectral patterns supplied to the central nervous system by the auditory periphery rather than on direct time-domain estimation of fundamental periodicity. Both the place-rate and temporal-rate representations are candidates for such peripherally generated spectral patterns. In order to support pitch estimation, these representations must show peaks at the harmonics of the fundamental frequency and troughs between. It is then up to the central processor to extract the pitch from these spectral patterns. The rate profiles shown in Figs. 6 and 7 do not show any clear pitch-related structure; that is, there are no clear peaks at the harmonics of the 128 Hz fundamental frequency. This conclusion needs to be tempered by pointing out that data for CFs below about 250 Hz are sparse, so that peaks at the first two harmonics could be missed. On the other hand, the lowest harmonics need not be present in order for a complex stimulus to produce a quite well-defined pitch sensation (27). The rate profiles for stop consonant onset in Fig. 11 have been smoothed by a weighting function which would wash out pitch-related peaks if they did exist. However, unsmoothed versions of these profiles do not show pitch-related peaks (23). No statement can be made about the relevance of the low spontaneous fibers in representing pitch because the data from this small population are just too sparse. The ALSR plot in Fig. 10, on the other hand, does reflect the pitch-related peaks in the spectrum of the stimulus shown above. Using cepstral analysis (21) we have shown (23) that there is adequate information in these ALSR spectral displays to allow precise tracking of a varying pitch throughout a CV syllable. Precise pitch estimates can also be made from the ALSRs for vowels computed from PST histograms.

Conclusion

Rate-place profiles provide good representations of formant frequencies for vowels at low and moderate stimulus levels. At levels above about 60 dB SPL formant frequencies are well represented only in the small population of fibers with low spontaneous rates (less than one per second). Temporal-place profiles provide stable representations of formant frequency even at high stimulus levels. Gross features of the vowel spectra (e.g., compact versus diffuse) are maintained even at high levels by both rate- and temporal-place representations. Formant transitions of stop consonants are preserved in a temporal-place representation. At least for /da/, formant frequencies are well represented by a rate-place profile during the consonant but not during the vowel portion. Differences in shape of consonant onset spectra are clearly represented in either temporal- or rate-place profiles. Pitch of consonants and vowels are precisely represented in temporal profiles but not in rate profiles.

Thus, the temporal-place representation generally seems to provide a more precise and stable representation of speech spectra than does the rate-place representation. However, there may be enough information in a rate representation to code most features of speech. Pitch is an important exception. Finally, it is unlikely that a temporal code can represent speech features which have energy at high frequencies, such as the fricative consonants, whereas a rate code can represent such signals (28).

ACKNOWLEDGEMENT

This work was supported by a grant from the National Institute of Neurological and Communicative Disorders and Stroke.

REFERENCES

1. Sachs, M. B. and Young, E. D. (1979). J. Acoust. Soc. Am. 66, 470.

2. Young, E. D. and Sachs, M. B. (1979). J. Acoust. Soc. Am. 66, 1381.

3. Miller, M. I. and Sachs, M. B. (1981). J. Acoust. Soc. Am. 70, S9.

4. Reale, R. A. and Geisler, C. D. (1980). J. Acoust. Soc. Am. 67, 891.

5. Liberman, M. C. (1978). J. Acoust. Soc. Am. 63, 442.

6. Kim, D. O. and Molnar, C. E. (1979). J. Neurophysiol. 42, 16.

7. Rose, J. E., Brugge, J. F., Anderson, D. J. and Hind, J. E. (1967). J. Neurophysiol. 30, 769.

8. Hind, J. E., Anderson, D. J., Brugge, J. F. and Rose, J. E. (1967). J. Neurophysiol. 30, 794.

9. Brugge, J. F., Anderson, D. J., Hind, J. E. and Rose, J. E. (1969). J. Neurophysiol. 32, 386.

10. Sachs, M. B. and Young, E. D. (1980). J. Acoust. Soc. Am. 68, 858.

11. Jacobson, R., Fant, C. G. M. and Halle, M. (1963). Preliminaries to Speech Analysis, MIT Press, Cambridge, Mass.

12. Gleason, H. A. (1961). Introduction to Descriptive Linguistics, Holt, Rinehart, Winston, New York.

13. Sachs, M. B. and Abbas, P. J. (1974). J. Acoust. Soc. Am. 56, 1835.

14. Evans, E. F. (1978). Audiology 17, 369.

15. Sachs, M. B. and Kiang, N. Y. S. (1968). J. Acoust. Soc. Am. 43, 1120.

16. Abbas, P. J. and Sachs, M. B. (1976). J. Acoust. Soc. Am. 59, 112.

17. Schalk, T. B. and Sachs, M. B. (1979). J. Acoust. Soc. Am. 67, 903.

18. Sachs, M. B., Young, E. D., Schalk, T. B. and Bernardin, C. P. (1980) in:
     G. van den Brink and F. A. Bilsen (Eds.), Psychophysical, Physiological
     and Behavioural Studies in Hearing, Delft University Press, Delft,
     Holland, pp. 281-291.

19. Rose, J. E., Kitzes, L. M., Gibson, M. M. and Hind, J. E. (1974). J.
     Neurophysiol. 36, 218.

20. Johnson, D. H. (1974). The Response of Single Auditory-Nerve Fibers in
     the Cat to Single Tones: Synchrony and Average Discharge Rate. Thesis,
     MIT, Cambridge, Mass.

21. Oppenheim, A. V. and Schafer, R. W. (1975). Digital Signal Processing,
     Prentice-Hall, Englewood Cliffs, N.J.

22. Smith, R. L. and Brachman, M. L. (1980) in: G. van den Brink and F. A.
     Bilsen (Eds.), Psychophysical, Physiological and Behavioural Studies in
     Hearing, Delft University Press, Delft, Holland, pp. 312-319.

23. Miller, M. I. and Sachs, M. B. (1982). J. Acoust. Soc. Am. (submitted)

24. Stevens, K. N. and Blumstein, S. E. (1978). J. Acoust. Soc. Am. 64, 1358.

25. de Boer, E. (1976) in: Keidel, W. D. and Neff, W. D. (Eds.), Handbook of
     Sensory Physiology, Vol. V, Part 3, Springer-Verlag, Berlin, pp. 479-583.

26. Goldstein, J. L. (1973). J. Acoust. Soc. Am. 54, 1496.

27. Ritsma, R. J. (1962). J. Acoust. Soc. Am. 34, 1224.

28. Delgutte, B. (1980). J. Acoust. Soc. Am. 68, 843.

29. Young, E. D. and Sachs, M. B. (1981) in: T. Myers, J. Laver and J. Ander-
     son (Eds.), The Cognitive Representation of Speech, North-Holland Pub-
     lishing Co., Amsterdam, pp. 75-92.

© 1982 Elsevier Biomedical Press
The Representation of Speech in the Peripheral
Auditory System, R. Carlson and B. Granström eds.

SOME CORRELATES OF PHONETIC DISTINCTIONS AT THE LEVEL OF THE AUDITORY NERVE

BERTRAND DELGUTTE

Centre National d'Etudes des Télécommunications, BP 40, 22301 Lannion (France).

INTRODUCTION

Speech discrimination must be based on information that is present at the level of the auditory nerve. In recent years, data on responses of auditory-nerve fibers to speech and speech-like stimuli have been reported [29, 30, 21, 44, 56, 8]. These results are being interpreted in the framework of models of peripheral auditory processing [28, 17, 10]. The purpose of this paper is to review some of the cues that are available in the responses of auditory-nerve fibers for various types of phonetic distinctions, and to discuss how these cues might be used by the central processor. The results are based on both electrophysiological data and model data. The physiological data are recordings from auditory-nerve fibers in anesthetized cats that have been described in preliminary form [9]. The model data were generated by a phenomenological analogue of the peripheral auditory system that simulates some of the characteristics of the responses of auditory-nerve fibers to speech-like stimuli.

Speech sounds can be organized along similar principles in many languages of the world [24, 13, 51, 52]. Classes of sounds that share certain acoustic properties constitute phonetic categories such as vowels, stop consonants, or fricatives. Distinctions between these major phonetic categories are generally based on the gross distribution of spectral energy and the time variations of energy in broad frequency bands. Distinctions of different speech sounds within each category usually involve more detailed spectral discriminations. Voicing distinctions and identification of prosodic features further require the detection of a low-frequency periodicity that listeners identify as voice pitch. The present paper follows this organization of speech sounds, treating successively distinctions between major phonetic categories, detailed spectral patterns, and voicing and fundamental frequency.

METHODS

Electrophysiological experiments. Methods to record responses of auditory nerve fibers in anesthetized cats were basically those of Kiang et al. [31], and were described in detail in [9]. Recordings were restricted to the most sensitive auditory-nerve fibers [34]. Processing of responses to speech-like stimuli is described separately for specific cases.

Model of the peripheral auditory system. The model of the peripheral auditory system is a computer program that takes as input the sampled pressure at the tympanic membrane, and produces simulated post-stimulus time (PST) histograms for a number of channels differing in tuning characteristics and sensitivity. Each channel represents the activity of a group of auditory-nerve fibers that innervate a restricted portion of the cochlea and are homogeneous with respect to sensitivity. Figure 1a illustrates the signal processing that takes place in any one of the channels. The first processing element is a linear bandpass filter whose magnitude characteristics are derived from tuning curves of auditory-nerve fibers [31, 30]. Figure 1b shows the tuning characteristics of all the model channels. The center frequency (CF) of a bandpass filter corresponds to the characteristic frequency of an auditory-nerve fiber.

The bandpass filter is followed by an envelope detector that smoothes out high-frequency components of the filter response, so that the model does not simulate fine time patterns of discharge.

The envelope detector is followed by one of three saturating, memoryless nonlinearities whose input-output characteristics are shown in Fig. 1c. The three nonlinearities differ in their sensitivity and their dynamic range. Each nonlinearity represents the normalized discharge rate vs sound level function for one of the three populations of auditory-nerve fibers that are defined on the basis of spontaneous discharge rate and threshold at CF [34]. Unless otherwise indicated, all model responses shown in the figures are for the most sensitive channels.

The last model element in each channel simulates the short-term adaptation and the refractoriness of auditory-nerve fibers. Some of these properties are illustrated in Fig. 1d, which shows discharge rate as a function of time in response to a burst of envelope presented at different levels. The decay in discharge rate following the onset of the stimulus is the superposition of a component with a time constant of 30 ms [50, 48], and a more rapid decay that is most prominent at high stimulus levels [49]. The time constant of recovery after the offset of the stimulus is greater than the adaptation time constant, and increases with the level of previous stimulation [18].

Because the model is based on linear bandpass filters, it does not simulate certain nonlinear properties of auditory-nerve fibers such as two-tone suppression and combination tones. Although these nonlinear phenomena seem to affect the responses of auditory-nerve to speech-like stimuli [56], the model in its current form suffices to discuss some aspects of speech coding.

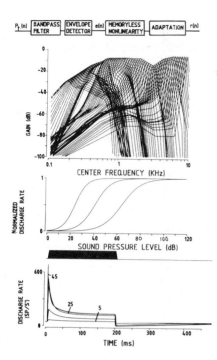

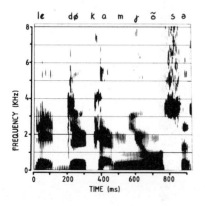

Fig. 1. a) Signal-flow diagram for one model channel. The input signal p(n) is the pressure at the tympanic membrane sampled at 20 kHz. The bandpass filter and the memoryless nonlinearity are as specified in Fig. 1b and 1c respectively. The envelope detector finds local maxima of the absolute value of the filtered signal, interpolates between these maxima, and reduces the sampling rate to 2 kHz. The adaptation element is the parallel combination of a linear memoryless component and two high-pass components with different cutoff frequencies. Each high-pass component is realized by a nonlinear, first-order difference equation. The output signal r(n) represents a PST histogram with a bin width of 0.5 ms and units of spikes/s.
(b) Magnitude characteristics of the minimum-phase bandpass filters of the model channels. The filter center frequencies (CF) are spaced every 1/12 octave between 0.2 and 10 kHz.
(c) Input-output characteristics of the model memoryless nonlinearities for the three populations of channels differing in sensitivity and dynamic range. The thresholds (5 % of maximum response) for the high, middle and low-sensitivity channels are respectively 10, 22, and 40 dB above best thresholds for cat auditory-nerve fibers [34]. The dynamic ranges (between 10% and 80% of maximum response) for the three populations of channels are 18, 24 and 30 dB respectively [45].
(d) Response of the combined memoryless nonlinearity and adaptation elements of the most sensitive channels to a stimulus presented at levels of 5, 15, 25, 35 and 45 dB above threshold. The top pannel shows the waveform at the input of the nonlinearity.

Fig. 2. Spectrogram of a French utterance produced by a male speaker. A broad phonetic transcription is given at the top.

RESULTS

Major phonetic categories

Figure 2 shows the spectrogram of an utterance produced by a male speaker. The waveform of this utterance is shown in the top panel of Fig. 3. This utterance includes representatives from many phonetic categories: the stop consonants [d] and [k], the fricative [s], the nasal consonant [m], the "glides" [l] and [j], and several vowels. These sounds can be further classified into two broad categories on the basis of their gross distribution of spectral energy. Sonorant sounds, which include vowels, glides and nasal consonants, have most of their energy in the narrow frequency bands associated with low-frequency formants. In contrast, obstruent sounds, which include stop, fricative and affricate consonants, do not always have clear spectral peaks associated with the formant frequencies, and have little energy below 1 kHz. Between the relatively steady-state portions of sonorants and obstruents, there are rapid spectral changes indicated by arrows in Fig. 3.

The bottom panels of Fig. 3 show model PST histograms obtained in response to this utterance presented at 75 dB SPL for 6 channels whose CF's are spaced every octave. In all channels, there are prominent peaks in discharge rate followed by a decay to relatively sustained activity. These peaks occur when there is a great increase in stimulus energy in one channel, so that peaks at the onset of groups of sonorants are found mostly in the low-CF channels, whereas peaks at the onset of group of obstruents are more in the high-CF channels. The distribution of these peaks across channels also depends on the preceding segment. For instance, at the onset of the initial group of sonorants [le], there is a peak in discharge rate in all channels up to at least 2 kHz. In contrast, at the onset of the sonorant [ə], which is preceded by the obstruent [s], a peak is found only in the 0.25 and 0.5-kHz channels. This reduction in the extent of peaks along the CF dimension resembles the effect of preceding context on responses of auditory-nerve fibers [9]. Similarly, the peaks at the release of the stop consonant [k], which is preceded by a silence, are more prominent and extend further into the low-CF region than the peaks at the onset of the fricative [s], which is preceded by a group of sonorants.

Sonorants and obstruents also differ in the spatial distribution of response patterns during the relatively steady-state portions. Specifically, as the stimulus energy in one channel increases, there is a gradation from background activity to a rapidly fluctuating response pattern to a relatively sustained

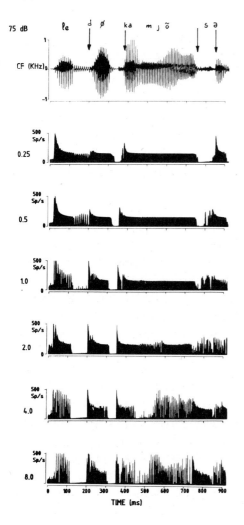

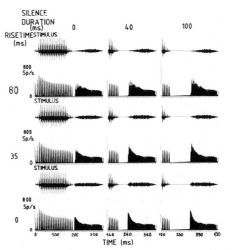

Fig. 3. Responses of 6 model channels to the utterance of Fig. 2 presented at a level so that the vowel [a] is at 75 dB SPL. The waveform of the utterance and a broad phonetic transcription are shown at the top. Arrows point to regions of rapid spectral changes.

Fig. 4. Portions of stimulus waveforms and responses of the 2.8-kHz model channel for nine [aša] or [ača] stimuli that differ in the rise time of the frication noise or the duration of the silence between the initial vowel and the onset of frication. The stimuli were generated by a formant speech synthetizer [33], and presented at a level so that the [a] was at 75 dB SPL. Stimuli on one column have the same silence duration (listed at the top), while stimuli on one row have the same rise time (listed at the left).

response. During sonorants, low and middle CF channels usually show sustained response, while high-CF channels have a rapidly fluctuating discharge rate. In contrast, for obstruents, high-CF channels have a more sustained response, while low-CF channels have little response or rapid fluctuations in discharge rate. Among sonorants, the nasal [m] is distinguished from vowels and glides by a drop in activity in the 4 and 8-kHz channels, and rapid fluctuations in discharge rate in the 2-kHz channel.

Speech sounds can also be classified on the basis of their onset characteristics. For instance, stop and affricate consonants tend to have an abrupt increase in amplitude of the frication noise preceded by an interval of silence, whereas the onsets of fricatives are more gradual and are not, in general preceded by a silence. Human listeners use both the rise time and silence duration cues for distinguishing the fricative [š] and the affricate [č] in postvocalic position [13]. Figure 4 shows portions of the waveforms of nine synthetic stimuli that range between [ašа] and [ača], differing in rise time of frication or in duration of the preceding silence. The stimuli on the top left of the figure are most appropriate for an [ašа] sound, while the stimuli on the bottom right are most appropriate for [ača]. The panels below each stimulus waveform in Fig. 4 show the response of one model channel to the nine stimuli presented at 75 dB SPL. The channel CF is in a frequency region where the frication noise has considerable energy. It is clear that both a decrease in rise time and a longer silence duration increase the amplitude of the peak in discharge rate at the onset of frication. Thus two different acoustic cues for the distinction between affricates and fricatives tend to produce similar effects on the response of the model of the peripheral auditory system.

In summary, there are many cues in the time variations of average discharge rate in the most sensitive channels to discriminate between stops, fricatives, affricates, nasal consonants and non-nasal sonorants (vowels and glides). The main internal cues are the gross distribution of response patterns across channels, particularly the prominent peaks in discharge rate that tend to occur at the release of stop consonants and at the rapid spectral changes between sonorants and obstruents.

Detailed spectral patterns

Sonorants. Distinctions among sonorants are based primarily on the frequencies of the first two or three formants [39, 41, 6, 3, 4]. A study of the coding of vowels with steady-state formant patterns [44] showed that, at moderate and high speech levels, the formant frequencies were not clearly apparent in the profiles of average discharge rate against characteristic frequency of the most sensitive auditory-nerve fibers. However, one cannot conclude that the rate profiles do not contain sufficient information for vowel identification because the study did not include a large sample of the least sensitive fibers. Figure 5b shows profiles of average discharge rate against CF for the most sensitive model channels in response to a synthetic [ε] vowel whose power spectrum is shown in Fig. 5a. In agreement with physiological results [44], the profiles show peaks corresponding to the formant frequencies at low stimulus levels, but these peaks become hard to detect above 50 dB SPL. However, the model profiles show a broad plateau at high stimulus levels, whereas the physiological profiles tend to slope downward for CF's above the place of the first formant, possibly because of suppression effects. Figure 5c shows rate profiles for the least sensitive model channels. At low stimulus levels, the profiles deviate little from the baseline, but at high levels there are clear peaks corresponding to the formant frequencies. Rate profiles for the least sensitive auditory-nerve fibers also have formant peaks at high stimulus levels [44]. Figure 5d shows weighted sums of the rate profiles from the three populations of channels. At each stimulus level, the greatest weight is given to the population of channels for which the slope of the rate vs level function at the place of maximum rate is greatest. Thus, the profile from the most sensitive channels receives the greatest weight at low levels, while the least sensitive channels receive the greatest weight at high levels. The weighted rate profiles are similar throughout the 60-dB range of stimulus levels, and show clear peaks at the formant frequencies. This result holds for 10 synthetic vowels whose formant frequencies roughly cover the range of variation found in language. Thus, an appropriate weighting of the profiles of average discharge rate against CF from the three population of channels provides essential cues for distinctions between vowels over a broad range of stimulus levels.

Considerable information about the spectra of vowels is also available in fine time patterns of discharge [56]. Fourier analysis of interval or period histograms has been used to identify the main components of the synchronized response [37, 25, 56]. Figure 6b shows the power spectrum of the period histogram measured from an auditory-nerve fiber in response to a 75-dB, two-formant [ε] vowel whose spectrum is shown in Fig. 6a. The fiber CF is about one octave above the first formant frequency (F1). The largest component in the response spectrum is the harmonic closest to F1. Figure 7a shows averages of response spectra such as the one of Fig. 6b for fibers whose CF's are in consecutive narrow frequency bands. This display represents the frequency components to

138

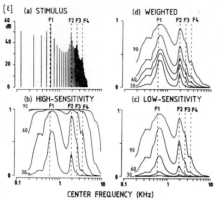

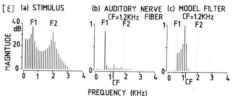

CENTER FREQUENCY (KHz)

FREQUENCY (KHz)

Fig. 5. (a)Power spectrum of an [ε] stimulus produced by a formant synthetizer [33].
(b) Normalized average discharge rate in response to the vowel [ε] against center frequency of the most sensitive model channels for stimulus levels of 30, 45, 60, 75 and 90 dB SPL.
(c) Same as (b) for the least sensitive channels.
(d) Weighted sums of the profiles of discharge rate against CF for the three populations of model channels in response to the [ε] vowel. For each stimulus level, the weighted rate profile is computed as follows: (1) the CF for which discharge rate is maximum is determined; (2) at this CF, the slope of the rate vs level function is computed for each of the three populations of channels; and (3) the weight given to the rate profile of each population of channels is proportional to the square root of the slope, with the constraint that the sum of weights be one.

Fig. 6. (a) Power spectrum of a two-formant [ε] stimulus with a fundamental frequency of 125 Hz [9].
(b) Normalized power spectrum of the period histogram obtained for a 1.2-kHz auditory-nerve fiber in response to the two-formant [ε] presented at 75 dB SPL. The power spectrum is plotted on with a linear amplitude scale, and normalized by the DC component which is omitted from the plot. The CF is indicated by an arrow below the frequency axis.
(c) Normalized power spectrum of the response of the 1.2-kHz model filter to the two-formant [ε]. The power spectrum is plotted with a linear vertical scale, normalized by its largest component, and is corrected by a first-order lowpass filter with a cutoff frequency of 1 kHz that simulates the decrease in synchrony of discharges with frequency [26].

which discharges are synchronized across the array of auditory-nerve fibers. There are broad CF regions over which the power spectra of different bands are similar. Over each of these regions, the largest response components are close to one of the formant frequencies. In contrast, there are rarely large components near the fibers CF's, except near the places of the formant frequencies and near 0.25 kHz. Such results are typical for 9 two-formant vowels whose formant frequencies cover a wide range, although large response components near the CF are also found between the formant frequencies when they are widely separated [9].

A comparison between these physiological results and model results can only involve model stages preceding the envelope detector because this element eliminates fine time patterns of response. Figure 6c shows the power spectrum of the output of the 1.2-kHz model filter in response to the two-formant [ε]. The largest component of the spectrum is the harmonic closest to the channel CF, in contrast with the response spectrum for the auditory-nerve fiber of Fig. 6b, which has a similar CF. Figure 7b shows power spectra of the outputs of model filters for channels covering a wide range of CF's. The largest components in the model spectra are similar to those of the physiological spectra for CF's near the formant frequencies and above 4 kHz. However, in the CF regions between F1 and F2, and between F2 and 4 kHz, components near the center frequency, which are characteristic of the outputs of narrow bandpass filters, are more prominent in the model spectra than in the physiological spectra. Thus, in response to intense vowel stimuli, auditory-nerve fibers behave as if they were not as sharply tuned as the model filters, although the transfer functions of the model filters are derived from fiber threshold tuning curves. This nonlinear effect resembles the decrease in the frequency selectivity of auditory-nerve fibers that has been observed at high stimulus levels [38, 56, 20]. Qualitatively similar changes in tuning have been obtained with a nonlinear model of cochlear mechanics [16].

In summary, fine time patterns of auditory-nerve fiber discharge provide a redundant representation of the formant frequencies of vowels since, for the majority of fibers, the largest response component is close to one of the formant frequencies. Several processing schemes that take advantage of this redundancy to efficiently estimate the formant frequencies of vowels form fine time patterns of auditory-nerve fiber responses have been proposed [56, 9].

Obstruents. Certain phonetic distinctions among obstruents are based on the gross shape of the stimulus spectrum [7, 22, 2]. Figure 8b shows profiles of average discharge rate against CF for the most sensitive model channels in res-

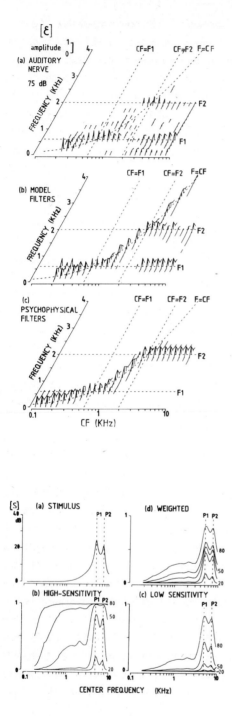

Fig. 7. (a) Pseudo-perspective representation of band-average power spectra for 17 bands of CF's in response to the two-formant [ε]. Each spectrum is obtained by averaging the normalized power spectra of period histograms for all auditory-nerve fibers whose CF's are in a 0.55-octave frequency band [9]. Each band-average spectrum is plotted with frequency along the oblique axis and amplitude along the vertical axis. Spectra of CF bands with center frequencies spaced every quarter octave are plotted at different positions along the horizontal axis. Horizontal dashed lines show the positions of the formant frequencies along the frequency axis, and oblique dashed lines mark the places of the formant frequencies along the CF dimension. The curved dashed line is the locus of points for which frequency is equal to CF.
(b) Pseudo-perspective representation of the normalized power spectra of the outputs of model filters with different CF's in response to the two-formant [ε].
(c) Same as (b) for filters whose equivalent bandwidths are equal to critical bandwidths [57]. The filter transfer functions have symmetrical, triangular shapes on log-frequency vs log-amplitude scales for CF's below 1 kHz. Above 1 kHz, the ratio of the high-frequency slope to the low-frequency slope increases to reach 2 at 2 kHz.

Fig. 8. (a) Power spectrum of a synthetic [s] stimulus [9].
(b) Normalized average discharge rate in response to the [s] stimulus plotted against CF of the most sensitive model channels for stimulus levels of 20, 35, 50, 65, and 80 dB SPL.
(c) Same as (b) for the least sensitive channels.
(d) Weighted sums of the rate profiles for the three populations of channels in response to the [s] stimulus. For each stimulus level, the computation of the weighted profile is as described in the caption of Fig. 5d.

ponse to a synthetic [s] stimulus whose power spectrum is shown in Fig. 8a. These rate profiles are roughly similar to those obtained in response to the same stimulus for the most sensitive auditory-nerve fibers [9]. Figure 8c shows rate profiles for the least sensitive channels. None of the profiles from the two populations of channels provides a good representation of the stimulus spectrum throughout the range of levels, although the profiles from each population do well over part of the range. Figure 8d shows the weighted rate profiles from the three populations of channels, using the same weighting scheme as in Fig. 5. The weighted profiles provide a good representation of the stimulus spectrum over the 60-dB range of stimulus levels. Results are similar for a set of 4 synthetic voiceless fricatives that are representative of the range of fricative spectra found in language. Thus the same scheme in which the rate profiles from the three populations of channels are weighted appropriately might be useful for phonetic distinctions among both sonorants and obstruents.

Some information for distinguishing among fricative consonants is also available in fine time patterns of auditory-nerve fiber discharges, particularly for stimuli that have considerable energy below 3 kHz [9]. However, unlike for vowels, the largest components in the power spectra of PST histograms do not in general correspond to the formant frequencies because synchrony of discharges becomes minimal for frequencies above a few kHz. Thus, temporal processing schemes that estimate the formant frequencies of vowels do poorly for fricative consonants [9].

Voicing and fundamental frequency

In the utterance of Fig. 3, the sonorants and the stop consonant [d] are voiced, whereas the fricative [s] and the stop [k] are unvoiced. For voiced sounds, there is always an interval during which the responses of certain model channels have a clear periodicity at the fundamental frequency, whereas the response patterns of unvoiced sounds are more irregular. For sonorants, the clearest periodicity cues are found in the high-CF channels, which have rapidly fluctuating response patterns. For the vowel [e], whose first two formant frequencies are widely separated, clear periodicity cues are also present in the 1-kHz channel. These results are consistent with auditory-nerve data for vowel-like stimuli at high stimulus levels [8, 9]. In contrast, for obstruents, the clearest cues for the distinction between voiced and unvoiced sounds are found in the low-CF channels. In particular, the 0.25 and 0.5-kHz channels show a low-frequency periodicity during the closure of the voiced stop [d], while only background activity is found during the closure of the voiceless [k].

For stop consonants, the model responses also show voicing cues that are related to voice onset time [36]. In Fig. 3, the peak in discharge rate at the consonantal release is less prominent in the low-CF channels for [d] than for [k], because of the adaptation from the low-frequency energy during closure. In addition, the response of the 1-kHz channel shows two peaks associated with the [k] sound, a first peak at the onset of the burst of noise, and a second, smaller peak at the onset of voicing. These two separate peaks are not found as clearly for the voiced [d], presumably because the onsets of burst and voicing more nearly coincide. For voiceless aspirated stops (which are not found in French) one would expect to find even more clearly separated peaks than for voiceless unaspirated stops because the onset of voicing occurs later after the release [36].

For voiced sonorants, the estimation of the fundamental frequency needs not be accomplished by periodicity cues alone. In principle, a response measure that would show peaks at the CF's corresponding to the harmonics of the fundamental frequency would provide "place" cues to fundamental frequency estimation. The model rate profiles of Fig. 5 do not show clear peaks at the harmonics of the 125-Hz fundamental frequency for any of the three populations of channels. This lack of harmonic peaks is also observed in rate profiles for the most sensitive auditory-nerve fibers [44]. Thus, the available evidence suggests that average discharge rate provides only mimimal place cues for estimating the fundamental frequency of male voices.

DISCUSSION

Average discharge rates and fine time patterns of discharge

The present results suggest that both average discharge rates and fine time patterns of auditory-nerve fiber discharges contain cues for distinctions between speech sounds. The time variations of average rate for the most sensitive channels provide information for classifying speech sounds into major phonetic categories, even at high stimulus levels. In particular, there are prominent dynamic cues to the rapid changes in amplitude and spectrum that are important for phonetic distinctions. If profiles of average rate against CF from the three populations of channels are combined appropriately, a good representation of the power spectra of both sonorants and obstruents can be obtained over a wide range of stimulus levels. However, one has to be cautious in interpreting these model results because the signal processing in the model is highly idealized, and in particular does not simulate the suppression of high-frequency formant peaks in rate profiles at high stimulus levels [44]. Moreover, the three-population weighting scheme has only been tested for steady-state, synthetic stimuli. In any case, the model results emphasize the necessity of studying responses of the least sensitive fibers in order to obtain a complete description of speech coding in the auditory nerve.

Fine time patterns of discharge also contain much information about the spectra of speech sounds, particularly those with intense low-frequency components such as sonorants. Schemes to estimate the formant frequencies of steady-state vowels from temporal patterns have been proposed [56, 9]. Some of these schemes have been shown to remain effective in broadband background noise [54, 9], and for other classes of stimuli such as whispered vowels [55] and the formant transitions of stop and fricative consonants [9, 43]. However, the proposed processing schemes do poorly for sounds that have considerable high-frequency components, such as certain obstruents [9]. Thus, although a scheme based on a combination of average rate profiles from the three populations of fibers could, at least in principle, be effective for all speech sounds, the proposed temporal processing schemes apply only to certain classes of stimuli.

The detection of the fundamental frequency imposes strong constraints on response measures based on average rates and fine time patterns of discharge. Model and physiological results suggest that the variations in discharge rate averaged over time intervals of about 1 ms show periodicities at the fundamental frequency of male voices. However, for intense speech stimuli, the high-CF fibers show the clearest periodicity cues, whereas psychophysical results suggest that low-frequency harmonics are dominant in pitch perception [40, 14]. Moreover, background noise considerably degrades these periodicity cues, even at signal-to-noise ratios at which the pitch of voiced sounds remains readily identifiable by human listeners [9]. These arguments suggest that identification of voice pitch would rather be based on place cues. The available evidence suggests that, for male voices, such cues are minimal in profiles of average discharge rate against CF, although more data are needed for the least sensitive auditory-nerve fibers. In contrast, some of the processing schemes based on fine time patterns of discharge that effectively estimate the formant frequencies of vowels can also provide place cues to the fundamental frequency provided they use filters that are sufficiently selective to resolve the low-frequency harmonics. Thus, periodicity cues for estimating the fundamental frequency of male voices are available in short-time average discharge rate, while place cues can be extracted from fine time patterns of discharge.

In summary, it is not possible at present to conclude as to the use of average discharge rates vs fine time patterns of discharge for speech coding. Although each response measure provides cues for discriminations between certain speech sounds, none of the measures has been shown to be effective for all aspects of speech. It is of course possible that some combination of the two schemes is used, or that each scheme is used predominantly in certain cases. Indeed, the ability of the central processor to use a variety of cues may be key in processing speech stimuli in conditions of severe degradations in the signal.

Comparison with psychophysical models of speech processing

Considerable efforts have been made to develop models of speech processing based on psychoacoustic data [41, 5, 58, 46, 32, 47, 1]. These models usually involve a bank of filters whose tuning characteristics are derived from critical-band or masking data. We have shown that linear filters based on threshold tuning curves of auditory-nerve fibers fail to predict certain aspects of responses to intense vowels. Figure 7c shows the power spectra of the responses of a set of psychophysical filters to the two-formant [ε] vowel. This diagram was obtained in the same manner as that of Fig. 7b, except the model filters were replaced by filters whose equivalent bandwidths were set to the critical bandwidths given in [57]. In the CF region between the two formant frequencies, the responses of the critical-band filters show more intense components near their center frequencies than the responses of auditory-nerve fibers. As argued previously, this result implies that, in response to intense vowel stimuli, auditory-nerve fibers are not as sharply tuned as the critical-band filters. In contrast, the responses of the model filters and of the psychophysical filters to the [ε] vowel are similar for center frequencies between the two formant frequencies. This result is consistent with the observation that effective bandwidths of cat auditory-nerve fibers measured near threshold have about the same values as human critical bandwidths [12]. This similarity breaks down in the CF region above F2 because the low-frequency skirts of these particular critical-band filters differ greatly from those of the model filters.   Thus, although critical bandwidths may have roughly the same values as threshold tuning curves bandwidths, critical bands do not change greatly with stimulus level [57], whereas auditory-nerve fibers appear to be less sharply tuned at high stimulus levels [38, 20]. The discrepancy between physiological responses to intense vowels and predictions of linear filter-bank models become even greater for filters based on pulsation-threshold or forward-masking data, which are more sharply tuned than critical bands [23].

In comparing physiological and psychophysical measures of frequency selectivity, one needs to consider possible differences between cats and humans. The question of species differences has been discussed previously [30, 27] with the general conclusion that the main features of peripheral auditory processing are likely to be similar in both species. Comparison of compound action potential tuning curves in cats [15, 22] and humans [19] give no evidence for great differences in frequency selectivity, although the data are limited to frequencies above 2 kHz.

In conclusion, psychophysical models of speech processing based on linear filter banks have a greater frequency selectivity than auditory-nerve fibers at high stimulus levels. Many models of speech processing also fail to simulate the dynamic aspects of fiber responses to the rapid changes in amplitude or spectral characteristics that occur in speech. Thus, some of the current psychophysical models can only provide a crude approximation to the coding of speech in the auditory nerve. However, more realistic psychophysical models are likely to be more consistent with physiological data. For instance, the model of Zwicker et al. [58] includes a nonlinear filter bank whose frequency selectivity decreases with stimulus level, and the model of Chistovich et al. [5] has dynamic characteristics that are qualitatively similar to those of auditory-nerve fibers.

Are speech sounds adapted to the peripheral auditory system ?

Some of the present results suggest that the aspects of speech that are important for phonetic distinctions are prominently represented in the responses of auditory-nerve fibers. For instance, it appears that, during continuous speech, responses of fibers in specific CF regions show prominent peaks in discharge rate at the rapid changes in amplitude and spectrum that occur at the release of stop consonants and at boundaries between sonorants and obstruents. Such rapid changes, which are found in all languages, are particularly rich in information for phonetic distinctions [7, 52].

A more specific instance of correspondence between perception and physiology is the result that both the rise time and silence duration cues for the distinction between fricatives and affricates tend to produce similar response patterns in the model of peripheral auditory processing. Because the two cues naturally cooccur in speech production, the fact that either of two apparently unrelated acoustic properties can evoke the same listener's response has been interpreted as evidence for a special mode of processing for speech sounds [11]. An alternative interpretation consistent with the present results is that there is considerable leeway in speech production because the auditory system is capable of integrating different cues at some stage of processing.

We have shown that, in response to intense vowels, the majority of auditory-nerve fibers discharge predominantly in synchrony with components close to one of the formant frequencies. This representation of the formants is both robust, because it is not strongly affected by moderate-level background noise, and distinctive, because broadband noise produces a different response pattern in which discharges are synchronized to components near the fiber CF's [38, 20]. It is noteworthy that formants are a universal property of speech and that their frequencies are of great importance in speech perception [39, 41, 6, 3, 4].

In conclusion, speech sounds seem to be well adapted to the properties of signal processing by the peripheral auditory system. This result provides some physiological arguments in favor of the notion that the auditory system imposes constraints on the types of sounds that can be used for speech communication [35, 52], although a causal link cannot, of course, be demonstrated. This is a natural idea from an evolutionary perspective since the general plan of the auditory system is similar among almost all mammals, whereas the speech production apparatus is more specific to humans.

ACKNOWLEDGEMENT

I wish to thank M. Stella for his generous assistance with the computer system, and C. Sorin for valuable discussions on psychophysical matters. The electrophysiological experiments were done at Eaton Peabody Laboratory in Boston, Massachusetts, and were funded by N.I.H. grants.

REFERENCES

1. Bladon, R.A.W. and Lindblom, B. (1981). "Modeling the judgement of vowel quality differences," J. Acoust. Soc. Am. 69, 1414-1422.

2. Blumstein, S.E., and Stevens, K.N. (1979). "Acoustic invariance in speech production: Evidence from measurements of the spectral characteristics of stop consonants," J. Acoust. Soc. Am. 66, 1001-1017.

3. Carlson, R., and Granstrom, B. (1980). "Model predictions of vowel dissimilarity," Speech Transmission Laboratories QPSR 3-4 (Royal Institute of Technology, Stockholm), pp 84-104.

4. Carlson, R., Granstrom, B., and Klatt, D.H. (1979). "Vowel perception: The relative perceptual salience of selected spectral and waveform manipulations," Speech Transmission Laboratories QPSR 3-4 (Royal Institute of Technology, Stockholm), pp 73-83.

5. Chistovich, L.A., Granstrem, M.P., Kozhevnikov, V.A., Lesogor, L.W., Shupljakov, V.S., Taljasin, P.A. and Tjulkov, W.A. (1974). "A functional model of signal processing in the peripheral auditory system," Acustica 31, 349-353.

6. Chistovich, L.A. and Lublinskaya, V.V. (1979). "The 'center of gravity' effect in vowel spectra and critical distance between the formants: Psychoacoustical study of the perception of vowel-like stimuli," Hearing Res. 1, 185-195.

7. Cooper, F.S., Delattre, P.C., Liberman, A.M., Borst, J.M., and Gerstman, L.J. (1952). "Some experiments on the perception of synthetic speech sounds," J. Acoust. Soc. Am. 37, 318-325.

8. Delgutte, B. (1980). "Representation of speech-like sounds in the discharge patterns of auditory-nerve fibers," J. Acoust. Soc. Am. 68, 843-857.

9. Delgutte, B. (1981). "Representation of speech-like sounds in the discharge patterns of auditory-nerve fibers," Ph.D. Thesis, Massachusetts Institute of Technology, Cambridge, Massachusetts.

10. Dolmazon, J.-M. (1982). "Representation of speech-like sounds in the peripheral auditory system in the light of a model" (this volume).

11. Dorman, M.F., Raphael, L.J. and Liberman, A.M. (1979). "Some experiments on the sound of silence in phonetic perception," J. Acoust. Soc. Am. 65, 1518-1532.

12. Evans, E.F. and Wilson, J.P. (1973). "The frequency selectivity of the cochlea," in Basic Mechanisms in Hearing edited by A.R. Møller (Academic, New York), pp 519-554.

13. Fant, C.G.M. (1973). Speech Sounds and Features (MIT Press, Cambridge).

14. Goldstein, J.L. (1978). "Mechanisms of signal analysis and pattern perception in periodicity pitch," Audiol. 17, 421-445.

15. Gorga, M.P., and Abbas, P.J. (1981). "Forward masking AP tuning curves in normal and in acoustically traumatized ears," J. Acoust. Soc. Am. 70, 1322-1300.

16. Hall, J.L. (1977). "Two-tone suppression in a nonlinear model of the basilar membrane," J. Acoust. Soc. Am. 61, 802-810.

17. Hall, J.L. (1980). "Frequency selectivity of the cochlea for formant peaks at high signal levels," J. Acoust. Soc. Am. 68, 480-481.

18. Harris, D.M., and Dallos, P. (1979). "Forward masking of auditory-nerve fiber responses," J. Neurophysiol. 42, 1083-1107.

19. Harrison, R.V., Aran, J.-M., and Erre, J.-P. (1981). "AP tuning curves from normal and pathological human and guinea pig cochleas," J. Acoust. Soc. Am. 69, 1374-1385.

20. Harrison, R.V., and Evans, E.F. (1982). "Reverse correlation study of cochlear filtering in normal and pathological guinea pigs," Hear. Res. 6, 303-314.

21. Hashimoto, T., Katayama, Y., Murata, K., and Taniguchi, L. (1975). "Pitch synchronous response of cat cochlear nerve fibers to speech sounds," Jap. J. Physiol. 25, 633-644.

22. Heinz, J.M., and Stevens, K.N. (1961). "On the properties of voiceless fricative consonants," J. Acoust. Soc. Am. 34, 179-188.

23. Houtgast, T. (1974). Lateral Suppression in Hearing (Academische Pers, Am-

sterdam).

24. Jakobson, R., Fant, C.G.M., and Halle, M. (1952). Preliminaries to Speech Analysis (MIT Press, Cambridge).

25. Johnson, D H. (1974). "The response of single auditory-nerve fibers in the cat to single tones: Synchrony and average discharge rate," Ph.D. Thesis, MIT, Cambridge.

26. Johnson, D.H. (1980). "The relationship between spike rate and synchrony in the response of auditory-nerve fibers to single tones," J. Acoust. Soc. Am. 68, 1115-1122.

27. Kiang, N.Y.S. (1980). "Processing of speech by the auditory nervous system," J. Acoust. Soc. Am. 68, 830-835.

28. Kiang, N.Y.S., Eddington, D.K., and Delgutte, B. (1979). "Physiological considerations in designing auditory implants," Acta Otolaryngol. 87, 204-218.

29. Kiang, N.Y.S. and Moxon, E.C. (1972). "Physiological considerations in artificial stimulation of the inner ear," Ann. Otol. Rhinol. Laryngol. 81, 714-730.

30. Kiang, N.Y.S, and Moxon, E.C. (1974). "Tails of tuning curves of auditory-nerve fibers," J. Acoust. Soc. Am. 55, 620-630.

31. Kiang, N.Y.S., Watanabe, T., Thomas, E.C., and Clark, L.F. (1965). Discharge Patterns of Single Fibers in the Cat's Auditory Nerve, MIT Research Monograph No 35 (MIT Press, Cambridge).

32. Klatt, D.H. (1980). "Speech perception: a model of acoustic-phonetic analysis and lexical access," in Perception and Production of Fluent Speech, edited by Cole, R.A. (Erlbaum, Hillsdale, N.J.), pp 243-288.

33. Klatt, D.H. (1980). "Software for a cascade/parallel formant synthesizer," J. Acoust. Soc. Am. 67, 971-995.

34. Liberman, M.C. (1978). "Auditory-nerve response from cats raised in a low-noise chamber," J. Acoust. Soc. Am. 63, 442-455.

35. Lindblom, B.E.F. (1971). "Phonetics and the description of language," 7th Intern. Congr. Phon. Sci., 22-28.

36. Lisker, L., and Abramson, A.S. (1964). "A cross-language study of voicing in initial stops: Acoustical measurements," Word 20, 384-422.

37. Littlefield, W.M. (1973). "Investigation of the linear range of the peripheral auditory system," Sc.D., Washington Univ., St. Louis.

38. Møller, A.R. (1977). "Frequency selectivity of single auditory-nerve fibers in response to broadband noise stimuli," J. Acoust. Soc. Am. 62, 135-142.

39. Peterson, G.E., and Barney, H.L. (1952). "Control methods used in a study of the vowels," J. Acoust. Soc. Am. 24, 175-184.

40. Plomp, R. (1976). Aspects of tone sensations (Academic, London).

41. Pols, L.C.W. (1971). "Real time recognition of spoken words," IEEE Trans. C-20, 972-978.

42. Pols, L.C.W., van der Kamp, L. J. Th., and Plomp, R. (1969). "Perceptual and physical space of vowel sounds," J. Acoust. Soc. Am. 46, 458-467.

43. Sachs, M.B. (1982). "The encoding of vowels and stop consonants in the temporal patterns of auditory-nerve fiber discharges" (this volume).

44. Sachs, M.B. and Young, E.D. (1979). "Encoding of steady-state vowels in the auditory nerve: Representation in terms of discharge rate," J. Acoust. Soc. Am. 66, 470-479.

45. Schalk, T.B., and Sachs, M.B. (1980). "Nonlinearities in auditory-nerve fiber responses to bandlimited noise," J. Acoust. Soc. Am. 67, 903-913.

46. Schroeder, M.R., Atal, B.S. and Hall, J.L. (1979). "Objective measures of certain speech signal degradations based on masking properties of human auditory perception," in Frontiers of Speech Communication Research, edited by B. Lindblom and S. Ohman (Academic, London), pp 217-229.

47. Searle, C.L., Jacobson, J.Z., and Kimberley, B.P. (1980). "Speech as patterns in the 3-space of time and frequency," in Perception and Production of Fluent Speech, edited by Cole, R.A. (Erlbaum, Hillsdale, N.J.), pp 73-102.

48. Smith, R.L. (1979). "Adaptation, saturation and physiological masking in single auditory-nerve fibers," J. Acoust. Soc. Am. 65, 166-178.

49. Smith, R.L. and Brachman, M.L. (1980). "Operating range and maximum response of single auditory-nerve fibers," Brain Res. 184, 499-505.

50. Smith, R.L., and Zwislocki, J.J. (1975). "Short-term adaptation and incremental responses of single auditory-nerve fibers," Biol. Cybernetics 17, 169-182.

51. Stevens, K.N. (1980). "Acoustic correlates of some phonetic categories," J. Acoust. Soc. Am. 68, 836-842.

52. Stevens, K.N. (1981). "Constraints imposed by the auditory system on the properties used to classify speech sounds: Data from phonology, acoustics and psychoacoustics," in The Cognitive Representation of Speech, edited by T. Myers, J. Laver and J. Anderson (North Holland), pp 61-74.

53. Van Heusden, E. and Smoorenburg, G.F. (1981). "Eighth-nerve action potential tuning curves in cats before and after inducement of an acute noise trauma," Hear. Res. 5, 25-48.

54. Voigt, H.F., Sachs, M.B., and Young, E.D. (1981). "Effects of masking noise on the representation of vowel spectra in the auditory nerve," in Neuronal Mechanisms of Hearing, edited by J. Syko and L. Aitkins (Plenum).

55. Voigt, H.F., Sachs, M.B., and Young, E.D. (1981). "Represen .cion of whispered vowels in the temporal patterns of auditory-nerve fiber discharges," J. Acoust. Soc. Am. 69, S53(A).

56. Young, E.D., and Sachs, M.B. (1979). "Representation of steady-state vowels in the temporal aspects of the discharge patterns of populations of auditory-nerve fibers," J. Acoust. Soc. Am. 66, 1381-1403.

57. Zwicker, E. and Feldtkeller, R. (1967). Das Ohr als Nachrichtenempfanger (Hirzel, Stuttgart).

58. Zwicker, E., Terhardt, E., and Paulus, E. (1979). "Automatic speech recognition using psychoacoustic models," J. Acoust. Soc. Am. 65, 487-498.

© 1982 Elsevier Biomedical Press
The Representation of Speech in the Peripheral
Auditory System, R. Carlson and B. Granström eds.

REPRESENTATION OF SPEECH-LIKE SOUNDS IN THE PERIPHERAL AUDITORY SYSTEM IN LIGHT OF A MODEL

JEAN-MARC DOLMAZON
Laboratoire de la Communication Parlée, I.N.P.G./E.N.S.E.R.G., 23 avenue
des Martyrs, 38031 GRENOBLE Cédex, (FRANCE)

INTRODUCTION

There have been a number of attempts to characterize the responses of auditory-nerve fibers to single tones and to more complex stimuli and to relate them to the well known nonlinear properties of the cochlea (1, 2, 3, 4, 5).

In recent years physiological studies on animals have progressed to a state that enables the study of how speech sounds are coded in the auditory nerve. Nevertheless discussions are presently focused on the periphery of central nervous system because our knowledge about more central mechanisms is not at a comparable level of detail.

The purpose of this paper is to review, in the light of a model of the peripheral auditory system, some of the nonlinear properties of the cochlea and to consider their effects on the peripheral encoding of speech-sounds. For this purpose we have used synthesized speech-like sounds consisting of complexes of harmonics with one or two constant spectral peaks. Such stimuli are a considerable simplification of natural stimuli but they allow to extend the properties of auditory nerve fiber responses to single tones and pairs of tones, to broadband tonal complexes such as vowels. It must be mentioned here that the phonetic content of our stimuli has no signification in our experiments, and we only consider their physical characteristics (even if they correspond to a phonetic reality).

After reviewing the general structure of the model we have used, we shall present simulated responses to a one-formant speech-like sound showing the effect of basic nonlinearities on the coding of such a sound. Then the responses obtained with a two-formant vowel-like stimulus will be analyzed. At last, a voiceless stimulus having an equivalent spectral envelope (fricative sound) will be considered in order to show the harmonic structure loss effect in the responses of our simulated auditory-nerve fibers.

METHODS

The results relating to speech encoding presented in this paper are obtained
by recording simulated responses of auditory nerve fibers to computer-generated
stimuli. The model used and some of the results of these experiments have been
described in detail in our previous papers (6, 7, 8) ; the model will be described here only briefly.

Figure 1 shows the general structure of the digital computer simulated model.
The electrical analog of sound pressure at the tympanic membrane passes through
an association of first and second order filters (M.E) which simulate the
transfer function of the middle-ear. These filters allow to reproduce the
middle-ear transfer coefficient changes as a function of the input frequency.
The middle-ear model is linear, assuming that input levels are, for all
frequencies, low enough to insure an inactive acoustic reflex.

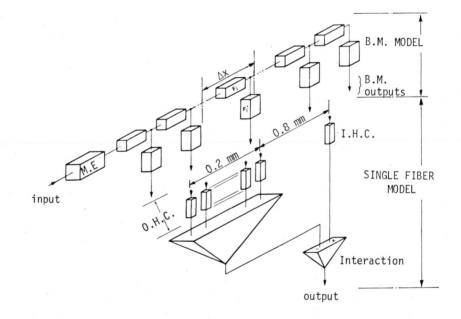

Fig. 1. The model of basilar membrane motion (upper part) and the model
of a single auditory-nerve fiber (lower part).

Then the signal passes through a double bank of filters which is a one-
dimensional linear model for the motion of the basilar membrane. Each section
Δx, representing a constant length portion of the cochlear partition, consists
mainly of two filters : a second-order damped low-pass filter (F_i) which

simulates the variations of the pressure difference across the cochlear partition, and a second-order resonant low-pass filter (F_i') which gives, as output, the electrical analog of the instantaneous position of the corresponding point of the basilar membrane. The central frequencies of the filters F_i and F_i' slightly differ from each other, and decrease monotonically with the abscissa according to experimental data. The complete model of the basilar membrane consists of a cascade of 128 such sections, allowing to use input frequencies in the range : 25 - 9000 Hz.

At each point of the basilar membrane model, a single auditory nerve fiber model can be connected as shown in the bottom part of figure 1. Each hair cell (I.H.C., O.H.C.) is modeled separately by a component giving an output logarithmically related to input, with an input threshold and an output saturation. This component transmits the instantaneous movements of the basilar membrane for low frequency vibrations, whereas we suppose that only the vibration envelopes are transmitted for frequencies exceeding some kilohertz. Connections between both kinds of hair cells (always connected on the basilar membrane model with a gap of .8 mm) are made according to innervation patterns found in animals (9) up to the interaction component where we suppose that information issued from O.H.C. and I.H.C. may interact electrically. The output of this component is supposed to drive a spike generator (not drawn on figure 1) whose output frequency is proportional to the analog signal delivered by the interaction component. The complete model output has been shown to be equivalent to the discharge probability density (elicited from PST histograms) of the auditory nerve fibers (6).

This model has been tested with various kinds of input signals. For a single tone stimulus the output is a function of amplitude and frequency with reasonably well fitted tuning curves and rate versus level functions. However, because of the linearity of the basilar membrane model, the tuning curve broadening according to the input level is perhaps not so important as usually found in animals (10). For pairs of tones the model has strong nonlinear behavior. It shows distortion products and two-tone suppression effects which are in very good agreement with experimental data. We have shown in previous papers that two-tone suppression areas of the model are very similar to those observed in the chinchilla (6, 7), and that the fractional responses proposed by ABBAS and SACHS (12) or the two-tone suppression measurement proposed by JAVEL *et al* (5) are quantitatively well reproduced (6). For click stimuli or inferred trapezoidal movements of the basilar membrane the simulated responses are generally in good agreement with most of the experimental data. These results lead us to study more complex stimuli such as speech-like sounds.

The computer generated stimuli were obtained with Klatt's serial synthesizer and presented digitally. Each voiced-sound is a periodic wave with a fundamental frequency (F_0) and one or two spectral peaks (called formants and defined by the amplitude A_i, the frequency F_i and the bandwidth B_i). For voiceless sounds the periodic source is replaced by a random noise generator with a flat spectral content modulated by the formant peaks.

RESULTS

One-formant stimulus. All the results presented in this paragraph are obtained with a static synthetic speech-like sound composed of a one-formant signal having a fundamental frequency (F_0) of 100 Hz. The frequency of the formant is taken at 1 kHz with a 70 Hz bandwidth. The total number of harmonics in the signal is near 30 (the higher order harmonics being attenuated enough to be considered as missing). Figure 2 shows the main characteristics of the responses, at different levels of the model for such a stimulus. The left column curves give the responses observed at the basilar membrane outputs (a), at the hair-cell outputs (b) or at the nerve fiber outputs as a function of abscissa along the basilar membrane (BM). Curve (a) shows that the fundamental frequency (first peak) and mainly nine harmonic components are present in the vibration pattern of the basilar membrane. Because of the tuning properties of the basilar membrane, the frequency components of higher order do not lead to noticeable responses. Responses obtained at the hair cell outputs (curve b) are a logarithmic picture of the BM vibration pattern with a saturation effect near the place corresponding to the formant of the stimulus. Responses obtained at the level of simulated nerve fibers (c) present several interesting characteristics : responses of fibers having a characteristic frequency (CF) corresponding to a harmonic component give a strong activity whatever the order of the harmonic is. At this level the action of the formant is not so prominent as at the BM level. The main explanation of this fact lies in the logarithmic behavior of the mechano-receptors transducing BM vibrations into nervous activity, combined with the nonlinear action of the interaction component. It is clear that these effects contribute to a great increase of the valley region surrounding the response of fibers whose CF corresponds to an F_0 multiple. Curve (c) also shows the abnormally low responses of the fibers whose CF correspond to the number eight and nine harmonics of the input signal. The decrease of these responses is due to the two-tone suppression effect that concurs to a significant reduction of the response. Suppression effect is more pronounced on the

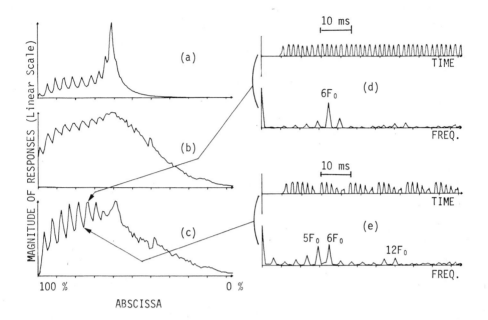

Fig. 2. Simulated responses obtained with a one-formant input sound.

high frequency side of the tuning curve of each fiber so harmonic ten (corresponding to the formant) has a strong reducing effect on the response to harmonic nine and a smaller but effective one on the response to harmonic eight.
For the two-tone suppression effect our model has an optimal frequency separation of 1.1 (in accordance with experimental data) which leads to the most
effective effect between harmonics ten and nine. The order of the two harmonics
which give the best two-tone suppression effect can be changed by modifying
fundamental frequency or formant frequency. This nonlinearity has also a side
effect on the responses observed beyond the best response to formant. The slope
of the response envelope is more pronounced. We can summarize these findings by
remarking that the main result of the two-tone suppression effect seems to be
an increase of the overall contrast in the responses to favour the responses to
the harmonic components and specially that of the formant.

The right part of figure 2 shows two typical responses observed in our nerve
fibers. For each response we give the temporal pattern (upper curve) and the
corresponding spectral content (lower curve). The upper response (curves d) is
typical of a fiber which responds to a harmonic component (number 6 in this
case) : after a delay, due to the propagation of travelling waves along cochlear partition, the temporal pattern is very regular with a periodicity quite

entirely determined by the CF of the fiber. The corresponding spectral content (obtained by Fourier transform) shows a main component at $6F_0 = CF$ and two secondary components at $5F_0$ and $7F_0$ but with a very low magnitude. The lower response (curves e) is typical of fibers which do not respond to a harmonic component (valley region of curve c) : the temporal pattern is now very irregular, it has a strong amplitude modulation at the fundamental frequency. The spectral content of such a response has two components of nearly the same magnitude (here $5F_0$ and $6F_0$). The two components are obviously accompanied by distorsion products, the main of them being the difference at frequency F_0.

So, the spectral content of each response is of great interest because it shows the frequencies on which the activity of the fibers can be synchronized. The results of the systematic investigation of the responses obtained with a one-formant sound are summarized on figure 3. This figure shows a three-dimensional picture which gives the spectral content of the response for each fiber. The horizontal axis (linear scale) corresponds to the Fourier analysis frequency (FAF), the oblique axis corresponds to abscissa (x) along cochlear partition and the vertical axis corresponds to the magnitude of the frequency components. For FAF = 0 the Fourier analysis gives the mean activity of the fibers :

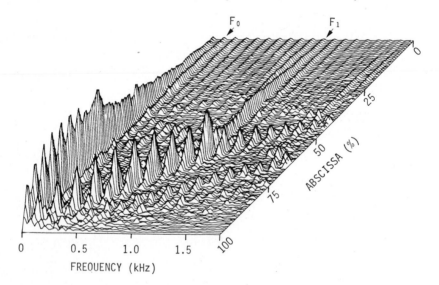

Fig. 3. Fourier analysis of responses obtained with a one-formant sound.

this oblique curve is identical to curve c in figure 2. For fibers connected near apex (x > 60 %) the responses are mainly driven by the harmonic frequency which is near fiber CF : when CF corresponds exactly to a harmonic frequency, no component at F_0 is seen in the response. When CF does not corresponds so exactly there is a not insignificant component at F_0. It can also be seen in this region that nonlinearities such as threshold and saturation can contribute to the generation of an activity synchronized to twice the best frequency component. A great number of fibers have an activity synchronized to the formant frequency (FAF = 1000 Hz). This fact cannot be explained by looking at the only tuning properties of such fibers. It is necessary to involve a nonlinear mechanism which increases the role of the most prominent frequency component. As seen previously this effect seems to be two-tone suppression which allows fibers with CF >> 1 kHz to have synchronized activity to formant frequency. It is also worth pointing out that nonlinearities generate distortion products in almost all the fibers leading to the presence of synchronized activity at frequency F_0 (sometimes $2F_0$) in the great majority of the fibers even for fibers whose CF is higher than 5 kHz.

In summary, the simulated nerve fiber responses suggest that information about fundamental frequency and formant frequency is present in the discharge patterns of fibers over a wide range of characteristic frequencies. The tuning properties of the fibers cannot explain such a spread of information and it is necessary to include the role of the nonlinearities to explain the response patterns. For a one formant speech-like sound, interaction phenomena take place between harmonics of the fundamental frequency with a prominent effect near the formant only because it corresponds to the highest harmonic component (if the formant frequency is chosen just between two harmonic frequencies the results do not change basically). In order to confirm this last remark we have analyzed the responses of the model with two-formant vowel-like sounds.

Two-formant stimulus. The results presented in this paragraph are issued from a systematic investigation on the responses obtained with two-formant vowel-like sounds covering the classical vowel triangle defined in the F_1/F_2 plane. We have chosen the vowel /æ/ which has two clearly distinct spectral peaks (right most position on the above mentioned triangle) to illustrate our findings. For this sound F_0 = 100 Hz, F_1 = 0.8 kHz and F_2 = 1.8 kHz (B_1 (formant F_1 bandwidth) = 70 Hz ; B_2 (formant F_2 bandwidth) = 120 Hz and A_2/A_1 (formant magnitude ratio) = - 6 dB). Figure 4 illustrates the characteristics of the responses obtained in our simulated fibers. The left panel shows, as on figure 3, the Fourier transform of the temporal patterns of the responses along the cochlear partition. Each Fourier transform is plotted with the analysis frequency along the horizontal axis, and the amplitude along vertical axis. The oblique axis gives the

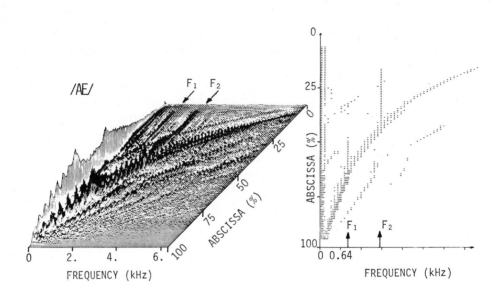

Fig. 4. Fourier analysis of responses obtained with the vowel /AE/.

abscissa from which the corresponding response is issued. The right panel
gives a section of the previous surface obtained by plotting all the points
superior to a given amplitude for each curve. This section is drawn with the
analysis frequency along the horizontal axis and the corresponding abscissa
along the vertical axis. The oblique curve, obtained by joining the points corresponding to FAF = 0 on each curve of the left panel, gives the mean activity
of the fibers. As observed in animals when analyzing the mean discharge rate of
the fibers (10) the general shape of this curve has two significant peaks which
correspond to the formant frequencies F_1, F_2. These peaks rise up from the
responses clearly driven by the harmonic structure of the input sound. When
increasing the input level, the peaks in the rate profiles disappear beginning
with the high frequency side of the spectrum. This effect is similar to those
observed in animals, where increasing the input level contributes to a loss of
the second formant peak followed by a loss of all the spectral content (10).
Nevertheless this effect is not preceded in our model by such an effective
broadening of the spectral peaks which leads to the conclusion that when increasing the input level two phenomena will take place : a loss of selectivity
due to BM responses (14) and saturation effects joined with two-tone suppression effects. Since two-tone suppression in each fiber is generally more effective for frequencies above CF it is conceivable that the regions concerned by
the second formant will be affected before the regions concerned by the first
formant.

Figure 4 also shows the spread of the information concerning the formant frequencies. This phenomenon is basically the same as that observed for a one-formant sound except for a small region near $CF = F_2$ where synchronized information at $F = F_1$ disappears. Table 1 summarizes, for all the different sounds we have tested, the frequencies where one can expect the nervous activity to be synchronized as a function of the unit CF considered. This table shows that the activity of the fibers is greatly influenced by F_0 and CF for all locations,

TABLE 1

SYNCHRONISATION OF THE NERVOUS ACTIVITY ACCORDING TO THE FIBER CF

CF	25 Hz	F_1		F_2	4 kHz
$m\ F_0$	YES $(1 < m < 8)$	YES $(m=8)$	YES $(m=1)$	YES $(m=18)$	YES $(m=1,2)$
$n\ F_1$	NO	YES $(n=1)$	YES $(n=1)$	NO	YES $(n=1)$
$k\ F_2$	NO	NO	NO	YES $(k=1)$	YES $(k=1)$
$1\ CF$	YES $(1=1,2)$	YES $(1=1,2)$	YES $(1=1)$	YES $(1=1,2)$	YES $(1=1)$

whereas information about formant frequencies is more localized (as observed by SINEX *et al* (15),for a formant F_i the concerned fibers are generally those with $CF > F_i$). The low efficiency of threshold and saturation effects chosen to obtain the responses shown in figure 4 explains the lack of multiples for the different components of the responses (by modifying saturation coefficients we have observed responses driven by multiples 6 or 7 of a formant frequency).

The temporal patterns of the unit-responses are not basically different from the one-formant sound : if the fiber responds to a main component of the input signal the temporal pattern is very regular (whatever the component will be) and if the fiber responds to several components the temporal pattern is irregular with generally a pronounced amplitude modulation at $F = F_0$.

This Fourier analysis of the responses obtained with our model for a two-formant vowel sound confirms that the temporal coding provides a more robust and more precise representation of the vowel characteristics than the rate coding does (10, 11). In presence of background noise the temporal representation usually retains all information about vowel spectra. The experiments that we

have made by adding broad-band noise to our stimuli confirm the conclusions of
VOIGT *et al* (16) even if our sensory receptors are presently too simple to
reproduce exactly their experiments. Anyhow, information about vowel spectra
disappears in the mean activity profile much before than in the Fourier analysis.

Fricative stimulus. To study more in detail the role of the formant frequencies, it is interesting to use a fricative-like sound because such a stimulus
has formant frequencies but no harmonic complexes. Formants are defined as the
spectral peaks of a broad-band noise. The results presented below are issued
from a study of sounds /f/, /S/, /CH/ in our model. Figure 5 shows the characteristics of the responses obtained for the two-formant sound /S/. The formant
frequencies of this sound are F_1 = 5 kHz (bandwidth = 0.8 kHz), F_2 = 7,5 kHz
(bandwidth = 1 kHz).

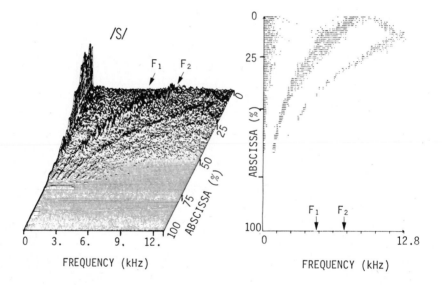

Fig. 5. Fourier analysis of responses obtained with the fricative /S/.

The left panel in figure 5 shows the Fourier transform of the temporal patterns of the responses along cochlear partition (same drawing as in figure 4).
The right panel gives a horizontal section of the previous surface (same drawing as in figure 4). These pictures show clearly that, for such a stimulus,
the temporal pattern of the activity of a fiber is only determined by the CF of
the fiber, and that no synchronized activity is observed at the formant

frequency. The mean activity of the simulated fibers (FAF = 0) gives a representation of the spectral content of the stimulus, but this representation is not more robust than with vowel stimuli and will disappear if the input level is rather increased to saturate a great number of fibers. Nonlinearities such as two-tone suppression effect do not seem to be of primary importance in such conditions : we have changed the efficiency of this effect on the model without any noticeable improvement of the overall contrast of the response, and we have never observed synchronized activity at formant frequencies. The fine Fourier analysis of responses always shows activity synchronized to F = CF or multiples of CF due to rectifier distortion products generated by threshold and saturation nonlinearities. These results are conform to the experimental data of DELGUTTE (17) and correspond to the analysis made by SINEX et al (15).

The temporal patterns of our simulated responses are different from the responses obtained with a vowel-like sound. The temporal pattern is always very irregular with an envelope modulation which does not display a clear periodicity.

CONCLUSIONS

The results which we have presented in this paper describe the internal representation of the characteristics of some typical speech-like sounds at the level of the auditory nerve. It is reasonable to assume that such a representation is a first step in the perception of speech. Our results indicate that there must be cues in the neural discharge patterns other than average discharge rate which are useful and more resistant to stimulus manipulations. These cues may be related to synchrony, some others may involve the distribution of activity among different populations of fibers. These issues appear to be resolvable by further research using presently available methods. Among them, models will play an important role because they allow to relate accurately the acoustic features of sounds to the responses of nerve fibers. In order to be really useful, a model must reproduce all the known experimental data for various kinds of stimulus and take into account all the anatomical and physiological data. In this respect we think that our model must be improved especially at the level of the sensory receptors where our description is not accurate enough, and at the level of basilar membrane where the nonlinearities seem to play an important role in the observed fusion of formants as input level is increased.

The ultimate understanding of such a representation of sounds requires more knowledge of how the information contained in auditory nerve activity is processed by the central nervous system. Our results indicate that it is reasonable to think that the central nervous system can process the neural data in, at least, two ways depending upon the presence or the lack of a synchronized activity in the discharge patterns of auditory-nerve fibers. Central mechanisms must be now studied and our knowledge about the periphery will be improved by analysing the functional role played by the Central Nervous System to process the data observed in nerve fibers.

ACKNOWLEDGEMENTS

The author wishes to acknowledge the work and the fruitful advice of Dr. M. BOULOGNE concerning the experiments, the design of software and the collection of data. Whithout his help this work would not have been done. This research is supported by C.N.R.S. (E.R.A. 366) and by Agence de l'Informatique (Convention N° 80/379).

REFERENCES

1. GEISLER, C.D., RHODE, W.S. and KENNEDY, D.T. (1974) Responses to Tonal Stimuli of Single Auditory Nerve Fibers and their Relationship to Basilar Membrane Motion in the Squirrel Monkey, J. Neurophysiol. 37, pp 1156 - 1172.

2. KIANG, N.Y.S. (1965) Discharge Patterns of Single Fibers in the Cat's Auditory Nerve, MIT Press, Cambridge MA.

3. SACHS, M.B. and ABBAS, P.J. (1974) Rate Versus Level Functions for Auditory-Nerve Fibers in Cats : Tone-Burst Stimuli, J. Acoust. Soc. Am. 56, pp 1835 - 1847.

4. JAVEL, E., GEISLER, C.D. and RAVINDRAN, A. (1978) Two-Tone Suppression in Auditory Nerve of the Cat : Rate-Intensity and Temporal Analyses, J. Acoust. Soc. Am. 63, pp 1093 - 1104.

5. JAVEL, E. (1981) Suppression of Auditory Nerve Responses I : Temporal Analysis, Intensity Effects and Suppression Contours, J. Acoust. Soc. Am. 69, pp 1735 - 1745.

6. DOLMAZON, J.M. (1980) Contribution aux recherches sur l'appareil auditif : élaboration et exploitation d'un modèle de fonctionnement du système périphérique, Thèse d'Etat, I.N.P.G. Grenoble (France).

7. DOLMAZON, J.M. and BOULOGNE, M. (1982) Interaction phenomena in a model of mechanical to neural transduction in the ear, to be published in Speech Communication, North-Holland Publ. Comp.

8. BOULOGNE, M. and DOLMAZON, J.M. (1981) Simulated auditory nerve fiber responses to speech signal, J. Acoust. Soc. Am. 69 S1, pp S54.

9. SPOENDLIN, H. (1974) Neuroanatomy of the cochlea, in ZWICKER, E. and TERHARDT, E. (Ed.), Facts and Models in Hearing, Springer-Verlag, Berlin, pp 18 - 32.

10. SACHS, M.B. and YOUNG, E.D. (1979a) Encoding of Steady-State Vowels in the Auditory Nerve : Representation in Terms of Discharge Rate, J. Acoust. Soc. Am. 66, pp 470 - 479.

11. YOUNG, E.D. and SACHS, M.B. (1979b) Representation of Steady-State Vowels in the Temporal Aspects of the Discharge Patterns of Populations of Auditory Nerve Fibers, J. Acoust. Soc. Am. 66, pp 1381 - 1403.

12. ABBAS, P.J. and SACHS, M.B. (1976) Two-tone Suppression in Auditory Nerve Fibers : Extension of a Stimulus Response Relationships, J. Acoust. Soc. Am. 59, pp 112 - 122.

13. DELGUTTE, B. (1980) Representation on Speech Like Sounds in the Discharges of Auditory-Nerve Fibers, J. Acoust. Soc. Am. 68, pp 843 - 857.

14. RHODE, W.S. (1978) Some Observations on Cochlear Mechanics, J. Acoust. Soc. Am. 64, pp 158 - 176.

15. SINEX, D.G. and GEISLER, C.D. (1981) Responses of Auditory Nerve Fibers to Consonant-vowel syllabes, J. Acoust. Soc. Am. 69 S1, pp S54.

16. VOIGT, H.F., SACHS, M.B. and YOUNG, E.D. (1980) Effect of Masking Noise on the Representation of Vowel Spectra in the Auditory Nerve. Personnal Communication.

17. DELGUTTE, B. (1981) Representation of Speech-Like Sounds in the Discharge Patterns of Auditory-Nerve Fibers, PH Thesis, M.I.T., Cambridge, MA.

18. SACHS, M.B. and YOUNG, E.D. (1980) Effect of Nonlinearities on Speech Encoding in the Auditory-Nerve, J. Acoust. Soc. Am. 68, pp 858 - 875.

19. KIANG, N.Y.S. (1980) Processing of Speech by the Auditory Nervous System, J. Acoust. Soc. Am. 68, pp 830 - 835.

© 1982 Elsevier Biomedical Press
The Representation of Speech in the Peripheral
Auditory System, R. Carlson and B. Granström eds.

TEMPORAL PROCESSING OF PERIPHERAL AUDITORY PATTERNS OF SPEECH

L.A. CHISTOVICH, V.V. LUBLINSKAYA, T.G. MALINNIKOVA, E.A. OGORODNIKOVA,
E.I. STOLJAROVA AND S.JA. ZHUKOV
Pavlov Institute of Physiology, the Academy of Sciences of the USSR,
Nab. Makarova 6, Leningrad, 199164, USSR

This paper is dedicated to the memory of the late Professor Valerij
Kozhevnikov who was a leader of one of the two areas in speech perception
research carried out at the Pavlov Institute of Physiology. This area is
concerned with building a signal processing system simulating some phenomena believed to be important for peripheral auditory processing and with
studying the representation of speech signals at the output of this system.
The other area's aim is to gain at least a preliminary understanding of the
principles of the central auditory processing of the peripheral speech pattern. Our attempts to achieve the last goal are based on the assumption
that the problems inherent in automatic speech recognition and made explicit by research in this field also are the fundamental problems of the theory of central auditory processing. We treat the alternative ways of a
possible solution of some of these problems as the working hypotheses, and
we try to test them by experiments on speech-like stimuli perception. It
is clear that the system simulating peripheral auditory processing is an
obligatory tool in studying central processing. The study of central processing includes modelling: on the one hand, models are to be fed by the
output signals of the peripheral auditory system; on the other hand, the
knowledge about central procedures of the peripheral pattern processing
could help to decide whether the peripheral model is good or bad. In simulating the peripheral system one has, in fact, to invent some schemes re-
producing the empirical phenomena observed in a quite restricted set of
stimuli situations. It is, a priori, unclear whether the combination of
such schemes will lead to meaningful results in a complex real speech situation.

Fig. 1 and Fig. 2 present the results of incorporating the blocks of
"two-tone suppression" (from high-to-low frequencies) and the blocks of
"short-term adaptation" (independent adaptation in each channel) in the
model of peripheral processing.

Fig. 1A shows the dynamic spectrogram and the spectrum shape contour
registered at the output of a multichannel analyzer (1-3) representing the

linear part of the model. Fig. 1B shows the dynamic spectrogram and the spectrum shape contour at the output of the layer of "two-tone suppression" blocks (4). A comparison of A and B makes it clear that the signal processing in the "two-tone suppression" layer results in sharpening the spectrum shape pattern.

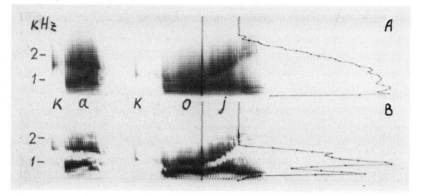

Fig. 1. The word /kakoj/. Vertical lines indicate the moments of registration of spectrum shape contours.

Fig. 2A and Fig. 2B show the dynamic spectrograms obtained at the output of the "two-tone suppression" layer and at the output of the "short-term adaptation" layer. Each "short-term adaptation" block receives the signal from the output of the corresponding "two-tone suppression" block. The obvious effect of adaptation consists of flattening the spectrum shape at the steady-state portions of the vowels. Only the transitional parts of the patterns seem to possess the contrastive spectrum shape.

If a similar effect of adaptation is inherent in real peripheral auditory processing, the conventional "continuous extraction of the parameters" approach would be hardly applicable in the case of speech perception. A more compelling alternative is to treat the speech flow as a temporal sequence of events, but the acceptance of this point of view leads to many questions concerning the inventory of events, their role in phonetic interpretation and so on. Our attempts to find some approach to these problems will be described below.

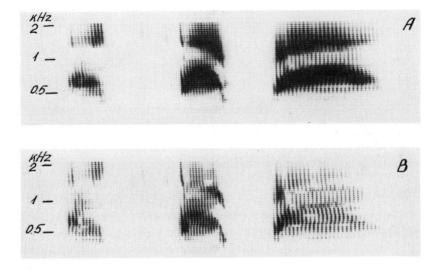

Fig. 2. The word /ašxabat/.

SIMULATION OF ON- AND OFF-RESPONSES, POSSIBLE ROLE OF THESE RESPONSES IN SPEECH PROCESSING

The minimal perturbations of the stimulus which are sufficient to transform it from a single sound into a sequence of rhythmically organized sounds have been studied (5-7). The results suggested that the processing responsible for this transformation must be based on detection of the amplitude changes in the frequency channels of the auditory system. A model for the envelope in the channel processing has been developed (6); the output signals of the model can be treated as the equivalents of the on- and off-responses of the higher order phasic auditory neurons. Up to this moment, the situations we have tested the system (8,9) on are those in which the envelope processing blocks are fed with half-wave rectified and compressed waveforms originating from the frequency channels of the analyzer (1,2). Neither the "two-tone suppression" blocks nor the "short-

term adaptation" blocks have been interposed till now between the analyzer
and the envelope processing scheme.

Fig. 3A shows the response of the system to the sentence /žŏska kắk
na kŏčk'i/. Fig. 3B shows the dynamic spectrogram of the same sentence
registered at the output of the analyzer. The on-responses (black dots)
and off-responses (white dots) mark the onsets and offsets of the vowel
segments as well as onsets of the bursts. The temporal dispersion of the
dots in different channels is rather small -- the dots form almost vertical lines. It appears that mere combining of responses over the frequency channels might be sufficient for formation of segment boundary markers.

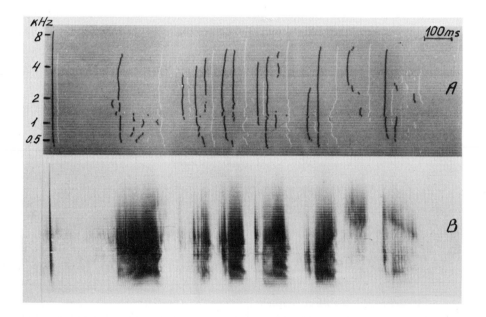

Fig. 3. Dynamic spectrogram (B) and the output of the envelope processing blocks (A). The sentence /žŏska kắk na kŏčk'i/.

Assumption of the reality of segment boundary markers seems to be a
crucial point for the development of the theory of the central auditory
processing of speech, music and various other natural sounds. Without this
assumption, one cannot virtually describe extraction and processing of the

durational information (stress, rhythmic pattern, tempo). The markers seem to be the most appropriate candidates for control signals in spectral and temporal integration, sorting and sampling all kinds of auditory information.

The tonotopically organized subsystem, indicating by on- and off responses the moments of amplitude changes in the frequency channels, might also provide the answer to one of the troublesome problems concerning phoneme identification. It is known that identification of diphones is based not only on the spectral patterns of the constituent segments, but also either on the "contrast" between these patterns (10) or on the pattern of the spectrum change from the first to the second segment.

The identification data (Table 1) for stimuli S1 and S2, shown in Fig. 4, can serve as a good example. The stimuli are made of two steady-state segments, the first segment being the same in both stimuli. Both stimuli are perceived as syllables, but the first phoneme in S1 is a nasal consonant and the first phoneme in S2 is a vowel. The results are highly reliable -- they were obtained for a group of 17 subjects with 500 responses accumulated for each stimulus (11).

TABLE 1

IDENTIFICATION OF S1 AND S2 STIMULI

Responses:	Vn	Vm	nV	mV	V	mn	Vw
% S1			0.6	91.4	8.0		
S2	67.2	28.6				3.8	0.4

The first step to get a probable explanation of these data is to assume that the first segment processing does not result in a phoneme decision but gives rise to a set of phoneme-candidates similar to the segment. The second step is to find a reason why the VV combination predicted by the above-mentioned assumption was never observed as a response to the S1 stimulus. Inspection of real speech points to a possible reason: an abrupt change in the spectrum or the amplitude of the signal is incompatible with the VV combination. Experiments on perception of synthetic vowels or two-tone complexes subjected to amplitude modulation confirm this explanation. Stimuli with a step-like intensity increment are perceived as CV (in case of decrement - as VC); smoothing of the step results in VV perception (5,12).

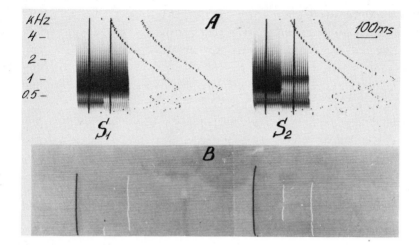

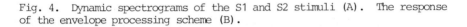

Fig. 4. Dynamic spectrograms of the S1 and S2 stimuli (A). The response
of the envelope processing scheme (B).

Temporal distribution of on- or off-responses could apparently be
used to differentiate between an abrupt and a gradual change in the peripheral auditory pattern. Fig. 4B suggests that even the choice between
the nasal-vowel and the vowel-nasal diphones might be influenced by the
subsystem generating on- and off-responses. Off-responses in the S2 representation are concentrated in a mid-frequency region, while off-responses in the S1 representation are concentrated in a low-frequency region.

Thus, it is tempting to speculate that the human auditory-to-phonetic
transformation procedure is based on some combination of segment-by-pho-
neme recognition and diphone recognition approaches. Each element corresponding to a diphone has two phoneme (allophone) inputs and one or more
additional inputs excited by some specific properties of on- and off-response patterns.

To suggest a speech perception model based on this idea, one first
has to gain some understanding of the temporal processing of spectral information inside the segments. Perception of vowels seems to be the most
appropriate object for the study.

FORMANT TRANSITION PERCEPTION

The experiments described in this and in the next section have been
inspired by the idea that the auditory dynamic spectrum of a vowel might
be subjected to two parallel procedures of processing, one dealing with
the spectrum shapes and the other dealing with the spectrum changes.

The spectrum changes occurring in the natural vowel segments are simple enough and consist in rather slow movements of spectral (formant)
peaks along the frequency scale. The first experiment (13) was aimed to
find out whether the spectral peak movement - the formant transition - is
important for the identification of at least some of the vowels. Short
(80 ms) two-formant stimuli with steady-state F1 fixed at 300 Hz and with
linearly rising or falling F2 were used in the experiment. The subjects
were asked to identify the stimuli as one of four vowels: [u], [ʉ], [i],
[ɨ].

The initial frequency of the F2 contour, $F2_i$, and the final frequency,
$F2_f$, are used as the stimuli parameters in Fig. 5. The filled and open circles represent the boundary between the [ʉ] and [ɨ] categories obtained
for one subject in two experiments. A similar shape of the boundary
($F2_f - F2_i + A = 0$) was found for each of 8 subjects participating in the experiments, but the value of the constant A slightly varied from subject to
subject and could be either positive or negative. The results suggest
that falling F2 and rising F2 are consistently associated with different
vowel categories by Russian subjects. It is rather safe to assume that
one of these categories really corresponds to the cardinal vowel [ɨ] which
is treated by the Leningrad phonetic school as a phoneme in the Russian
language. As to the second category, we are not so sure that [ʉ] is an
appropriate symbol.

The range of average frequencies of F2-contours eliciting [ʉ] and
[ɨ] responses is approximately delimited by 1.1 and 1.7 kHz. More recent
data to be described below have been obtained for this frequency range.
The influence of the stimulus duration on the response distributions was
studied at first for three kinds of two-formant stimuli (F1=0.3 kHz): F2
was either steady-state or rising or falling. The duration has been varied from two to eight glottal pulses, the fundamental period being equal
to 8 ms. The second formant frequency has been changed in steps of 40 Hz
from pulse to pulse. The subjects (16 Russian adults) were allowed to use
[u], [ʉ], [ɨ], [i] for identification responses.

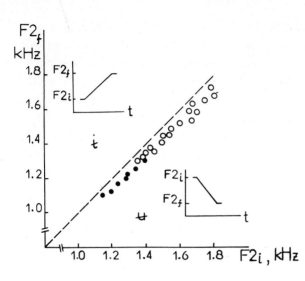

Fig. 5.   Boundary between [ʌ] and [ɨ] vowel categories.

In the case of a steady-state stimulus, the response distribution appeared to be practically uninfluenced by the increase of the stimulus duration.   This was true for the whole set of F2 frequencies tested in the experiment.

The continuous change of response distribution with the lengthening of the stimulus in the whole range of durations was observed for stimuli with moving second formant.   There was a gradual increase of [ʌ] responses for stimuli with falling F2, and there was a gradual increase of [ɨ] responses for stimuli with rising F2.   One possible explanation of [ʌ] or [ɨ] increase could be a widening of the frequency range over which the spectral peak is moving.   The next experiment was carried out to test this hypothesis.

The stimuli were made in a similar way, but two values of the step in F2 increase (or decrease) were used: 40 and 80 Hz.   The range of durations was the same for the stimuli with a different step value (with a different rate of the F2 transition).   To facilitate the [ʌ] and [ɨ] responses, the subjects were asked to select between these two alternatives and to answer "neither [ʌ] nor [ɨ]" only in the case when no resemblance to [ʌ] or [ɨ] could be found in the stimulus.

The results are shown in Fig. 6. It is evident that the open circles, representing the data for a 40 Hz step of the F2 change, and the filled circles, representing the data for 80 Hz step of the F2 change, form a single smooth [æ] identification function (or [ɨ] identification function) when the range of the F2 movement, $\Delta F2 = F2_f - F2_i$, is used as an independent variable. The duration itself does not seem to be important: arrows indicate the pairs of filled and open circles corresponding to the same frequency range with the stimuli durations differing by a factor of two.

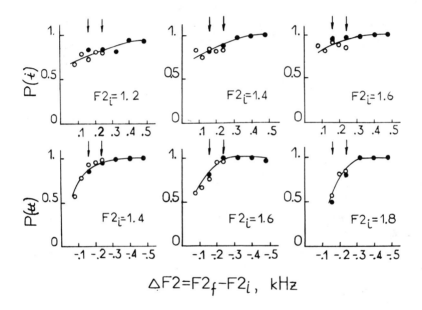

Fig. 6. Relative frequency of identification of [æ] and [ɨ] as a function of the frequency range of formant transition.

It might be interesting to mention that the model simulating the detection of rise or fall of F2 does not necessarily have to incorporate the formant extraction procedure. Fig. 7 shows the on- and off-response patterns representing the F2 transitions at the output of the envelope processing system which is virtually blind to the formants in a steady-state stimuli. Rather simple processing blocks based on comparison of

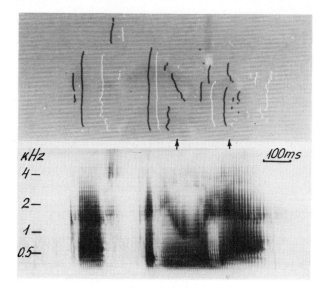

Fig. 7. Spectrogram of the word /kastriul'a/ (bottom) and output of the envelope processing model (top). Arrows mark the second formant transitions.

the outputs of three adjacent channels of this system could serve as local detectors of falling or rising of the spectral peak. Summing elements collecting the responses from the layer of local detectors would receive a stronger excitation when the range of the F2 movement increased and a larger set of local detectors were responding. To be compatible with the experimental data, the summing element has to have a rather long integration time, and it must be accessible to external control in reading out the accumulated information.

Inspection of the real speech patterns leaves no doubt that interpretation of the formant transition must depend on much additional information. The elements corresponding to diphones seem to be more appropriate receivers of the transition detectors' responses than the elements corresponding to phonemes. For instance, the data concerning [ɑ] and [ɨ] identification might be treated in such a way that the subjects were in

fact discriminating between the truncated C [u] and C [i] syllables with
C being the soft consonant in the first case and C being the hard consonant in the second case.

TEMPORAL PROCESSING OF THE SPECTRUM SHAPES

An identification of steady-state vowels is undoubtedly based on the
spectrum shape configuration. A number of hypotheses could be proposed
for spectrum shape processing in nonstationary vowels. Our strategy was
to start with the most simple hypotheses which do not require short-term
memory for the dynamic spectrogram of the segment. The first task (14)
was to test whether there exists an integration (averaging) of the spectral information over the vowel segment. The second task (15) was to select between two hypotheses concerning the nature of the integrated information: does it correspond to the spectrum shapes or to the results
of the running classification of the spectrum shape samples, for instance,
to the responses of the neurons tuned to specific spectral configurations?
If the dynamic spectrum is integrated over the vowel duration, it is reasonable to expect that the stimulus made of alternating one-formant F1-
pulses and two-formant F1, F2-pulses will give rise to the same integrated
spectrum shape as some two-formant stimulus with the first formant dominating in amplitude. The higher the proportion of F1-pulses in the first
stimulus, the greater must the difference between A1 and A2 in two-formant
stimulus be to make these stimuli equal in the integrated spectrum shape.
Assuming that the phoneme response distribution is determined by integrated spectrum shape, one could predict that the increase of the proportion of one-formant pulses in the stimulus with alternating one-formant and
two-formant pulses would be phonetically equivalent to the increase of the
amplitude of the corresponding formant in two-formant stimulus.

Short tonal pulses with F1 and F2 frequencies and with triangular en-
velope-shape were synthesized to simulate F1- and F2-pulses. Two-formant
pulses were synthesized by adding with proper coefficients the wave-forms
of F1- and F2-pulses. Stimuli were made as trains of 8 pulses with
$T_0 \approx 20$ ms. The formant frequencies (F1=0.75 kHz, F2=2.5 kHz) were chosen
to make two-formant stimulus with A1=A2 clearly dissimilar in phonetic
quality from each of the one-formant stimuli. The subjects were asked to
use the following symbols for identification: [u], [ʉ], [o], [ø], [a],
[æ], [ɛ], [e], [ɨ], [i].

176

The processing of the response data was based on the assumption that the theoretical response distribution, R_i, corresponding to the two-formant stimulus with a given A1-A2 ratio, can be treated as a weighted sum of three "basic" distributions: P1 and P2 corresponding to the one-formant F1 and F2 stimuli, and P0-response distribution corresponding to the "best" of the two-formant stimuli. P1 and P2 were based on a great number of responses and they were believed to be equal to the theoretical distributions

$$R_i = a_i P1 + b_i P2 + c_i P0.$$

It was assumed that a similar treatment is valid for the distributions corresponding to stimuli with alternating one-formant and two-formant pulses.

Fig. 8A shows a, b, c as functions of the formant amplitudes in two-formant stimuli. Fig. 8B shows a, b, c as functions of the proportion of one-formant pulses in stimuli with alternating one-formant and two-formant pulses. The approximation appeared to be equally good for both sets of stimuli.

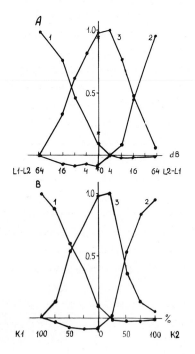

Fig. 8. Coefficients of three components (a – curve 1, b – 2, c – 3) used to approximate the response distributions corresponding to test stimuli.
A. Data for two-formant stimuli. L1-L2 – the level difference between the first and the second formant; L2-L1 – the level difference between the second and the first formant.

B. Data for stimuli with alternating one-formant and two-formant pulses. K1 – percent of F1-pulses, K2 – percent of F2-pulses in the stimulus.

The results indicate that an increase of the proportion of one-formant pulses and the increase of the amplitude of the corresponding formant in two-formant stimulus have the same effect on the vowel quality of the stimulus. This is in agreement with the dynamic spectrum integration hypothesis, but the data do not exclude the possibility of the running classification of the dynamic spectrum with the additional integration of the running classification results.

If the dynamic spectrum is immediately subjected to integration, the stimulus made of an equal number of alternating F1- and F2-pulses must give rise to the response distribution, P_m, roughly corresponding to the response distribution, P_s, elicited by the two-formant stimulus with equal amplitudes of the formants.

To explain what could be expected in a case of running classification, let us assume that the dynamic spectrum is sampled at the moments of peak response of the analyzer to each of the pulses. If the interval between the pulses is long enough in comparison to the pulse duration and to the response time of the filters, the sampled spectrum shapes will be close to those for one-formant stimuli. No spectrum shape with equally high maximum characteristics for two-formant stimulus would appear in the series of the sampled shapes. The data presented earlier in this paper (Table 1) suggest that the segment percept corresponds not to a single phoneme but to a list of the similar-to-segment phonemes with the magnitudes of similarity ascribed to indicated phonemes. Let us assume that eath sampled shape is transformed into such a list and that the segment percept is formed by accumulating all the lists appearing along the segment. Treating the response distribution as a direct empirical estimation of the segment percept, one could expect P_m to be close to a weighted sum of P1 and P2 but not to contain the phonemes specific to two-formant stimulus.

To test these predictions, one has to select such F1, F2 combinations which give rise to the most dissimilar P1, P2, and P_s distributions. Four F1, F2 combinations used in the experiments (15) were indicated in Fig. 9. The subjects had to identify the same 10 vowels as in the preceding experiments.

To check whether our choice of F1, F2 was a successful one, we approximated P_s by a sum of corresponding P1 and P2:

$$P_s = aP1 + bP2 + R_s$$

and inspected the residue R_2, both the R_s-pattern and the magnitude $\|R_s\|^2$.

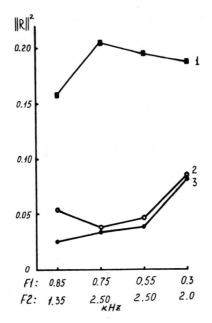

Fig. 9. Magnitude of the residue resulting
from approximation of the response distribution (see text).

The magnitude of the residue appeared to be very high for all four
F1, F2 combinations (curve 1 in Fig. 9); a clear maximum was observed in
all four R_s-patterns. The phoneme corresponding to this maximum was accepted as specific to a given two-formant stimulus.

The percentage of the specific phoneme in the response distribution
P_m, representing the stimulus with alternating F1- and F2-pulses was
quite low for all F1, F2 combinations: 17, 10, 5 and 3%.

A more sophisticated method of estimating the similarity of P_m and
P_s was based on comparison of the results of two types of P_m approximation:

$$1. \quad P_m = a_1 P1 + b_1 P2 + R_1$$
$$2. \quad P_m = a_2 P1 + b_2 P2 + c R_s + R_2$$

The magnitude of the residue $\|R_1\|^2$ is represented by curve 2 in Fig. 9,
the magnitude of $\|R_2\|^2$ - by curve 3 in Fig. 9. It is clear that the ad-
dition of R_s as a third basic component (type 2 of approximation) does not
noticeably improve the quality of approximation. Some decrease of $\|R\|^2$

is observed only for one of the F1, F2 combinations.

It is self-evident that the approximation of P_m by three components (P1, P2 and R_s) would reduce the approximation error if the spectrum integration hypothesis was true. Fig. 8A suggests that the exact similarity of the amplitude difference between maxima in the spectrum shapes corresponding to P_m and P_s is not necessary for this effect: a rather wide range of A1, A2 differences gives rise to a two-formant percept.

We must conclude that the data do not support the dynamic spectrum integration hypothesis and point to the running classification of "instantaneous" or sampled spectrum shapes with an additional accumulation of the running classification results.

CONCLUSION

As a conclusion we prefer to outline the sketch of the probable auditory processing of speech.

1. Two kinds of processing are applied in parallel to the output signals of the peripheral auditory system. One subsystem deals with the peripheral pattern itself, another deals with the changes in the pattern.

2. The processing responsible for the changes in the pattern extraction is based on amplitude (spike density) changes in the frequency channels. The output of the initial part of this subsystem is the spatial pattern of on-responses and, perhaps, off-responses.

3. The on- and off-patterns are, again, processed in a number of parallel ways. Some of them are short cut with the basic operation being the summation of the responses over wide ranges of the frequency scale. Some other branches (detection of the direction of transition) incorporate first the spatially local processing with accumulation of data over wide spatial and temporal ranges. The signals derived from on- and off-patterns are used for different purposes: to control the processing and to identify the speech elements.

4. Processing dealing with the form of the peripheral excitation patterns includes some preliminary local processing of the patterns (this was not discussed in this paper) and the running excitation of the restricted set of elements tuned to specific configurations of the transformed patterns. Responses of these elements integrated over the segment duration can be treated as the description of the segment in terms of similar-to-segment phonemes (allophones).

5. Both subsystems converge on elements close to diphones. These elements are activated by the inputs corresponding to constituent segments and they are either activated or inhibited by additional inputs responding to specific on- and off-patterns at the boundaries between the segments. This sketch based on speech-like stimuli perception data seems at least more compatible with the neurophysiological facts than the parameter extraction approach widely used in automatic speech recognition and in speculations based on current psychoacoustical theory.

REFERENCES

1. Shupljakov, V.S., Dolmazon, J-M. and Bastet, L. (1978) Fiziologich-eskij Zhurnal SSSF, 64, 12, pp. 1786-1802.

2. Borozdin, A.N., Goloveshkin, V.T., Kozhevnikov, V.A. and Shupljakov, V.S. (1980) Fiziologicheskij Zhurnal SSSR, 66, 1, pp. 125-131.

3. Kozhevnikov, V.A., Slepokurova, N.A., Stoljarova, E.I. and Chujkina, L.I. (1981) Issledovanie Modelej Recheobrazovania i Rechevosprijatia, Leningrad, pp. 94-103.

4. Kozhevnikov, V.A. and Chistovich (1980) Devise for transformation of frequency-dependent voltage. Avtorskoe svidetelstvo SSSR No. 822071, vudano 12 decabrja 1980 g.

5. Physiology of Speech. Speech Perception (1976), "Nauka", Leningrad.

6. Chistovich, I.A. (1978) Fiziologia Cheloveka, 4, 2, pp. 208-212.

7. Stoljarova, E.I. and Chistovich, I.A. (1977) Fiziologia Cheloveka, 3, 1, pp- 72-76.

8. Kozhevnikov, V.A. and Stoljarova, E.I. (1980) Fiziologicheskij Zhurnal SSSR, 66, 1, pp. 132-138.

9. Malinnikova, T.G., Ogorodnikova, E.A. and Stoljarova, E.I. (1980), Fiziologicheskij Zhurnal SSSR, 66, 1, pp. 139-145.

10. Bondarko, L.V. (1981) Phonetic Description of Language and Phonological Description of Speech. Izdatelstvo LGU, Leningrad.

11. Zhukov, S.J. and Shukova, M.G. (1978) Fiziologia Cheloveka, 4, 2, pp. 220-224.

12. Lesogor, L.V. and Chistovich, L.A. (1978) Fiziologia Cheloveka, 4, 2, pp. 213-219.

13. Lublinskaja, V.V. and Slepokurova, N.A. (1977) Fiziologia Cheloveka, 3, 1, pp. 77-84.

14. Chistovich, L.A., Bedrov, Ja.A., Malinnikova, T.G. and Ogorodnikova, E.A. (in press) Traides de Symposium Franco-Sovietigue, Grenoble, 20-22 Novem., 1981.

15. Chistovich, L.A. and Ogorodnikova, E.A. (in press) Speech Communication.

© 1982 Elsevier Biomedical Press
The Representation of Speech in the Peripheral
Auditory System, R. Carlson and B. Granström eds.

SPEECH PROCESSING STRATEGIES BASED ON AUDITORY MODELS

DENNIS H. KLATT

Massachusetts Institute of Technology, Room 36-523, Cambridge MA
02139 (U.S.A.)

INTRODUCTION

In keeping with the theme of a conference on speech
processing in the auditory periphery, my contribution will focus on
two issues. One is the rather specific goal of improving the sound
spectrograph based on auditory constraints, if indeed that is
possible. The second objective is to look more broadly at current
speech recognition strategies (and current models of speech
perception) to ask whether knowledge of peripheral processing, and
knowledge of basic psychophysical relations can help constrain and
chose among models.

AN IMPROVED SOUND SPECTROGRAPH?

The broadband sound spectrograph machine has been used for
speech analysis for about 40 years. The spectrograph was
masterfully designed (Koenig, Dunn and Lacy, 1946; Presti, 1966) to
bring out as horizontal dark bands the natural resonant frequencies
(formants) of a male speaking voice while preserving sufficient
time resolution to detect sudden onsets, and also display each
glottal pulse as a vertical striation. The machine has proven to
be of great value in investigations of many speech production
processes.

However, in this paper, I am going to focus on the negative
aspects of the sound spectrograph. As far as speech perception
research is concerned, it is not inconceivable that the sound
spectrograph has had an overall detrimental influence over the last
40 years by emphasizing aspects of speech spectra that are probably
not direct perceptual cues (and in some cases may not even be
resolved by the ear).

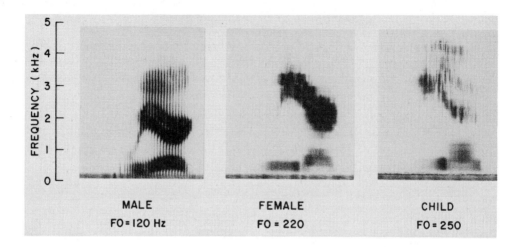

Figure 1. Broadband spectrograms of the words "we are".

An example of this problem is shown in Figure 1. Broadband
spectrograms are displayed of the same words, "we are", spoken by a
man, woman, and child. The woman and child speak with a much
higher fundamental frequency, have a more breathy voice quality,
and also have shorter vocal tracts, implying higher formant
frequencies. These changes result in rather different appearing
patterns for the same word: formant frequency motions are less
distinct than for the male voice, harmonics begin to appear as
horizontal dark bands, and some audible sounds disappear below the
marking threshold of the spectrogram paper (for example, the /w/ of
"we are").

All of these differences leave the observer with the
impression that either (1) the speech of women and children must be
harder to understand than that of men, or (2) listening to women
and children requires the invocation of different decoding
strategies. It may be the case that higher-pitched vowels are
slightly less intelligible (Sundberg, this volume), but we know
from intelligibility testing that overall, women's speech is as
intelligible, or even slightly more intelligible than man's.

Few people could be convinced that the second alternative, markedly different perceptual strategies for women, is true either. In fact, it seems to be generally believed that the speech patterns of men and women could be made to look more similar if minor modifications were made to the sound spectrograph. For example, one might make the analysis filter slightly wider in bandwidth than the present 300 Hz so that individual harmonics of a female voice would not be resolved, but not too wide so that closely spaced formants could still be resolved as individual horizontal dark bands.

Yet here we are, nearly 40 years later, and the sound spectrograph machine essentially has not changed. The reason, of course, is that these two goals conflict -- two formants often approach to within about 300 Hz in running speech, so any analysis filter with a bandwidth greater than 300 Hz will merge them into one broad energy concentration. Furthermore, researchers prefer to work with a formant-like representation, even if it means often restricting their data bases to male speakers, simply because one can quantify and compare the frequency motions of formant peaks. It is not as easy to quantify and compare the shapes of spectra that are highly smoothed. I'll return to this problem below.

The purpose of the following paragraphs, then, is to explore the desirability of replacing the conventional sound spectrograph analysis filter by a spectral representation based on fundamental auditory constraints, at least when the purpose of the spectral analysis is related to perceptual questions.

Auditory Models. There have been a number of auditory models proposed for speech processing (Zwicker et al., 1979, Searle et al., 1979, Dolmazon et al., 1977; Dolmazon, this volume, Chistovich et al., 1974; Chistovich et al., this volume) and other purposes. These models are based on behavior seen in physiological preparations and/or transformations inferred from psychophysical data. Most researchers seem to agree that the auditory system can be simulated to a first order by a functional model that includes:

1. A linear preemphasis filter to model the mid-frequency boost provided by the external ear canal and middle ear.

2. A set of more-or-less linear bandpass "critical-band" filters spaced equally along a Mel or Bark frequency scale to model basilar membrane mechanics.

3. Half-wave rectifiers to model the transformation that takes place at the hair cells.

4. Low-pass filters with rather short time constants, at least in the high-frequency channels.

5. Lateral suppression circuitry to sharpen peaks seen in the output spectra (Houtgast, 1977; Houtgast and van Veen, 1982; Sachs and Kiang, 1968).

6. Partial adaptation of filter outputs via time derivatives or other computations that emphasize onsets and perhaps offsets (Delgutte, this volume).

7. A log transformation of filter outputs to approximate the phone scale of loudness.

There are a number of refinements that might be added to the list, involving nonlinearities and other detailed phenomena. I present a few of them separately below in the hope that they are of lesser importance if the objective is to model speech processing:

8. Middle ear muscle activation at high stimulus intensities, which has the effect of attenuating low-frequency components by up to 30 dB and thus partially compensates for the upward spread of masking at high intensities.

9. Basilar membrane nonlinearities (Allen, 1980) that are the probable source of combination tones and the nonlinear upward spread of masking with increased stimulus intensity.

10. Signal-duration-dependent time constants characterizing the decay of excitation patterns (Zwicker et al., 1979).

An example of a spectrogram produced by a system incorporating factors 1 through 7 can be found in Chistovich (Figure 3b, this volume). The speech patterns thus produced do not seem to be easily interpretable in conventional terms. In part this may be due to unfamiliarity with a new display, but it seems to me that there are serious problems with this kind of display, and that it is not the answer we seek. In particular, the bandwidths of the critical band filters are too narrow, about 100 Hz, at low frequencies (Greenwood, 1961; Patterson, 1976) so that rising and falling frequency harmonics dominate the visual pattern in this region. Relative harmonic amplitudes, which determine formant locations and thus phonetic quality, are poorly represented (as has always been the case for the conventional spectrogram because of the minimal dynamic range of the spectrograph marking paper).

Unfortunately, there seems to be no way to justify increasing the analysis filter bandwidths based on physiological or psychophysical constraints characterizing peripheral processing. It may be that additional spectral smoothing is performed more centrally, for example when listening phonetically (Chistovich et al., 1979), but the evidence for such smoothing is conflicting (Klatt, 1982; Traunmuller, this volume). [It should be noted that if more smoothing were done, as I would advocate on practical grounds simply to make male-female spectral differences minimal, then the lateral suppression phenomena seen at the periphery has no clear role or advantage for speech processing.]

Simulation experiments that I have performed suggest that the analysis bandwidth would have to be increased to nearly double the critical bandwidth (resulting in a bandwidth of about 200 to 250 Hz at low frequencies, and 0.25 times the filter center frequency at high frequencies) in order to provide sufficient spectral smoothing to make the patterns for men and women look similar and be insensitive to harmonic locations. Unfortunately, we do not know

whether a system which performs that much additional smoothing
retains sufficient spectral resolution to make fine phonetic
distinctions. A critical-band vocoder study (Klatt, Seneff, and
Zue, 1982) suggests that there is some loss in intelligibility as
bandwidths exceed 200 Hz in the low frequencies. With a better
vocoder synthesizer design, this intelligibility loss may be
overcome, but until such time, or until the appropriate perceptual
experiments are performed:

> CONCLUSION 1. Peripheral auditory constraints are not
> sufficient to constrain the redesign the spectrograph machine
> if the primary purpose is to make the patterns of men and
> women look more similar and be less sensitive to fundamental
> frequency changes. In addition, there is insufficient
> perceptual evidence to justify building a speech analysis
> system with filter bandwidths wider than a critical band,
> although I am sorely tempted to do so.

Auditory Models that Include Interspike Interval Processing.
Thus far we have only been considering auditory models based on
average firing rate statistics gathered from primary auditory
neurons. The times between firings for a given neuron or
population of neurons contains additional information, at least
below about 5 kHz, which the central nervous system may be
processing.

Recent studies of the responses of auditory neurons to
vowel-like sounds suggests that the spectral pattern, as
represented by average firing rates versus frequency (place)
changes with stimulus level. The majority of fibers in the region
of the first and second formant frequencies saturate to their
maximum firing rate as level increases to 60 or 70 dB SPL (Sachs
and Young, 1980). Output invariance with changes in level is more
nearly preserved in the pattern of interspike intervals (Young and
Sachs, 1979), if these patterns are looked at properly. However,
interpretation of interspike interval data requires an
autocorrelation-like analysis over a delay interval near
one-over-the best frequency of the primary auditory unit in

question, and little is known about how or where such calculations are performed. At present, it is not known whether interspike interval data is used in vowel quality estimation, but (it) does seem to be implicated in pitch estimation (Sachs, this volume).

Carlson and Granstrom (this volume) have proposed a novel method based on interspike interval statistics for improving the representation provided by the sound spectrograph. Axis crossing counters are placed at the outputs of a set of critical-band filters, and a histogram of axis-crossing frequencies is scanned to find peaks in the distribution indicating the dominant frequencies present in the signal that and are near the formants. These are displayed as intense points superimposed on a spectrogram (Carlson and Granstrom, (Fig. 2&3, this volume).

For periodic vowel-like sounds, the dominant frequencies correspond to the strongest harmonics in the signal. However, this method of computing dominant frequencies is sensitive to general spectral tilt, and, as we will see below, vowel quality estimates are not influenced by moderate changes to spectral slope.

CONCLUSION 2: A central auditory process that estimates dominant frequency components in the output from the periphery is an appealing notion that fits well with the established perceptual importance of formant frequency locations for vowel identity, but details of the method for extracting and using this information at higher levels are yet to be worked out.

Thus we are left with two candidate improvements to the spectrograph, critical-band filtering and dominant frequency estimation, but we may not understand either well enough to implement them in detail.

SPEECH RECOGNITION AND MODELS OF SPEECH PERCEPTION

The most popular speech recognition techniques today generally use linear prediction spectra as input to a pattern-matching decision process (Itakura, 1975). There is clearly a potential benefit to be gained by switching to an input spectral analyzer more in tune with critical-band concepts, since it is known that the linear prediction representation does a less than ideal job of representing fricatives and nasalized spectra. The Mel frequency scale does a better job of weighting frequency components according to their perceptual importance (Kryter, 1962), and the spectral smoothing implied by a critical-band filter bank (Zwicker et al., 1979) ensures that spectral details unresolved by the ear and thus perceptually irrelevant are not acting like input noise

However, in a practical system, the input representation is only one of several factors that constrain recognition accuracy. In a pattern matching approach to speech recognition, it is just as important to have a good metric for comparing input spectra with stored spectral template sequences for the words to be recognized. The metric should give greatest weight to spectral changes that are phonetically important. While we know very little about the desired properties of such a metric (see below), it does appear that the linear prediction residual (Itakura, 1975) is quite competitive when compared with the kinds of Euclidean metrics commonly used with critical-band representations (White and Neeley, 1976; Blomberg et al., this volume).

In a final section, we will describe recent research conducted to discover aspects of an improved spectral distance metric. It suggests that both the linear prediction residual and the critical band Euclidean distance are seriously deficient, and that a new metric is badly needed if pattern-matching recognition devices are to be improved in performance (Klatt, 1982). Until such time, however, there does not appear to be a great practical advantage to replacing the linear prediction spectrum by a critical band spectrum.

Perceptual Models. So little is known about the processes involved is speech perception that the field is overwhelmed with alternative models, many of which are, unfortunately, not defined in great detail. Rather than review these models, which I have done elsewhere (Klatt, 1979), let me summarize the alternative

transformations that have been proposed to get from an input
representation such as a critical-band spectrum to a phonetic
representation (or directly to a lexical representation).

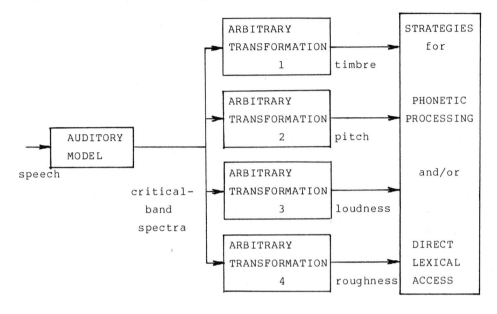

. . .

ADDITIONAL AND ALTERNATIVE ARBITRARY TRANSFORMATIONS
1. Smoothing in frequency
2. Smoothing in time
3. Time derivatives: emphasize spectral change
4. Formant frequency detection
5. Detection of F1 and F2', or dominant frequencies
6. Feature detectors: basic auditory
7. Feature detectors: specialized phonetic
8. Vocal tract shape versus time
9. Talker normalization, e.g. linear shift on Mel scale

Figure 2. Alternative models of speech perception that are all
consistent with an auditory model based on known properties of
peripheral processing.

   The alternatives, as I see them, are summarized in Figure 2.
At the top of the figure, four basic attributes of sounds, timbre,
pitch, loudness, and roughness (Zwicker et al., 1979) are computed
by black boxes labeled "arbitrary transformations 1 thorough 4".
While Zwicker describes tentative algorithms for computing these
candidate perceptual dimensions, the important points to be noted
here are that (1) they require additional computations on the
critical-band input, (2) currently, the details of these
transformations must be deduced from perceptual data since little
relevant physiological data exists, and (3) there is by no means
general agreement that these are indeed the primary perceptual
dimensions of all sounds, including speech.

   The biggest problem is with "timbre" (Plomp, 1970), which is
really a catch-all description of those perceptual dimensions that
remain when one factors out pitch, loudness, and roughness. If
timbre is thought of as the slowly changing smoothed spectrum of
the input, than it contains information about the speech sounds
uttered, the speaker who uttered them, and the channel over which
the speech arrived at the ear of the listener, among others. When
listening phonetically, the perceiver presumably ignores some of
these irrelevant dimensions. But how?

   Proposals abound. A list of candidate alternative arbitrary
transformations interposed between the hypothesized auditory model
and the strategies for phonetic processing are listed at the bottom
of Figure 2. They point out issues such as the amount of
additional smoothing in frequency over and above critical-band
smoothing that might be desirable to remove pitch ripple from the
representation, the amount of additional smoothing in time to
remove pitch-synchronous amplitude ripple from the spectra as a
function of time, and, finally, whether there are any more complex
transformations such as spectral change detectors, formant
frequency trackers, an F2' detector (Carlson, Fant and Granstrom,
1975) or dominant frequency detector (Carlson and Granstrom, this
volume)? Are there feature detectors that indicate the presence of
perceptually important basic auditory properties (Stevens, 1972) or
specialized detectors for phonetic contrasts (Eimas and Miller,

1978)? Is phonetic recognition mediated by a representational level involving articulatory dimensions (Liberman and Studdert-Kennedy, 1978) that involves estimation of vocal tract shapes from input spectra and constraints imposed by a model of the vocal tract (Atal, 1975)? Is talker normalization at least in part a low-level process such as a linear shift of the spectrum along the Mel frequency scale (Miller, 1982)? There are no answers to these questions as yet. All are viable theoretical alternatives.

Another important question is, "Should the auditory input be considered as a sequence of spectra or as a set of time functions?" One way to answer this question is to look at the ability of listeners to compare the timing of onsets occurring in different critical bands. If the JND is large, one must conclude that spectral snapshots are not as appropriate a representation as sets of time functions, one for each critical band. On the other hand, if the JND is small, as it is (Wier and Green, 1975), then both views of the input are equally valid.

CONCLUSION 3: Constraints imposed by the auditory periphery have little to say about strategies for phonetic processing of speech. There remain many candidate strategies to choose from.

PREDICTION OF PERCEIVED PHONETIC DISTANCE FROM SMOOTHED SPECTRA

Rather than end this paper on the negative note that peripheral constraints tell us little about how to improve the spectrograph or choose among models of speech perception, let me describe briefly some experiments concerned with relating spectral differences to perceived phonetic changes. Three experiments were performed to elicit from subjects estimates of phonetic change for pairs of synthetic vowel-like and fricative-like sounds, in which the stimulus variables that were changed included formant frequencies, formant bandwidths, spectral tilt, and filtering passband/stopband (Klatt, 1982). Related experiments involving judgements of "psychophysical distance" have been performed by Bladen and Lindblom (1981), Carlson, Granstrom and Klatt (1979), Carlson and Suchowersky (1977).

The results of my phonetic distance judgement experiments indicate that formant frequency changes were far and away the most important dimensions that caused subjects to report a change in phonetic quality. Changes in spectral tilt and filtering passband/stopband, while clearly audible, did not induce the impression of a phonetic change -- something else changed, such as the speaker or perceived transmission channel.

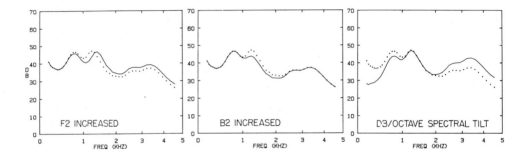

Figure 3. Smoothed spectra (1.8 times a critical band) of selected pairs of /a/-like stimuli. The reference stimulus is always the dotted line.

An example is shown in Figure 3. Comparing the pairs of curves, one might guess that the F2 (second formant frequency) and B2 (second formant bandwidth) changes were roughly comparable in subjective magnitude, while the spectral tilt change was greater. This is not the case at all. The F2 change produced a moderate change in phonetic quality, while the B2 and tilt changes resulted in essentially <u>no</u> change in phonetic quality.

How can one design a spectral distance metric that will predict these relations? The metric must be sensitive to changes in spectral peak locations while being relatively insensitive to changes in peak heights or average spectral tilt. [Peripheral adaptation may, to some extent, aid in neutralizing small differences in spectral tilt and channel filtering differences, but inclusion of adaptation in a processing system causes other problems because the pattern changes during the beginning of a stationary sound.] Let me conclude by considering two possible metrics that have some of the desired characteristics.

A Spectral Slope Metric. The first approach assumes that a smoothed spectral representation, such as the one illustrated in Figure 3, serves as input to the decision process. It compares the spectral slope differences between the two curves at each point along the frequency axis. Differences in spectral slope are great when a peak location moves, but not as great if a peak increases in height or the spectrum tilts gradually. A computational simulation of this metric (Klatt, 1982) revealed that, in order for the distances predicted by the metric to correlate well with the perceptual data, one had to devise a weighting function that said, in essence, only slope differences very near the peaks of one or the other spectrum were perceptually important.

The optimal correlation between metric and data was quite high, about 0.93 for several sets of data. This correlation is significantly higher than for Euclidean distance and the linear prediction residual. Unfortunately, the correlation was overly sensitive to details of the weighting function and the amount of spectral smoothing in the input. In addition, the metric attends very little to places of large spectral slope, the "edges" in the spectrum that are perhaps most clearly defined aspects of the spectra. My feeling is that there must exist a better metric, but I haven't been able to think of one -- at least not given the assumption that smoothed spectra form the input to this decision process.

A Dominant Frequencies Metric. An alternative, proposed by Carlson and Granstrom in this volume, is to assume that the histogram of dominant frequencies in the stimulus forms the input to the decision process. Such an assumption does not immediately solve all the problems -- peak heights in the dominant frequencies histogram are clearly sensitive to changes in formant amplitudes or spectral tilt, and, in fact, individual low-frequency harmonics of a female voice are clearly resolved in this representation.

The hypothesis, as yet untested, is whether a computation such as smoothing coupled with a slope metric might work better in the dominant frequencies domain. On the other hand, dominant frequencies processing may simply be the way that the auditory system solves the problem of producing a spectral representation whose shape is more-or-less insensitive to input level, and engineering systems that do not have the severe dynamic range problem seen in the average firing rate behavior of a primary auditory neuron need not go to the trouble of computing dominant frequencies.

CONCLUSION 4. Currently used spectral distance metrics all have serious flaws. Additional experiments that try to characterize aspects of phonetic distance between static (and dynamic) speech-like sounds are needed if we are to make progress in this promising line of research.

ACKNOWLEDGEMENTS

The research described herein was supported in part by an NSF grant.

REFERENCES

Allen, J.B. (1980), "Cochlear Micromechanics -- A Physical Model of Transduction", J. Acoust. Soc. Am. 68, 1660-1670.

Atal, B.S. (1975), "Toward Determining Articulator Positions from the Speech Signal", in Speech Communication, G. Fant (Ed.), Vol. I, 1-9, Almqvist and Wiksell, Stockholm.

Bladon, R.A.W. and Lindblom, B. (1981), "Modeling the Judgement of Vowel Quality Differences", J. Acoust. Soc. Am. 69, 1414-1422.

Carlson, R., Fant, G., and Granstrom, B. (1975), "Two-Formant Models, Pitch, and Vowel Perception", in Auditory Analysis and Perception of Speech, (G. Fant and M.A.A. Tathem, Eds), Academic Press, London, 55-82.

Carlson, R., Fant, G., and Granstrom, B. (1975), "Two-Formant Models, Pitch, and Vowel Perception", in Auditory Analysis and Perception of Speech, (G. Fant and M.A.A. Tathem, Eds), Academic Press, London, 55-82.

Carlson, R. and Granstrom, B. (1979), "Model Predictions of Vowel Dissimilarity", Speech Transmission Laboratory Quarterly Progress and Status Report STL-QPSR 3-4/1979, 84-104.

Carlson, R., Granstrom, B. and Klatt, D.H. (1979), "Vowel Perception: The Relative Perceptual Salience of Selected Acoustic Manipulations", Speech Transmission Laboratory STL-QPSR 3/4, Royal Institute of Technology, Stockholm, 73-83.

Chistovich, J.A., Grostrem, M.P., Kozhevnikov, V.A., Lesogor, L.W., Shupljakov, V.S., Taljasin, P.A., and Tjulkov, W.A. (1974), "A Functional Model of Signal Processing in the Peripheral Auditory System", Acoustica 31, 349-353.

Chistovich, L.A., Sheikin, R.L., and Lublinskaja, V.V. (1979), Centers of Gravity and Spectral Peaks as the Determinants of Vowel Quality", in Frontiers of Speech Communication Research, (B. Lindblom and S. Ohman, Eds.), Academic Press, London, 143-158.

Dolmazon, J.M., Bastet, L., and Schupljakov, V.S. (1977), A Functional Model of Peripheral Auditory System in Speech Processing", IEEE Int. Conf. Acoust. Speech, and Signal Proc. Conference Record, 261-264.

Eimas, P.D. and Miller, J.L. (1978), "Effect of Selective Adaptation on the Perception of Speech and Visual Patterns: Evidence for Feature Detectors", in Perception and Experience, R.D. Walk and H.L. Pick (Eds.), Plenum Press, New York, 307-345.

Greenwood, D.D. (1961), "Auditory Masking and the Critical Band", J. Acoust. Soc. Am. 38, 484-502.

Houtgast, T. (1977), "Auditory Filter Characteristics Derived from direct Masking Data and Pulsation Threshold Data with a Rippled-Noise Masker", J. Acoust. Soc. Am. 62, 409-414.

Houtgast, T. and van Veen, T.M. (1982), "On the Just-Detectable Modulation on the Spectral Envelope on a Log-f Scale", J. Acoust. Soc. Am. 71, Suppl. 1, S37.

Itakura, F. (1975), "Minimum Prediction Residual Principle Applied to Speech Recognition", IEEE Trans. Acoust. Speech and Signal Proc. ASSP-23, 67-72.

Klatt, D.H. (1979), "Speech Perception: A Model of Acoustic-Phonetic Analysis and Lexical Access", J. Phonetics 7, 279-312.

Klatt, D.H. (1982), "Prediction of Perceived Phonetic Distance from Critical-Band Spectra: A First Step", Proc. IEEE International Conference on Speech, Acoustics, and Signal Processing, 1278-1281.

196

Klatt, D.H., Seneff, S., and Zue, V.W. (1982), "Design Considerations for Optimizing the Intelligibility of a DFT-Based, Pitch-Excited, Critical-band-Spectrum Speech Analysis-Resynthesis System" Speech Communication Group Working Papers, MIT Research Lab of Electronics, Cambridge, MA.

Kryter, K.D. (1962), "Methods for the Calculation and Use of the Articulation Index", J. Acoust. Soc. Am. 34, 1689-1697.

Liberman, A.M. and Studdert-Kennedy, M. (1978), "Phonetic Perception", in Handbook of Sensory Physiology, Vol. VIII, R. Held, H. Leibowitz, & H.-L. Teuber, (Eds.), Springer-Verlag, Heidelberg.

Koenig, W., Dunn, H.K., and Lacy, L.Y. (1946), "The Sound Spectrograph", J. Acoust. Soc. Am. 18, 19-49.

Patterson, R.D. (1976), "Auditory Filter Shapes Derived with Noise Stimuli", J. Acoust. Soc. Am. 59, 640-654.

Plomp, R. (1970), "Timbre as a Multidimensional Attribute of Complex Tones", in Frequency Analysis and Periodicity Detection in Hearing, R Plomp and G.F. Smoorenburg, Eds.), Sijthoff, Leiden.

Presti, A.J. (1966), "High-Speed Sound Spectrograph", J. Acoust. Soc. Am. 40, 628-634.

Sachs, M.B. and Kiang, N.Y.-S. (1968), "Two-Tone Inhibition in Auditory Nerve Fibers", J. Acoust. Soc. Am. 43, 1120-1128.

Sachs, M. B. and Young, E.D. (1980), "Effects of Nonlinearities on Speech Encoding in the Auditory Nerve", J. Acoust. Soc. Am. 68, 858.

Searle, C.L., Jacobson, J.Z., and Rayment, S.G. (1979), "Stop Consonant Discrimination Based on Human Audition", J. Acoust. Soc. Am. 65, 799-809.

Suchowersky, W. (1977), "Beurteilung von Unterschieden zwischen aufeinanderfolgenden schallen", Acoustica 38, 131-139.

White, G.M. and Neeley, R.B. (1976), "Speech Recognition Experiments with Linear Prediction, Bandpass Filtering, and Dynamic Programming", IEEE Trans. Acoust. Speech and Signal Proc. ASSP-xx, xx-xx.

Wier, C.C. and Green, D.M. (1975), "Temporal Acuity as a Function of Frequency Difference", J. Acoust. Soc. Am. 57, 1512-1515.

Young, E.D. and Sachs, M.B. (1979), "Representation of Steady-State Vowels in the Temporal Aspects of the Discharge Patterns of Populations of Auditory Nerve Fibers", J. Acoust. Soc. Am. 66, 1381-1403.

Zwicker, E., Terhardt, E., and Paulus, E. (1979), "Automatic Speech recognition using Psychoacoustic Models", J. Acoust. Soc. Am. 65, 487-498.

© 1982 Elsevier Biomedical Press
The Representation of Speech in the Peripheral
Auditory System, R. Carlson and B. Granström eds.

EXPERIMENTS WITH AUDITORY MODELS IN SPEECH RECOGNITION

MATS BLOMBERG, ROLF CARLSON, KJELL ELENIUS AND BJÖRN GRANSTRÖM
Department of Speech Communication and Music Acoustics, KTH
S-100 44 Stockholm (Sweden)

INTRODUCTION

The aim of the following experiment was to test different auditory models in the context of a straightforward isolated word recognition system. The underlying assumption is that a good ear-model should result in better recognition performance than a less elaborated one. However, we have to keep in mind that only the peripheral processes of sound perception are included in the models used.

THE RECOGNITON SYSTEM

The recognition system is based on ordinary isolated word recognition techniques using pattern matching and dynamic programming. We use the "normalize and warp" procedure (1,2). The Euclidean metric is used for calculation of distances between word patterns.

Figure 1 shows a block diagram of the recognition system. First the speech signal is fed through a 4.0 kHz sampling filter to an A/D-converter. The sampling rate is 10 kHz. This low passing is arbitrary and is expected to limit the recognition performance somewhat, especially for consonants. The digitized signal is then processed according to different auditory models resulting in a 95-channel spectral representation of the speech.

Since the words used for the experiment were all recorded under good signal to noise conditions the endpoint detector is very simple. An amplitude threshold is set at the mean of the maximum and the minimum energy of the speech signal. The threshold is the main feature for defining word boundaries. Temporal constraints are used on silent intervals to include stop gaps to the words sampled.

When a word has been detected, the length of it is linearly normalized to a fixed length of 32 sample points. Though a linear

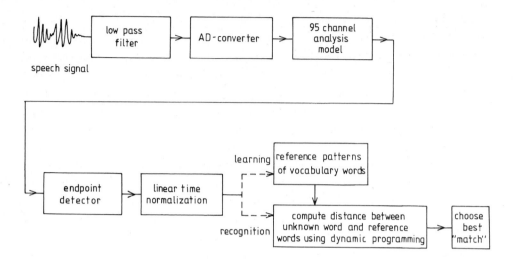

Fig. 1. Block diagram of the recognition system.

transformation is not enough to account for all of the speech tempo variations, it is a good first approximation. Besides, it will give all words the same length facilitating the subsequent calculations. A word is now described by 32 feature vectors, each one consisting of 95 features.

Each word in the reference vocabulary is built from ten utterances. The first learning sample of each word is used for a dynamic time alignment of the second one and a mean is calculated. The third utterance is warped to this mean giving a new reference, and so on. In the recognition phase the unknown word is matched to all the references by use of dynamic programming and the reference resulting in the best match is chosen. We have used no rejection threshold to discard bad matches.

The intention with this set-up is not to make a speech recognition machine with the best possible performance. Rather we want a flexible, standard framework to compare different recognition preprocessors and recognition strategies.

THE VOCABULARY

Two vocabularies were tested. One consisting of the 9 long Swedish vowels in an hVl-context and the other of the 18 Swedish consonants in an aCa-context. They were read by one male speaker. What really is tested, since the context is constant, is the consonant and vowel discrimination ability of the system though there is no segmentation into phonemes of the words used. The ten reference samples of each word were read in a normal way while the test samples were read in different manners. The vowels were read as follows: normal, fast, slow, normal with a different angle to the microphone, and normal with increased distance to the microphone. The consonants were read as: normal, fast, slow, emphatic and relaxed. There was only one sample of each condition resulting in 5*9 test samples of the vowels and 5*18 samples of the consonants. The recordings were made in a relatively silent office.

THE MODELS

The speech has been processed according to different models. First an ordinary FFT-transformation is included for reference. The FFT-spectrum has 85 channels from 0 to 5 kHz but the reduction of 10 channels compared to the 95 channels of the other representations should not be very crucial. The auditory models are based on the critical band scale and they are all described in another paper in this volume (3). In the BARK model, 95 one-Bark wide channels are spaced at a 0.2 Bark increment covering 19 Barks. In the MASK model the Bark representation is modified by a psychoacoustic masking filter. Adding a loudness measure to the MASK model results in the PHON representation (phon/Bark) and a SONE model (sone/Bark) has also been tested. In the DOMIN model, the dominant frequency (see 3) at 95 points along the Bark scale is used. Finally, in the DOMPHON model every other point of the 95-element feature vector comes from the DOMIN model while, the others are sampled from the PHON model.

It should be noted that these models do not include any temporal masking effects. However, an experiment by Zagoruiko and Lebedev (4) has tentatively shown some positive results of using such effects in a speech recognition system.

RESULTS AND DISCUSSION

The collected performance figures for the different models are presented in table 1. The number of incorrect responses are given along with the corresponding percentages in brackets. It should be noted that the entire experiment is a small one, and we are not claiming any high significance to differences of only a couple of percent. Some general tendencies seem to be clear, however. The Bark representation is somewhat better than the normal FFT looking at both consonants and vowels. Bark scaling has recently become more or less a standard in research speech recognition systems. With increasing complexity of the auditory models the performance drops rather quickly, especially for consonants.

TABLE 1

RECOGNITION RESULTS

Number of errors and percentages of errors for the different models tested

MODEL	VOWELS (45 stimuli)		CONSONANTS (90 stimuli)	
	Errors	%Errors	Errors	%Errors
FFT	6	13	9	10
BARK	4	9	6	7
MASK	6	13	20	22
PHON	9	20	20	22
SONE	10	22	33	37
DOMIN	2	4	30	33
DOMPHON	3	7	15	17

One exception to this trend is the DOMIN, the dominant frequency model, which has got the best recognition results for vowels but almost the worst for consonants. Considering the function of the model, it is not that surprising. The DOMIN model emphasizes spectral peaks, i.e., formants, which are known to be of paramount importance in discriminating vowels. However, this model totally disregards the overall energy. The recognition system is therefore making confusions between consonants of especially the same place of articulation.

The possible conclusion from this preliminary experiment could be that it is no value in including models of the human auditory system in automatic speech recognizers. From an evolutionary perspective, that conclusion is, however, against our intuition. It is very conceivable that in the long history of spoken communication, the speech code has been optimized both with respect to the sound production and reception capabilities of humans. The alternative conclusion that we want to draw is that we rather need better models of hearing, that are based on complicated real life signals, such as speech.

The rather ad hoc combination of DOMIN and PHON to DOMPHON shows, for consonants, a significant performance increase over the two constituent models. This suggests that it pays to combine different types of analysis in the speech recognition process, as humans obviously do.

REFERENCES

1. Myers, C.S., Rabiner, L. R. and Rosenberg, A. E. (1980) Performance Tradeoffs in Dynamic Time Warping Algorithm for Isolated Word Recognition, IEEE Trans. Acoust., Speech and Signal Proc. ASSP-28, pp 623-635.

2. Elenius, K. and Blomberg, M. (1982) Effects of Emphasizing Transitional or Stationary Parts of the Speech Signal in a Discrete Utterance Recognition System, Proc. IEEE ICASSP-82, Paris.

3. Carlson, R. and Granström, B. (1982) Towards an Auditory Spectograph, in: Carlson, R. and Granström, B. (Eds.), The Representation of Speech in the Peripheral Auditory System, Elsevier/North-Holland Biomedical Press, Amsterdam.

4. Zagoruiko, N. G. and Lebedev, V. G. (1975) Models for Speech Signal Analysis Taking into Account the Effect of Masking, Acustica, 31, pp 346-348.

PERCEPTUAL RELEVANCE OF COARTICULATION

LOUIS C.W. POLS[1] AND M.E.H. SCHOUTEN[2]

[1]Institute for Perception TNO, Soesterberg (The Netherlands) and [2]Dept. of English, University of Utrecht, Utrecht (The Netherlands)

INTRODUCTION

If we talk about the auditory representation of speech, the theme of this symposium, then we may wonder what hearing research can tell speech science about the peripheral process of speech perception. It is quite clear that most hearing research is devoted to simple, stationary, signals because only then can all parameters be kept under control and studied in detail. This has resulted in a basic understanding of the process of perceiving loudness, pitch, duration, and timbre (9). However, speech, like most every-day-like sounds, is a very dynamic, variable, and complex physical signal. At the acoustic-phonetic level, where the meaning of speech is not yet apparent, there are already many questions to be solved. In this contribution we want to focus attention on some acoustical (spectral) and perceptual aspects of *coarticulation*. Coarticulation can be defined as the mutual interaction of speech events. At the acoustic level this interaction is apparent as a spreading out of spectral properties between neighbouring sounds (e.g. formant transitions as visible in a spectrogram). In spectrograms of conversational speech one often wonders if there is anything which is not a transitional event, and if stationary, stable, segments are ever reached or do exist at all. This impression is further strengthened when one tries to gate out certain parts of an utterance. These isolated segments are quite frequently not understandable at all.

Recently there has been considerable interest in the question of whether coarticulation is merely an ambiguating factor we have to live with as listeners, or whether these transitions bear information about neighbouring sounds in such a way that they can ease identification. If, as we assume, the second statement is true, then the speech signal could perhaps be described as a succession of more or less context-independent and context-dependent segments. The more or less context-independent, or invariant, segments are short (plosive burst) or long (fricative noise), and contain stationary/average cues (18), or dynamic/time-varying cues (7). The context-dependent segments are the actual transitions which are influenced by preceding and following sounds, but also bear information about those sounds.

Under certain conversational or acoustic conditions it could happen that, because of fast or sloppy pronunciation or because of masking and reverberation, certain aspects of speech sounds are absent or undetectable. This loss of redundancy could cause a "secondary" feature, like transitional information, to be the only information left over on which phoneme and word recognition would have to rely. We have an ongoing research project to study spectral and perceptual aspects of coarticulation (10, 11, 12, 13, 14, 15). That project approaches the problem from the "speech side", some recent results along that line of research will be presented later on in this paper. But one can also look at the problem from the "hearing side": Coarticulation can only have perceptual relevance if we are able to hear, detect, discriminate, and interpret transitional spectral information or sweeps.

DETECTION, DISCRIMINATION, AND IDENTIFICATION OF FREQUENCY SWEEPS

In its simplest form a formant transition can be described as a frequency jump or a frequency sweep. However, a formant is not a single frequency but a filter band, so the study of band sweeps seems to be closer to reality. In fact even this is a simplification since in real speech we do not have just one formant but simultaneously moving formants, not necessarily all moving in the same direction. The signal leading towards the sweep, or continuing from the final frequency of the sweep probably also plays a role in interpreting the sweep. Finally, the interpretation of a sweep could very well be influenced by our speech and language training. A signal which by itself is a sweep of which it is difficult to say whether it goes up or down, could in a speech context easily be interpreted as /b/ or /d/, perhaps related to loci (3).

A frequency sweep has different attributes: initial, final and midfrequencies, frequency range, speed of sweep or sweep rate, sweep mode (linear, cubic, exponential, etc.), and signal duration. If a band is swept, bandwidth and shape or slope, as well as fundamental frequency in relation to spectral envelope may also play a part, as may filter output level. It is difficult to interpret the effect of one specific attribute at a time, because most of them are linked together, like sweep height, sweep rate, and sweep duration. Some of these aspects have been studied in the literature but only incidentally and not systematically, for instance with only one specific duration or bandfilter slope.

According to Flanagan (4) the just-discriminable changes in frequencies of the first and second formants, using synthetic stationary 750-ms vowel sounds, was 3-5% of the formant frequency. For single-formant signals and highly trained listeners, Horst (6) found much lower values (between 0.15 and 1% depending on the filter slope). He also studied the influence of signal-to-noise ratio on frequency discrimination. Just-noticeable frequency *sweeps* in synthetic two-formant CV-syllables (250 ms duration, with a sweep in the first 100 ms) were 3-4% of the reference frequency (2). Mermelstein (8) found that 9-14% frequency differences in symmetric formant trajectories in 200-ms synthetic CVC-syllables were just detectable. Horst (6) found lower thresholds for bell-shaped sweeps with identical initial and final frequencies: 0.4-2% for sweep-detection threshold and 1-3.5% for the sweep-discrimination threshold, depending on sweep height and filter slope. His subjects were highly trained. He suggests that the discrimination mechanism treats frequency sweeps as quasi-stationary input. A review of the psycho-physical literature about frequency discrimination vs. frequency-sweep dis-crimination shows that discrimination of frequency differences is far supe-rior to discrimination based on differences in sweep-rates (6). Neverthe-less, some psychophysical studies (using adaptation techniques) suggest the existence in the auditory system of channels specific to upward or down-ward frequency modulation (5).

Experimental results

We started some research on *sweep identification*, which is more difficult than sweep discrimination. Subjects were asked whether a single sweep went up or down. A single pure tone was swept around a centre frequency of 400, 1300, or 2700 Hz, with rates of 0, 5, 10, 20, 40, or 60 oct/s (unidirection-al and exponential, which means linear on a log frequency scale, see (17)). The duration of the signal varied between 20 and 50 ms, in steps of 10 ms. It was surprising to see that, within the chosen range of variables, which in our opinion covered most transitions in actual speech, several subjects could not do the task at all, whereas for those who showed some consistent performance, the interindividual differences were large. In Fig. 1[a] some re-sults for the sweeps around 1300 Hz are presented. There was a gradual in-crease in performance from 20- to 50-ms signal duration without an asymptotic value having been reached yet. With respect to increased rate, performance gradually improved and reached an asymptotic value around 40 oct/s. A com-plicating, and until now not fully understood, factor was the large re-sponse bias effect: Subjects showed a great preference in the forced-choice task to call any unidentifiable sweep "downward", even about 80% of all

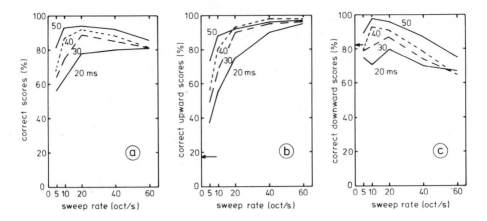

Fig. 1. The left-hand panel gives the overall percentage correct scores, averaged over 12 subjects, for frequency sweeps around 1300 Hz, as a function of sweep rate and sweep duration. The right-hand panels give the scores for the upward and downward sweeps separately. The arrow at 0 oct/s (stationary signal) indicates the average percentage upward or downward scores for that signal.

stationary signals (sweep rate 0 oct/s) were labeled as downward sweeps, see arrow in Fig. 1[b] and 1[c]. Besides that, several subjects had a strong tendency to label any detectable sweep (either going up or down) as "upward". This effect is the reason why the curves in Fig. 1[c] decline again.

We have just started similar identification experiments with double sweeps at frequencies around 400 and 1300 Hz, or around 1300 and 2700 Hz, with both sweeps going in the same or in opposite directions. The same "downward" preference was apparent here again. Subsequent steps will be 1) to combine these sweeps with stationary tones like those in CV- and VC-syllables, 2) to use bandfilter sweeps instead of tone sweeps, and 3) to ask for labeling as speech signals instead of identifying sweeps as going up or down.

PERCEPTUAL RELEVANCE OF TRANSITIONAL INFORMATION IN SPEECH

Apparently considerably more work has to be done before we can understand at a psychophysical level the mechanism for detecting, discriminating, and identifying frequency sweeps occurring for instance in vocalic transitions caused by coarticulation. Meanwhile, we will go on studying in real speech the perceptual relevance of transitional information for the identification of neighbouring speech sounds. This knowledge will perhaps also allow us to improve automatic speech recognition systems. As an example we give some experimental results for plosive identification. The results of a more detailed study about identification of all Dutch initial, medial, and final consonants in words spoken in isolation, as well as taken from conversational speech, are forthcoming. In the plosive experiment 11 subjects identified the three plosive consonants per $C_i VC_m VC_f$ word embedded in a short carrier phrase, like "attentie poebiek over". C_i and C_m are /p, t, k, b, d/ and C_f is /p, t, k/, and this was also the response set, 45 different words were used. Through digital tape splicing any specific part of the words (burst (B), 3-periods vocalic transition (T), or stationary vowel (S)) could be presented. Various combinations of B, T, and S resulted in a total of 13 conditions. Percentage correct identification of place of articulation for three particularly interesting conditions (burst alone (B), transition alonge (T), and burst plus transition (B+T)) are given in Fig. 2.

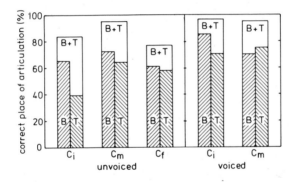

Fig. 2. Percentage correct identification of place of articulation of voiced and unvoiced Dutch initial (C_i), medial (C_m), and final plosives (C_f) in CVCVC words when only specific parts of the words are presented (burst alone (B), transition alone (T), or burst plus transition (B+T)).

Recently a great deal of emphasis has been put on the invariant cues which are supposed to be present in the static or dynamic onset spectra of plosive bursts in CV-syllables (1, 7). These papers more or less suggest that contextually variable formant transitions are unimportant or only "secondary" cues to plosive identification or identification of place of articulation. Our results, as well as those of others (19), contradict that view. It is clear from Fig. 2 that, at least for Dutch (unaspirated) plosives, adding the vocalic transition to the burst significantly improves correct plosive (or place of articulation) identification. More details as well as further results can be found in Schouten and Pols (16).

REFERENCES

1. Blumstein, S.E. and Stevens, K.N. (1980) Perceptual invariance and onset spectra for stop consonants in different vowel environments, J. Acoust. Soc. Am. 67, 648-662.

2. Danaher, E.M., Osberger, M.J. and Pickett, J.M. (1973) Discrimination of formant frequency transitions in synthetic vowels, J. Speech Hearing Res. 16, 439-451.

3. Delattre, P.C., Liberman, A.M. and Cooper, F.S. (1955) Acoustic loci and transitional cues for consonants, J. Acoust. Soc. Am. 27, 769-773.

4. Flanagan, J.L. (1972) Speech analysis synthesis and perception, Springer-Verlag, Berlin, 2nd Edition, p. 280.

5. Gardner, R.B. and Wilson, J.P. (1979) Evidence for direction specific channels in the processing of frequency modulation, J. Acoust. Soc. Am. 66, 704-709.

6. Horst, J.W. (1982) Discrimination of complex signals in hearing, PhD thesis, University of Groningen.

7. Kewley-Port, D. (1982) Representation of speech change as cues to place of articulation in stop consonants, Technical Report No. 3, Dept. of Psychology, Indiana Univ., Bloomington, Indiana.

8. Mermelstein, P. (1978) Difference limens for formant frequencies of steady-state and consonant-bounded vowels, J. Acoust. Soc. Am. 63, 572-580.

9. Plomp, R. (1976) Aspects of tone sensation. A psychophysical study, Academic Press, London.

10. Pols, L.C.W. (1979) Coarticulation and the identification of initial and final plosives, In: ASA*50 Speech Comm. Papers, Eds. J. Wolff and D. Klatt, pp. 459-462.

11. Pols, L.C.W. and Schouten, M.E.H. (1978) Identification of deleted plosives, J. Acoust. Soc. Am. 64, 1333-1337.

12. Pols, L.C.W. and Schouten, M.E.H. (1981) Identification of deleted plosives: The effect of adding noise or applying a time window (A reply to Ohde and Sharf), J. Acoust. Soc. Am. 69, 301-303 (L).

13. Schouten, M.E.H. and Pols, L.C.W. (1979[a]) Vowel segments in consonantal contexts: a spectral study of coarticulation - Part I, J. Phon. 7, 1-23.

14. Schouten, M.E.H. and Pols, L.C.W. (1979[b]) CV- and VC-transitions: a spectral study of coarticulation - Part II, J. Phon. 7, 205-224.

15. Schouten, M.E.H. and Pols, L.C.W. (1981) Consonant loci: a spectral study of coarticulation. Part III, J. Phon. 9, 225-231.

16. Schouten, M.E.H. and Pols, L.C.W. (1983) Perception of plosive consonants: The relative contribution of bursts and vocalic transitions, in press.

17. Smoorenburg, G. and Coninx, F. (1980) Masking of short probe sounds by tone bursts with a sweeping frequency, Hearing Res. 3, 301-316.

18. Stevens, K.N. and Blumstein, S.E. (1978) Invariant cues for place of articulation in stop consonants, J. Acoust. Soc. Am. 64, 1358-1368.

19. Walley, A.C. and Carrell, T.D. (1980) Onset spectra versus formant transitions as cues to place of articulation, Progress Report No. 6, Dept. of Psychology, Indiana Univ., Bloomington, Indiana, pp. 457-475, also in: J. Acoust. Soc. Am. 68, S49-50 (A).

© 1982 Elsevier Biomedical Press
The Representation of Speech in the Peripheral
Auditory System, R. Carlson and B. Granström eds.

SPEECH PERCEPTION BASED ON NON-SPEECH SIGNALS.

ARNE RISBERG AND EVA AGELFORS, Department of Speech Communication and Music Acoustics, Royal Institute of Technology (KTH), S-100 44, Stockholm, Sweden.

INTRODUCTION

Research and development around a type of hearing prostheses based on electrical stimulation of the auditory nerve (cochlear implant), either with a single extra cochlear electrode, a single or multiple electrode inserted in the cochlea, or with an electrode inserted in the VIIIth nerve have been going on at several laboratories during the last ten years. It has generally been assumed that in order to obtain a reasonably good ability to understand speech, such systems must be based on the stimulation of 10 to 20 separate channels along the basilar membrane (1). Experiments with single channel intra cochlear systems have been made by the group in Los Angeles since 1960 (2). The poor speech perception ability of subjects fitted with these systems (3, 4, 5) seems to support the opinion that in single channel systems only some time-amplitude information can be transmitted. Recently, however, the group in Vienna that is working on cochlear implants has reported on very good speech perception results with a single channel system (6). Results are given for four subjects. With only implants, these subjects got between 50 and 100 per cent correct on a test that consisted of 12 trained two-syllable nouns. On a test with the numerals between 13 and 99, they got between 50 and 90 per cent correct, and on unknown short sentences they got between 16 and 80 per cent correct.

The results reported by the Vienna group seem to be in conflict with the accepted function of the peripheral auditory system. Studies with cochlear implant subjects have, however, shown that they with a single electrode can discriminate gross frequency changes (7, 8) and scale pitch, at least up to 250 Hz (3), and sometimes up to 1000 Hz (6, 7, 8). They can also perceive the presence of a signal above 1000 Hz but cannot use the frequency information in this region (3). Signals with different time structure, e.g., periodic-aperiodic, can be identified (3). If a good coding system for amplitude is used, it seems also likely that the normal amplitude variations in the speech signal can be transmitted through a single channel system.

A possible explanation of the good results on different speech tests reported by the group in Vienna is that they have optimized the speech coding to the time domain properties of the auditory system. To get some insight into the possible speech perception ability when such a system is used, the following experiment was designed.

METHOD

Speech coding. The speech coding system used was a system developed by Traunmuller for tactile stimulation (9). In this system the energy in a highpass and a lowpass filter is weighted against each other to get a signal that is proportional to the center of gravity in the frequency spectrum. The signal derived in this way is used to control the frequency of an oscillator. For tactile stimulation, the frequency of the oscillator varies between 30 and 300 Hz. The amplitude of the signal is modulated by the total speech energy. In the experiment described here, the frequency of the oscillator was changed to vary between 250 and 2500 Hz. As the frequency of the oscillator varies with the spectral balance, this frequency is influenced by the micro-phone used, the frequency response of the amplifying system, etc. In the experiment, the frequency response of the amplifier was adjusted until the signal sounded as "natural" as possible.

The signal that the subjects listen to is a sine wave with the same amplitude variations as in the original speech signal and with a frequency that is an approximation to the variation in the center of gravity of the spectral energy. Fig. 1 shows a sonagram of an original word "lista två" (list two) and superimposed on the sonagram the derived signal is traced. A better approximation to a signal proportional to the center of gravity in the spectrum, shown in fig. 1, is possible by a more optimal adjustment of the frequency response of the system. It is apparent that the resemblence between the original speech signal and the coded signal is small. The information reduction might, at least to some extent, approximate the information transmission properties of a single channel cochlear implant prosthesis.

Speech material and subjects. As test material lists of 12 spondee words and lists with the numerals between 13 and 99 were used. Five randomizations of the test words were read by a female speaker. The words and the numerals were read twice after each other. The lists were played through the coding system. In the experiment the subjects listened to the words at a comfortable level over earphones. Noise with a slope of 3 dB/oct was added to reduce the possibility that lowfrequency energy leaked through to the listeners. The signal-to-noise ratio was 25 dB. Experiments after training with one subject showed that no detoriation of the result was obtained when the signal-to-noise ratio was lowered to 10 dB. This indicated that the information the subjects are using is the frequency and amplitude variation in the sine wave.

The subjects were told that they were going to hear a signal that sounded very peculiar but that it was derived from the acoustic signal

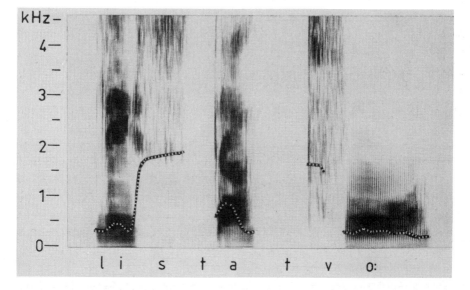

Fig. 1. Sonagram of the phrase "lista två" (list two). Superimposed on the sonagram is the frequency variation of the coded signal.

212

of the 12 spondee words or consisted of the numerals between 13 and
99. Their task was to try to guess which one of the spondees or
numerals that was presented. None of the subjects had difficulties
with the task. The subjects were not informed about the correct answer
but after each test list they were informed about how they had scored.

RESULTS

In figs. 2 and 3 results of the listening tests are shown. In the
test with spondee words six subjects were participating. Four of them
were employees from the laboratory. In the figure they are called
"trained". They are trained in the sense that they are used to participate in different listening tests but they had not earlier listened
to the type of signals used in the experiment. Two "naive" subjects
were also tested. They were visitors at the laboratory and had not
before been subjects in listening tests.

In the first test session, the subjects heard a coded word and had
two response alternatives. In test session two, the number of response
alternatives was three. From test session three, the number of response alternatives was 12.

In fig. 3 the results from the test with the numerals are shown. In
this test the subjects were only informed that they were to hear coded
numerals between 13 and 99. The figure shows the per cent identified
numerals. In many cases a part of a numeral was identified as, e.g.,
"sixty" in "sixtytwo". Only totally correct answers were scored.

DISCUSSION

It is apparent that the subjects in the experiment could identify
the 12 spondee words with good accuracy. Two of the subjects obtained
70 per cent correct already on test list three. The best subject
obtained almost 90 per cent correct after seven lists. The numerals,
fig. 3, were more difficult to identify and two subjects did not score
better than 20 per cent correct. The best subject got a score better
than 50 per cent correct after four lists.

The experiment shows that the coded signal contains enough of the
acoustic information in the test words to make them identifiable in a
forced choice situation. The information that the listeners are using

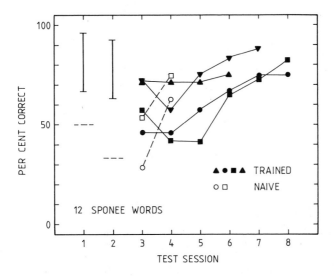

Fig. 2. Results on listening tests with coded spondee words. On test-list one the number of response alternatives were two, on testlist two the number of alternatives were three and on the following testlists the number of response alternatives were 12.

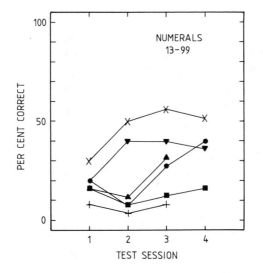

Fig. 3. Results on listening tests with the coded numerals from 13 to 99.

is probably mostly a timing information. To be able to perceive timing, a starting point and an end point have to be given. It is apparent that the coded signal gives start and end points that are in agreement with the traditional start and end points in the stimuli. The subjects probably also quickly learned to associate a highpitched sound with a fricative (see fig. 1). To what extent they also got formant frequency information from the coded signal is more difficult to say, but it seems necessary that they also to some extent could use the frequency of the sinusoidal to identify some of the vowels and some of the formant transitions.

Experiments with sinusoidal speech have also been reported by Remez, et al (10). They describe an experiment where they by means of LPC-analysis extracted the formant frequencies and amplitudes of the three first formants in a sentence. Based on this analysis they then generated a synthetic sentence, where the formants were replaced by sinusoidal signals with the same frequency and amplitudes as the original formants. Seven different versions were generated, differing in the number of formants that were included.

Different experiments were made with the generated stimuli. When naive listeners were asked to spontaneously describe the stimuli, only a few of them described them as speech. When the listeners were informed that they would hear a sentence generated by a computer, a large number of the subjects identified the sentence when Fl, F2, and F3 or Fl and F2 were replaced by sinusoids but not when only one simulated formant was heard.

Based on the results of the reported experiment, the results of the experiment by Remez, et al (10) and the known time domain analyzing capacity of the auditory system, the results reported by the cochlear implant group in Vienna seem plausible. The fact that so poor results have been obtained in other experiments, where a single channel system has been used, must be explained by the type of coding system used (2).

The Vienna group also report very good results on tests using open speech. Such results cannot be obtained with the coding system tested in this experiment. To obtain the reported results (6), it must be assumed that more information is transmitted to the implanted subjects than to the subjects in this experiment. It seems likely that these are intonation changes and a better transmission of the frequency of the first formant. It is also likely that a better transmission is obtained of friction information, especially in short segments.

AKNOWLEDGMENTS

The research reported in this article is supported by the Swedish Board for Technical Development.

REFERENCES

1. Kiang, N.Y.S., Eddington, D.K. and Delgutte, B. (1979) Fundamental considerations in designing auditory implants, Acta Otolaryng, 87, pp. 204-218.

2. House, W.F. (Ed) (1976) Cochlear implants, Annals Oto, Rhino, Laryngol, Suppl 27, 85.

3. Bilger, R.C. (1977) Psychoacoustic evaluation of present prostheses, Annals Oto, Rhino, Laryngol, Suppl 38, 86, pp. 92-140.

4. Bilger, R.C. and Hopkinson, N.T. (1977) Hearing performance with the auditory prostheses, Annals Oto, Rhino, Laryngol, Suppl 38, 86, pp. 76-91.

5. House, W. F., Berliner, K.I., Eisenberg, L.S. (1979). Present status and future directions of the ear research institute cochlear implant program, Acta Otolaryngol 91, pp. 176-184.

6. Hochmair-Desoyer, I.J., Hochmair, E.S., Burian, K. and Fisher, R.E. (1981). Four years of experience with cochlear implants, Medical Progress through Technology, 8, pp. 107-119.

7. Fischer, R. (1981) Methodik und Experimente zur psychoakustischen Evaluation des durch Cochlearprothesen wiedererlanbaren Hörvermögens in sensorineural Ertaubten. (Method and experiments for evaluation of the auditory ability restorable to the sensorineural deaf by a cochlear prostheses), Thesis, Technische Universität, Wien.

8. Simmons, F.B., Mathews, R.G., Walker, M.G. and White, R.L. (1979) A fuctioning multichannel auditory nerve stimulator, Acta Otolaryng, 87, pp. 170-175.

9. Traunmuller, H. (1980) The Sentiphone: A tactile speech communication aid, J Com Disorders, 13, pp. 183-193.

10. Remez, R.E., Rubin, P.E., Pisoni, D.B. and Carrell, T.D. (1981) Speech perception without traditional speech cues, Science, 212, pp 947-950.

© 1982 Elsevier Biomedical Press
The Representation of Speech in the Peripheral
Auditory System, R. Carlson and B. Granström eds.

PERCEPTUAL DISCRIMINABILITY OF NONEXPONENTIAL/EXPONENTIAL DAMPING OF THE
FIRST FORMANT OF VOWEL SOUNDS

T.V. ANANTHAPADMANABHA, LENNART NORD, AND GUNNAR FANT
Department of Speech Communication and Music Acoustics, Royal Institute of
Technology (KTH), S-100 44 Stockholm, Sweden

INTRODUCTION

In vowel production, the vocal tract resonances and bandwidths undergo
continuous modulation over the glottal open phase due to the coupling to the
subglottal system and the time-varying nonlinear glottal impedance. This
coupling is strong, especially for the first formant. The instantaneous
bandwidth over a glottal cycle is shown schematically in Fig. 1 for two
vowels. The impulse response of the first formant circuit has an exponential ringing over the glottal close phase and is nearly truncated over the
open phase due to the increased glottal damping (see Fig. 2). Henceforth,
we shall refer to this type of response as the 'true response' of the first
formant because of its resemblance to the first formant responses found in
natural speech. The true response of the first formant is calculated with
an interactive source-filter model which uses physiological parameters, such
as lung pressure, glottal area function and pitch as input source parameters and the vocal tract input impedance as system parameter (1). The log
spectrum of the true response has a typical $(\sin(x)/x)$ shape centered at
the first formant frequency and there are clearly identifiable side lobe
peaks. Conventionally, an exponentially damped first formant response is
used in vowel synthesis. The 'exponential impulse response' is compared
with the 'true response', both in the time and the frequency domains in
Fig. 3.

An interesting problem in vowel synthesis is concerned with the ability
of the auditory system to discriminate between different types of envelopes
of first formant ringing. In the present work we have conducted perceptual experiments on the discriminability between the 'true' impulse response,
i.e., the response of a resonance system with varying bandwidth, and the exponential (=constant bandwidth) impulse response of the first formant. An
effective bandwidth was chosen for the exponentially damped stimuli to obtain the same loudness level for the two types of responses (2). Perceptual tests were conducted in an ABX paradigm. The same ABX test stimulus

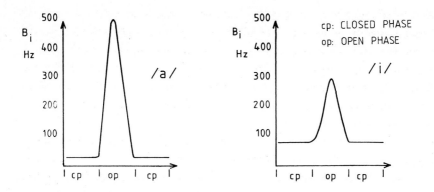

Fig. 1. Typical instantaneous first formant bandwidth over a glottal cycle.

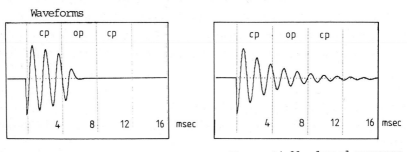

Fig. 2. True response of first formant circuit

Waveforms

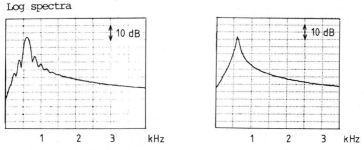

True response   Exponentially damped response

Log spectra

Fig. 3. Comparison of true and exponentially damped resonanses.

was repeated once more giving the listener a choice to indicate the level
of confidence or to reverse his judgment. The test lists were separated
so that the listeners heard the same first formant frequency throughout a
given test list. The stimuli were presented over headphones. A test list
consisted of randomly ordered ABX stimuli, where A, B, or X could be the
true response or the exponentially damped response. Experienced listeners participated in the test.

We have used three types of signals: (a) impulse response of a single
formant circuit, (b) single formant sounds, and (c) vowels. By this means
we approach the complex vowel sound in a stepwise manner thus studying the
discriminability as a function of the complexity of the signal.

TESTS ON IMPULSE RESPONSES

To simulate different degrees of glottal damping, three values of peak
glottal area, viz., 30, 20, and 10 sq mm were used. As the peak glottal
area decreases, the envelope of the true response approaches an exponential. For each glottal area, the effective bandwidth was calculated and
used for the exponentially damped response so as to ensure the same loudness level of the stimuli. The results of the perceptual tests are shown
in Table 1. It can be seen that as the peak glottal area decreases, the
discriminability also decreases, that is, the perceptual similarity between the two types of responses increases. But, for the stimuli with high
F_1, the discriminability is high, even for a peak glottal area of 10 sq mm.

TABLE 1
RESULTS OF PERCEPTUAL TEST: IMPULSE RESPONSES
Number of errors in judgment for different peak glottal areas (of 20 samples
each)

Formant frequency in Hz	Peak Glottal Area in sq mm		
	30	20	10
660 (/a/)	1	2	2
524 (/o/)	4	1	4
269 (/i/)	0	5	7

TESTS ON SINGLE FORMANT SOUNDS

Single formant sounds were synthesized with a constant pitch. Conventionally, a sequence of impulses is used as the driving source in the synthesis of vowel sounds. But, here we use source pulses specifically computed with the source-filter model mentioned earlier (1). Single formant sounds are more complex than simple impulse responses owing to the presence of several signal components (3): (i) Glottal pulses in a differentiated form appear in the waveform, (ii) There may be an additional excitation at the glottal onset, (iii) due to the superposition effect tail ends of the damped waves from previous periods may add in arbitrary phase to the main response of the present period. The presence of these additional components could mask the discriminability between the two types of impulse responses being compared. A peak glottal area of 20 sq mm, and a lung pressure of 8 cm H_2O were used as source parameters. Two values of pitch, $F_0=F_1/N$ and $F_0=F_1/(N-0.5)$, N=integer, were used for each sound. These two cases correspond to a pitch harmonic coinciding with the formant peak or to the pitch harmonics lying on either side of the formant peak, respectively. The results of the perceptual tests are shown in Table 2. The results once again show the easy discriminability for sounds with a high value for the formant frequency. It may be noted that for stimuli with $F_0=F_1/(N-0.5)$, the discriminability is relatively better.

TABLE 2

RESULTS OF PERCEPTUAL TEST: SINGLE FORMANT SOUNDS

Number of errors in judgment with repetition (of 144 samples each)

Formant frequency in Hz	Pitch	
	$F_0=F_1/N$	$F_0=F_1/(N-0.5)$
660 (/a/) (N=7)	24	6
444 (/ɛ/) (N=4)	41	26
269 (/i/) (N=3)	34	45

TESTS ON VOWELS

In the synthesis of vowels, five formants were used. A natural intonation pattern was used. Intensity variation was obtained by varying the peak glottal area keeping the lung pressure constant. For vowels with an exponentially damped first formant, a constant effective bandwidth considered to be a good average fit was used. Due to the 'speech mode' of listening, we expected the task to become more difficult. However, the perceptual tests (Table 3) show the same general trend as for the impulse responses and the single formant sounds. That is, the listeners made fewer mistakes for vowels with a high first formant frequency.

TABLE 3

RESULTS OF PERCEPTUAL TEST: VOWELS

Number of errors in judgment of 80 trials

Vowel	Number of errors
/a/	12
/o/	21
/ɛ/	27
/u/	37
/i/	42

CONCLUSION

The philosophy of vocoders and terminal analogue synthesizers is based on the assumption that finer temporal details in the signal may not be perceived in a complex signal, such as a vowel sound, though for simple signals, such as AM/QFM, the auditory system is known to be sensitive to the differences in the wave forms (4). In vowel production, the coupling of the vocal tract to the time-varying glottal impedance gives rise to a fine temporal structure, the formant damping being non-exponential. When comparing this type of signal to a signal with an exponential damping, corresponding to an excited resonance with a constant bandwidth, we have found that these two types of responses are discriminable even for a complex signal, such as a vowel sound.

This could have some bearing on the design of speech synthesizers. However, continuous synthesized speech samples should first be tried in order to ascertain the relative importance of using a more complex model for speech synthesis.

A more detailed discussion on the probable mechanism behind the processing of such complex signals and results from preference tests comparing the two types of signals will be presented elsewhere (5).

222

REFERENCES

1. Ananthapadmanabha, T.V. and Fant, G. (1982) Calculation of true glottal flow and its components, STL-QPSR 1/1982 (Dept. Speech Comm. & Music Acoustics, KTH, Stockholm).

2. Fant, G. and Liljencrants, J. (1979) Perception of vowels with truncated intraperiod decay envelopes, STL-QPSR 1/1979 (Dept. Speech Comm. & Music Acoustics, KTH, Stockholm).

3. Fant, G. (1979) Vocal source analysis - a progress report, STL-QPSR 1/1979 (Figs. II-A-6-10) (Dept. Speech Comm. & Music Acoustics, KTH, Stockholm).

4. Lozhkin, V.N. (1971) Monaural phase effects, Sov.Phys.Ac., 17, 1-14.

5. Nord, L., Ananthapadmanabha, T.V., and Fant, G. (1982), forthcoming article; to appear in STL-QPSR.

© 1982 Elsevier Biomedical Press
The Representation of Speech in the Peripheral
Auditory System, R. Carlson and B. Granström eds.

AMPLITUDE OF THE VOICE SOURCE FUNDAMENTAL AND THE INTELLIGIBILITY OF SUPER PITCH VOWELS

JOHAN SUNDBERG AND JAN GAUFFIN

Department of Speech Communication and Music Acoustics, KTH, S-100 44 Stockholm 70, Sweden

INTRODUCTION

The intelligibility of high pitched vowels has been investigated by several authors (1-8). It has been shown that a reasonable vowel intelligibility (better than 50% correct identification as an average over vowels) can be maintained in isolated vowels up to phonation frequencies of about 500 Hz, and at least up to 1000 Hz in a CVC context. In soprano singing the voice fundamental frequency may be as high as 1500 Hz.

In the investigations mentioned above which studied the singing voice, the intelligibility tests were carried out with vowels produced by singers. However, in such vowels, the formant frequencies may be far from their normal values. For instance, the first formant frequency is generally adjusted to the vicinity of the pitch frequency in cases where the fundamental is higher than the normal first formant value (9).

The voice source characteristics are generally regarded as personal factors while the phonetic value is determined by formant frequency information. However, in vowels where the fundamental frequency is very high, a perceptual separation of formants and voice source characteristics is unlikely. For instance, in cases where there are only one or two partials in the frequency region of the first formant, the relative amplitude of the lowest spectrum partial must be decisive to vowel quality.

Depending on the type of phonation the amplitude of the voice source fundamental can be varied independently within 15 dB or more (10, 11). Therefore, in high pitched vowels, a change of the voice source fundamental amplitude can be expected to affect vowel identification. In vowels with a first formant frequency as low as 300 Hz, this would occur at fundamental frequencies near or above 200 Hz. Still, as was mentioned above, several vowels can be correctly identified up to about 500 Hz fundamental frequency.

The present paper is an attempt to discover the effect of the voice source fundamental amplitude on vowel intelligibility, using synthetic vowels with realistic formant frequencies in the pitch range of a soprano singer.

EXPERIMENT

A set of six isolated vowels were produced at four fundamental frequencies on the singing synthesizer MUSSE (12). The formant frequencies were taken from previous measurements on a professional soprano singer (9). The vowels had a 6 undulations/second sinusoidal vibrato of $\pm$ 3% which made the stimuli sounds natural without affecting the vowel intelligibility and identity (8).

Each vowel was recorded with two different voice sources. In one source the amplitude of the fundamental was 10 dB higher than in the other source. These stimuli were recorded four times on four test tapes in random order at a constant overall amplitude. Each stimulus was 2 sec long, had a gradual 100 msec onset and decay, and was followed by a silent interval of 4 seconds. The first two tapes contained stimuli generated with both types of voice sources, while each of the last two tapes contained stimuli synthesized one voice source, only. In all, the four tapes took about 20 minutes to play.

The tape was presented to 14 phonetically trained observers who tried to identify the sounds as one of 12 vowels: [u, o, ɑ, a, ae, ɛ, e, i, y, ʉ, ø, oe]. In this way a relatively detailed information was obtained regarding the subject's perception of the vowels. The subjects found the sound of the stimuli to be natural. A total of 56 votes (14 subjects, 4 presentations) was collected for each of the 48 vowel stimuli (6 vowels, 4 pitches, 2 sources).

RESULTS

Following the procedure in a similar investigation (8) the responses were evaluated in the following way. A set of formant frequencies was ascribed to each of the 12 response vowels. These formant frequencies were taken from Fant's data on Swedish vowels and converted into the Mel unit (13). They will be referred to as apparent formant pitches. Mean apparent first and second formant pitches were computed for all responses given to each stimulus.

These mean apparent formant pitches do not necessarily correspond to the formant frequencies used in the synthesis; the formant frequencies of a vowel have to change with fundamental frequency if vowel quality is to remain constant. Because of the same reason the mean apparent formant pitches of the responses do not necessarily relate in a simple fashion to the formant frequencies which the subjects "heard". Still, changes in mean apparent formant pitch pertaining to stimuli with identical fundamental and formant frequencies and differing with respect to voice source will give information about the perceptual effect of this voice source difference on vowel quality.

In the first two test tapes both types of voice sources were mixed, while in each of the last two test tapes all vowels had the same type of voice source.

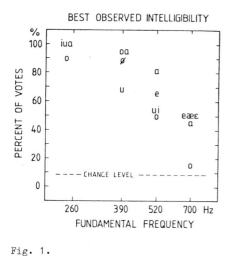

Fig. 1.

The responses given to identical stimuli in the first two test tapes were
pooled in order to minimize context
effects. The same was done with the
responses collected from the last two
test tapes. It turned out that the
effect on the mean apparent formant
pitches of our source spectrum difference was greater when both source
spectra were represented in the tape
than when all stimuli with the same
source spectrum was presented in a
sequence; 13 and 6 significant shifts
of the mean apparent formant pitch,
were obtained, respectively, out of
48. This differen that in some instances our subjects were actually normali-
zing with respect to the voice source spectrum when all stimuli generated with
the same source spectrum were presented in a sequence.

The highest number of votes received for a specific vowel at a given fundamental frequency is shown in Fig. 1. A 50% intelligibility of vowels such as [u]
and [o] can be obtained with a fundamental frequency of 520 Hz and formant
frequencies that are between 30 and 90 % higher than in normal speech. However, as these are only the best observed intelligibility data in our test, a
singer may be capable of producing an even better intelligibility.

The influence of an amplitude shift in the source spectrum fundamental on
vowel perception was studied. This was realized by comparing the mean appa-

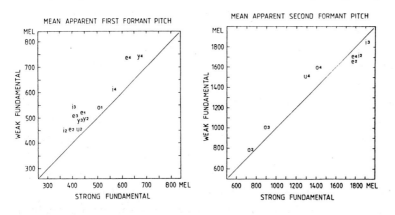

Fig. 2a.   Fig. 2b.

rent formant pitches for responses to stimuli differing in this stimulus
parameter only. Here, all reponses were pooled, regardless of where the stimulus appeared in the test tapes. The differences in the mean apparent formant
pitches, that were significant at a 99% level are shown in Fig. 2. It can be
seen that a strong source spectrum fundamental produced lower mean apparent
first formant pitches in all significant cases, most of which were front
vowels. With respect to the second formant, an increase of the amplitude of
the fundamental lowers the mean apparent formant pitch in some back vowels and
raises it in some front vowels. We conclude from these results that an
increase in the amplitude of the source spectrum fundamental is mostly interpreted as a <u>lowering</u> of the first formant frequency and, in the case of back
vowels, as a <u>lowering</u> also of the second formant frequency.

DISCUSSION

The results shown in Fig. 2a suggest that the subjects interpreted an increase of the amplitude of the fundamental as a drop in the first formant
frequency. An interpretation of this would be that the "perceived" first
formant is higher than the fundamental frequency; in such cases a lowering of
the first formant frequency increases the amplitude of the fundamental. The
case of the second formant in back vowels (Fig. 2b) can be explained by the
fact that in such vowels the frequency distance between the two lowest formants is rather small; a lowering of the second formant must then lead to an
increase of the amplitude of the fundamental. The reason why the front vowels
do not conform with the back vowels in this respect is hard to explain. It may
be relevant that the mean first apparent formant pitch also changed significantly in all these cases.

The accuracy with which our vowel stimuli were identified as specific vowels
is remarkably high in view of the pitches used. As suggested by Carlson & al.
(14) the "perceived" first formant frequency seems to correspond to a weighted
mean of adjacent harmonics rather than to the frequency of a single partial.
Our results support the same hypothesis. Indeed, all significant shifts in the
mean apparent formant pitches resulting from an increase of the amplitude of
the source spectrum fundamental are hard to explain if the "perceived" formants were locked to prominent partials. On the other hand, the weighting of
spectrum partials is not likely to be performed in a unique way. This can be
inferred from the fact that in some cases the effect of an increase in the
amplitude of the fundamental was different when all stimuli generated with
the same source spectrum was presented in a sequence on the test tape. Similar
effects have been observed previously by Lindqvist (Gauffin) and Pauli (15) in

a study which also evaluated a source spectrum difference. Such long term effects cannot be accounted for by a straight-forward weighting of spectrum partials.

The last mentioned observation suggests that in some cases our listeners were able to distinguish contributions from the voice source from those of the formant frequencies even in stimuli with a very high fundamental frequency. However, the stimuli with 260 Hz fundamental frequency and the first formant at 620 Hz may have been decisive for this result. Therefore, no conclusion should be drawn regarding our subjects´ ability in this respect at fundamental frequencies higher than 260 Hz. In a normal listening situation formant frequency changes between vowels and consonants may be important to the listener´s ability to separate source and filter characteristics.

According to Chistovich and Lubinskaya the perceptually relevant formant parameter is the ´center of gravity´ of the lowest two spectral peaks, as long as the distance between the corresponding two formants is smaller than 3 or 3.5 Barks (16). In vowels with normal fundamental frequencies there are several partials per formant. In our high pitched back vowel stimuli there is only one partial for each of the two lowest formants. Thus, each of the two lowest formants constitutes a separate spectrum peak. In the fundamental frequency range considered in the present study the pitch separation of the lowest two partials varies; approximately, it is 2 Barks in vowels with a fundamental frequency of 260 Hz and 4 Barks in vowels with a fundamental frequency of 700 Hz. Still, a weighting of the amplitudes of spectrum partials seems to be relevant to the subjects´ perception of vowel quality even at fundamental frequencies of 700 Hz (cf 17).

CONCLUSIONS

Our data support the conclusions that

1. the frequency corresponding to the apparent first formant pitch is higher than the fundamental even in super pitch vowels;

2. a 50% intelligibility of vowels can be maintained at fundamental frequencies up to 520 Hz, if appropriate formant frequencies are chosen (which may involve values that are 30 to 90 % higher than in normal speech);

3. a weighting of the amplitudes of spectrum partials seems perceptually relevant to vowel quality even at fundamental frequencies of 700 Hz.

REFERENCES
1. Delattre, P. (1958) Vowel Color and Voice Quality, National Association of Teachers of Singing Bulletin, October, pp. 4-7

2. Howie, J. and Delattre P. (1962) An Experimental Study of the Effect of

228

Pitch on the Intelligibility of Vowels, National Association of Teachers of Singing Bulletin, May, pp. 6-9

3. Triplett, W. (1967) An Investigation Concerning Vowel Sounds on High Pitches, National Association of Teachers of Singing Bulletin, February, pp. 6-8

4. Nelson H. and Tiffany, W. (1968) The Intelligibility of Song, National Association of Teachers of Singingy Bulletin, December, pp. 22-28

5. Smith L. A. and Scott, B. L. (1980) Increasing the Intelligibility of Sung Vowels, JASA 67, pp. 1795-1797

6. Fujisaki, H. and Kawashima, T. (1968) The Roles of Pitch and Higher Formants in the Perception of Vowels, IEEE Transactions on Audio and Electroacoustics, AU-16, pp.73-77

7. Tenenholtz, E. (1979) Vowel Identification as a Function of Increasing Fundamental Frequency, in Experiments in Speech Perception, Phonetic Research Seminar 1978-1979, Phonetic Experimental Research at the Institute of Linguistic, University of Stockholm, Report I, pp. 38-48

8. Sundberg, J. (1977) Vibrato and Vowel Identification, Archives of Acoustics, 2, 4, pp. 257-256

9. Sundberg, J. (1975) Formant Technique in a Professional Female Singer, Acustica 32, pp. 89-96

10. Sundberg, J. and Gauffin, J. (1979) Waveform and Spectrum of the Glottal Voice Source, in: Frontiers of Speech Communications Research, Lindblom, B. and Öhman, S. (Ed.), Academic Press, London, pp. 301-320

11. Sundberg, J. and Gauffin, J. (1980) Data on the Glottal Voice Source Behavior in Vowel Production, Speech Transmission Laboratory Quarterly Progress and Status Report 1977/1, 2-3/1980, pp. 61-70

12. Larsson, B. (1977) Music and Singing Synthesis Equipment (MUSSE), Speech Transmission Laboratory Quarterly Progress and Status Report 1977/1, pp. 38-40

13. Fant, G. (1973) Speech Sounds and Features, The MIT Press, Cambridge, Massachusetts

14. Carlson, R., Fant, G. and Granström, B. (1975) Two-formant Models, Pitch and Vowel Perception, in: Auditory Analysis and Perception of Speech, Fant, G. and Tatham M. A. A. (Ed.), Academic Press, London, pp. 55-82

15. Lindqvist(Gauffin), J. and Pauli, S. (1968) The Role of Relative Spectrum Levels in Vowel Perception, Speech Transmission Laboratory Quarterly Progress and Status Report 1977/1, pp. 12-15

16. Chistovich, L. A. and Lubinskaya, V. V. (1979) The ´Center of Gravity´ Effect in Vowel Spectra and Critical Distance between the formants: Psychoacoustical Study of the Perceptionof Vowel-like Stimuli, Hearing Research 1, pp. 185-195

17. Traunmueller, H. (198) Essentials of a Psychoacoustic Model of Spectral Matching (Work in Progress), in Experiments in Speech Perception, Phonetic Research Seminar 1978-1979, Phonetic Experimental Research at the Institute of Linguistic, University of Stockholm, Report I, pp. 49-63

© 1982 Elsevier Biomedical Press
The Representation of Speech in the Peripheral
Auditory System, R. Carlson and B. Granström eds.

PERCEPTUAL EVALUATION OF NATURALNESS OF VOWELS FROM TERMINAL ANALOG SYNTHESIS

UNTO LAINE[1] AND TAPANI RAHKO[2]
[1]Dept. of Speech Communication and Music Acoustics, KTH, S-10044 Stockholm
(Sweden) and [2]Dept. of Audiology, Tampere University Central Hospital (Finland)

INTRODUCTION

In text-to-speech synthesis a central question is how to control the
terminal analog speech synthesizer to generate natural sounding phonemes,
words and sentences with a minimum amount of control information. In the
synthesis of vowel sounds usually most attention is paid to control the
formant frequencies, while formant bandwidths (BWs) are determined by some
simple rule from their frequencies. However, the formant BWs do affect directly the formant intensities and also the naturalness of the vowels. Instead
of using more complicated rules for formant BWs (or intensities) we can also
change the structure of the synthesizer so that the formant peaks in the
spectrum are located approximately at right levels without any complex BW
controls. This was one of the motivations for the new design of a terminal
analog model called PARCAS (a PARallel-CAScade structure) (1).

The quality and naturalness of the synthetized vowel sound depends on the
terminal analog model and the type of control strategy used. How then do the
modelled spectra compare with measured spectra of natural vowel sounds? How
then do the synthesized vowel sounds compare with natural sounds perceptually?
These questions motivated the present study.

TEST MATERIAL

Four different synthesis strategies were simulated by digital computer:
1. Cascade model with constant formant bandwidths (BW_i = 100 Hz, i=1,...,5)
2. PARCAS model with BWs= 100 Hz
3. Cascade model with rule:

   BW = SQRT(2500 + $(FX/20)^2$), where FX is formant frequency
4. PARCAS model with constant Q-values (Q2=15, Q3=25, Q4=35, Q5=45).

The models were simulated with 16 kHz sampling frequency and floating point
arithmetic. A 12-bit D/A-converter with 6 kHz anti-aliasing filter was used
and the master tape recorded with TEACH A-33405 tape recorder. All models had
five controllable formant filters. The cascade models had two extra filters
for higher pole correction. The excitation signal used was a train of simple
exponential pulses. All formant circuits were standard all-pole digital

filters. So, the PARCAS models did slightly differ from the analog reali-
zation published earlier (1). In the PARCAS model with constant Q strategy
the BW of the first formant (constant value of 100 Hz) was the only exception.
The Q-values for the other formants were chosen so that all BWs of the neutral
vowel [ɜ] (FX = (2n-1)*500 Hz) had value of 100 Hz.

   Formant frequencies for the vowels were estimated from speech samples of one
male speaker by using spectrograms and inverse filtering. The synthesized
vowels were 460 ms in duration including 30 ms onset and offset segments (Fig.
1). Formant frequencies were held fixed over the entire duration of each
vowel. The pitch contour decreased linearly over the vowel from 110 to 100 Hz.
The neutral vowel [ɜ] was used for tuning the gains in models 2 and 4 so as to
correspond nearly to model 1. There was no audible difference between those
models in the case of this vowel. The model 3 differed from the other ones
slightly because of its narrower first formant BW and larger BWs for higher
modes.

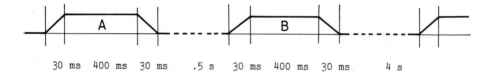

       30 ms   400 ms   30 ms   .5 s   30 ms   400 ms   30 ms   4 s

Fig. 1. Timing of the stimulii

   The test material consisted of 7 Finnish vowels: [a], [e], [i], [o], [u],
[y] and [ae]. The formant frequencies and intensities of the vowels used in
the test are listed in Table 1. Fig. 2 shows two variants of [y] vowel
synthesized by the strategies 3 and 4.

   The models were compared for all the seven vowels pairwise as: 1-2, 2-4, 4-
3, 3-1. The test was done as double blind test, consisting of 56 AB (BA)
vowel pairs in pseudo random order. The timing sequence of the stimulii is
shown in Fig. 1. The task of the listener was to indicate his preference for
the stimulus A or B for naturalness. Forty judges evaluated the models for
their preference. The judges were naive listeners who were native speakers of
Finnish language. The listening conditions were well controlled. The
listeners did not know how many different synthesis strategies of which type
were used in the material.

TABLE 1

TEST VOWELS

Number of the variant refers to the synthesis startegy used

[a]	F1 660	F2 1060	F3 2340	F4 3400	F5 4400	Hz		[e]	F1 480	F2 1900	F3 2500	F4 3500	F5 4300	Hz
1.	30.0	25.5	8.0	1.5	-4.5	dB		1.	25.5	18.5	18.0	11.5	5.0	dB
2.	31.5	27.0	7.0	7.5	0.0			2.	26.0	15.0	13.5	9.0	0.0	
3.	33.5	27.5	6.0	-2.5	-10.0			3.	29.0	18.5	16.0	6.5	-1.0	
4.	31.5	29.0	7.5	8.0	0.0			4.	26.0	13.0	16.5	9.0	0.5	

[i]	F1 300	F2 2100	F3 2700	F4 3700	F5 4500	Hz		[o]	F1 450	F2 800	F3 2200	F4 3200	F5 4200	Hz
1.	25.0	10.5	11.5	7.5	3.0	dB		1.	28.5	21.0	-4.0	-11.0	-12.0	dB
2.	25.5	13.0	15.0	10.0	1.0			2.	30.0	24.5	6.0	6.5	-1.0	
3.	28.5	9.5	9.0	2.0	-3.5			3.	31.5	23.5	-5.0	-14.5	-24.0	
4.	26.0	10.5	14.0	10.0	1.0			4.	30.0	28.0	7.0	7.5	-0.5	

[u]	F1 320	F2 660	F3 2000	F4 3000	F5 4100	Hz		[y]	F1 300	F2 1600	F3 2100	F4 3400	F5 4100	Hz
1.	27.0	17.0	-12.0	-21.0	-	dB		1.	26.0	10.0	7.0	-4.4	-10.0	dB
2.	29.0	21.0	5.0	5.0	-3.0			2.	26.0	13.0	12.5	8.0	1.5	
3.	30.5	19.5	-13.0	-24.5	-			3.	29.0	10.5	5.5	-9.5	-15.5	
4.	29.0	26.0	6.5	6.5	-2.0			4.	26.0	12.5	13.5	8.5	2.0	

[ae]	F1 640	F2 1600	F3 2500	F4 3500	F5 4200	Hz
1.	27.5	21.5	17.5	13.5	8.0	dB
2.	27.5	18.5	10.5	9.5	2.5	
3.	30.0	21.5	15.0	9.0	2.0	
4.	27.5	18.0	10.5	9.5	3.0	

232

RESULTS AND DISCUSSION

The listeners' scores are summarized in the Table 2. The results show that there is no significant difference amongst the models in the naturalness of the vowels synthesized. Every model obtained a score between 23.2 - 26.0 %. None of the models produced acceptable vowel quality sounds for all the vowels. Whereas, model 4 is prefered for vowels [a], [i] and [y], model 3 is prefered for vowels [e] and [u], and models 1 and 2 are prefered for vowels [ae] and [o] as seen in the detailed scores of Table 3.

TABLE 2
AVERAGE SCORES OF THE VOWEL TEST

1. Cascade model/BWs=100 Hz	25.2 %	total score	
2. PARCAS model/BWs=100 Hz	25.6 %	"	"
3. Cascade model/BW-by-rule	23.2 %	"	"
4. PARCAS model/const. Q	26.0 %	"	"

Does the randomness in the average results mean that the individuals were not able to make any systematic decissions? We can not say so. Upon a closer examination of the answers the listeners' responses grouped themselves into two conflicting trends (Table 3). The two main trends were found by computer analysis applying pattern clustering algorithms. A distance measure was designed to define the similarity/dissimilarity between any two answers. It was found that among the material of the 40 listeners, 24 pairs of answers did not have similar features (a maximal dissimilarity). By choosing anyone of those 24 pairs to form the starting centres of the clusters, we were able to group the material into two main clusters (A & B). Every answer was first compared with the members in both cluster and the average distance from the clusters calculated. Then the answer was included into the nearest cluster. Listeners in group A, quite consistently prefered vowels with clear timbre (more intense F2 and/or F3) irrespective of which model generated that quality. On the other hand, listeners in group B quite consistently prefered vowels with dark timbre.

Changes in the intensity balance between two closely spaced formants seems to produce relatively large changes in the psycho acoustical responses. In [a] from model 4, the spectral envelope has a strong second formant and consequently gets highest score whereas the same vowel in model 1 has weakest second formant and, was evaluated to be less natural. Also in [e] and [ae] the most natural variants were those with most intense second formant. For vowels [y] and [i] variants with F3 having more energy than F2 were prefered.

Generally speaking the intensity balance between the neighbouring formants
seems to be of importance expecially in the frequency range close to the F2′
formant of the two formant model proposed by Carlson et al (2).

TABLE 3
DETAILED SCORES AND RESULTS OF PATTERN CLASSIFICATION ALGORITHM
Line * : total scores of 40 listener
Line A : group A of 21 listener (more intense F2/F3 prefered)
Line B : group B of 19 listener (less intense F2/F3 prefered)

		1 - 2		2 - 4		4 - 3		3 - 1	
	*	37	43	35	45	52	28	46	34
[a]	A	12	(30)	19	23	(36)	6	24	18
	B	(25)	13	16	22	16	(22)	22	16
	*	42	38	50	30	35	45	43	37
[e]	A	(28)	14	27	15	13	(29)	20	22
	B	14	(24)	23	15	(22)	16	23	15
	*	34	46	38	42	48	32	29	51[a]
[i]	A	12	(30)	15	27	27	15	14	28
	B	(22)	16	19	19	21	17	15	23
	*	33	47	43	37	43	37	45	35
[o]	A	6	(36)	20	22	(29)	13	25	17
	B	(27)	11	23	15	14	(24)	20	18
	*	41	39	39	41	36	44	41	39
[u]	A	22	20	21	21	(24)	18	23	19
	B	19	19	18	20	12	(26)	18	20
	*	35	45	39	41	59	21[a]	30	50
[y]	A	10	(32)	18	24	38	4	13	29
	B	(25)	13	21	17	21	17	17	21
	*	51	29	42	38	36	44	35	45
[ae]	A	32	10	23	19	12	(30)	14	28
	B	19	19	19	19	(24)	14	21	17

[a]see Fig. 2
[o]note the conflicting trends

233

234

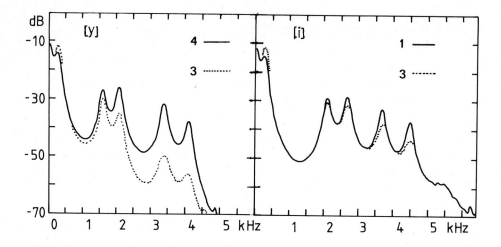
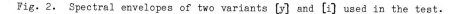

Fig. 2. Spectral envelopes of two variants [y] and [i] used in the test.

CONCLUSIONS

The results show that the naturalness of a vowel is a subjective attribute which is different for different listeners. Hence no single modelling strategy used in this work seems to satisfy all the listeners. Perhaps, suprasegmental features, such as intonation, durational aspects and spectral dynamics may be more important aspects in determining the naturalness of synthetic speech.

ACKNOWLEDGEMENTS

The authors are gratefull to Dr. M. Karjalainen at Helsinki University of Technology for organizing a part of the listening tests. The authors are indebted to the staff in Dept. of Speech Communication and Music Acoustics, KTH, Stockholm expecially to Dr. J. Liljencrants for the modifications needed in his simulation programs and Dr. T. Ananthapadmanabha for revision of the manuscript. This study has been supported by the Academy of Finland, Nordiska Forskarstipendier and Cultural Foundation of Finland.

REFERENCES
1. Laine, U.K. (1982) PARCAS, a New Terminal Analog Model for Speech Synthesis, Proc. ICASSP 82 Paris, IEEE Catalog No. 82CH1746-7, pp. 940-943.
2. Carlson, R., Fant, G. and Granström, B. (1975) Two-formant Models, Pitch and Vowel Perception, in: Auditory Analysis and Perception of Speech, Fant, G. and Tatham, M. A. A. (Ed.), Academic Press, London, pp. 55-82.

© 1982 Elsevier Biomedical Press
The Representation of Speech in the Peripheral
Auditory System, R. Carlson and B. Granström eds.

ANALYSIS OF NON-STATIONARY VOICED SEGMENTS IN SPEECH SIGNALS

T.V. SREENIVAS[*] AND P.V.S. RAO
Speech and Digital Systems Group, Tata Institute of Fundamental Research,
Homi Bhabha Road, Bombay 400 005, INDIA

INTRODUCTION

First level signal processing has attracted considerable amount of research
in developing speech processing systems as well as understanding human auditory
analysis. Spectral representation, in particular, has played a key role in
characterizing speech signals and the human system is supposed to perform
more than one level of frequency analysis. Because of the complexity of the
human auditory system, most of the stimulous signals considered are stationary.
These results are extended to speech on the widely assumed basis that speech
signals are stationary atleast over short durations of the order of 30 msec.
(linear model) In reality speech signals are more complex than supposed by
the above model due to fast variations of the sound in continuous speech and
due to interference signals of the transmission medium.[1] Under such non-
stationarity the existing notions of signal spectrum and the related parameters
such as pitch, formant, etc., are insufficient. The present study confines
to the short-time spectra of aperiodic signals.

SOURCES OF NON-STATIONARITY

The sources of non-stationarity (aperiodicity in the case of voiced sounds)
in speech are of the types (a) signal specific and (b) non-signal-specific.
While signal specific aperiodicity is caused by the underlying processes
generating the signal, non-signal-specific aperiodicity results from the transmission media. The causes of aperiodicity underlying the production of speech
are: (i) changes in periodicity of vocal-fold vibration, called period transition, (ii) variations in air flow resulting in loudness variation, called
amplitude transition, (iii) continuous variation of supra-laryngeal articulators
to produce different sounds, called formant or bandwidth transition and
(iv) constrictions in the vocal-tract causing additional noisy excitation
(e.g., /z/), called additive noise. The interference of the transmission
media affecting the signal can be really complex. For the present, only
additive noise is considered; this is similar to case (iv) above.

---

* now at Electronics and Radar Development Establishment, Bangalore 560 001.

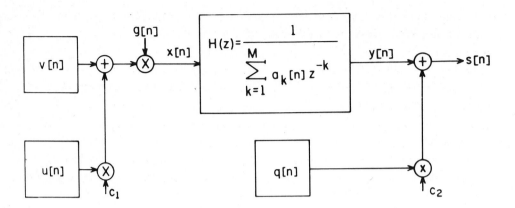

(a) source-filter model for aperiodic speech

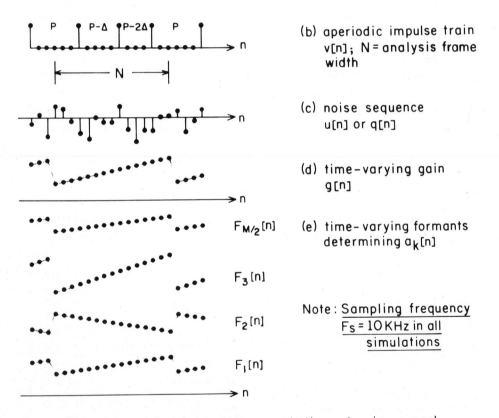

(b) aperiodic impulse train $v[n]$; N = analysis frame width

(c) noise sequence $u[n]$ or $q[n]$

(d) time-varying gain $g[n]$

(e) time-varying formants determining $a_k[n]$

Note: Sampling frequency $F_S = 10$ KHz in all simulations

Fig. 1 Model for synthesizing aperiodic and noisy speech

To study the properties of aperiodic signals, it is necessary to generate such signals with controlled magnitudes of the transitions. Fig.1 shows an extension of the linear model of speech production [2]: the time varying functions $v[n]$ and $g[n]$ represent the irregular vocal-fold vibration and loudness control respectively; the time-varying linear prediction coefficients (LPCs) [2] $a_k[n]$ approximate the continuously changing vocal-tract shape; the noise sources $u[n]$ and $q[n]$ simulate mixed source excitation due to constriction in the vocal-tract and additive channel noise respectively. Since the interest is only in short-time aperiodicity, all parameters are assumed to be varying periodically beyond the frame of analysis. Thus the aperiodic signal is given by

$$s[n] = y[n] + c_2 \, q[n] \qquad \qquad \ldots(1)$$

where
$$y[n] = x[n] - \sum_{k=1}^{M} a_k[n] \, y_{n-k} \qquad \qquad \ldots(2)$$

$$x[n] = g[n] \, (v[n] + c_1 \, u[n]) \qquad \qquad \ldots(3)$$

The time-varying system $H(z)$ is specified by the formant contours $F_i[n]$ and bandwidth contours $B_i[n]$ as in Fig. 1(e). The LPCs are computed at every sampling instant using the relations

$$\sum_{k=0}^{M} a_k[n] \, z^{-k} = \prod_{i=1}^{M/2} (1 - 2X_i Y_i \, z^{-1} + X_i^2 \, z^{-2}) \qquad \ldots(4)$$

where
$$X_i = \exp(-\pi B_i[n]/F_s), \qquad Y_i = \cos(2\pi F_i[n]/F_s)$$

Thus the model provides for simulating all the four types of aperiodicity discussed earlier.

SPECTRA OF APERIODIC SIGNALS

Fig.2 shows comparative spectra of a periodic signal (a) and of signals with each of the aperiodicities. (parameter transition is specified over an analysis segment of three "periods") A 10% per cycle reduction in the period of the signal, shown in (b), causes noise all over the spectrum; feeble "pitch-peaks" [3] (dominant peaks appearing above the background noise in the region) are discernible only in three regions; this structure of alternate bunches of pitch-peaks and noise can be seen clearly in the spectrum of the corresponding excitation signal shown in (c). For larger transition rates, there occur more bunches and fewer pitch-peaks per bunch. It is interesting to note that under all magnitudes of period transition, the pitch-peak separation is exactly equal to

238

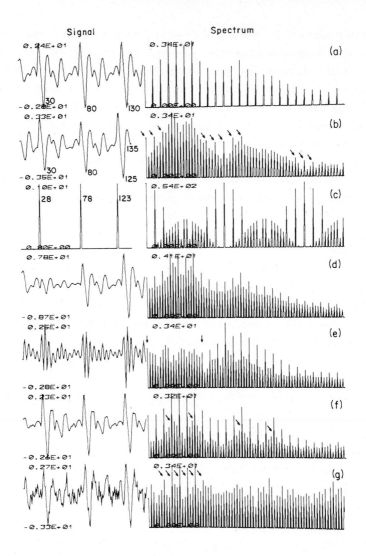

Fig.2. Aperiodic signals s[n] and their DFT spectra $|S[k]|^{1/4}$ compared with
that of a periodic signal; (a) periodic signal; (b) signal with 10%
period transition; (c) excitation signal x[n] of s[n] in (a) and the
spectrum $|X[k]|^2$; (d) signal with an amplitude transition of 6 dB;
(e) first formant transition of 200-1200 Hz; (f) transition of all
four bandwidths from 50-100 Hz; (g) signal with additive white noise
at 5 dB SNR. The spectra are plotted as discrete line spectra whereas
the signals are shown as continuous waveforms.

the arithmetic mean of the successive "periods" in the signal. Next, amplitude
transition affects the spectrum more uniformly; the envelope of the noisy
components exactly follows that of the harmonics, but at a lower amplitude
(see (d)). For a higher magnitude of transition the noise envelope level
increases. The example in (e) shows a first formant transition of 200-1200Hz;
this implies a transition in the transfer function, whose effect on the short-
time spectrum of the output signal could be quite complex. Interestingly, however, the effect on the spectrum is very systematic: only the spectral region
corresponding to the formant sweep is completely void of pitch-peaks; pitch-
peaks are discernible in the rest of the spectrum though amidst noise. The
effect of a bandwidth transition is quite small compared to that of a formant
(see (f)); note the larger magnitude of corruption in the region of the corresponding formant. In the two cases of formant and bandwidth transition, it is
quite surprising that the transfer function parameter transition is highly
correlated with the region of spectral corruption. Lastly, the effect of
additive noise is quite easily predicted; as shown in (g), the extent to which
the peaks in any region of the spectrum would get corrupted will depend on the
magnitude of noise only in that region.

DISCUSSION

The above spectral properties of aperiodic signals are quite important in
the context of estimating signal parameters such as pitch, formants, bandwidths,
etc. It also brings out some salient differences between the spectral analysis
of the human auditory system and the short-time spectral analysis resorted to
in speech processing systems. For example, when the signal has period transition, the aperiodicity is exactly reflected in the temporal displacement of the
basilar membrane at all points even at the basal end. This is because the
temporal resolution of the membrane displacement (duration of the impulse
response) is much larger compared to the aperiodicity occurring over several
"periods". Thus, instead of the alternate noise like and harmonic like
structure in the spectrum, the membrane displacement depicts aperiodicity at all
positions; the displacement amplitude nearly follows the spectral amplitude.
This property holds good also under amplitude transition in the signal. Under
formant or bandwidth transition of the signal, by virtue of band-pass filtering
at a given membrane point, the degree of aperiodicity is much less in the
membrane displacement. These specific responses of the human auditory system
to the aperiodic signals could provide further clues in discerning its
functioning.

REFERENCES

1. Flanagan, J.L. (1972) Speech analysis, synthesis and perception, 2nd edition, Springer Verlag, New York, pp. 184-185.

2. Rabiner, L.R. and Schafer, R.W. (1978) Digital processing of speech signals, Prentice Hall, New York.

3. Sreenivas, T.V. (1981) Pitch estimation of aperiodic and noisy speech signals, Ph.D. thesis submitted to Indian Institute of Technology, Bombay-76, Speech and Digital Systems Group, Tata Institute of Fundamental Research, Bombay-5.

© 1982 Elsevier Biomedical Press
The Representation of Speech in the Peripheral
Auditory System, R. Carlson and B. Granström eds.

HOW DO PITCH ERRORS AFFECT THE PERCEPTION OF LPC CODED SPEECH?

GUNNAR HULT

Chalmers University of Technology, Department of Information Theory,

S-412 96 Göteborg, Sweden

INTRODUCTION

Robust and accurate pitch extraction is an essential part of a speech
processing system. Unfortunately, it is a problem which still has not been
completely solved. We still do not know which features of the speech waveform
most readily lend themselves to a period (and hence pitch) measurement. We
also have incomplete knowledge of the relationship between this objective
interval measurement and the perceived pitch.

A large number of pitch extraction algorithms have been proposed (1)-(4)
and several comparative performance studies of such algorithms have been
carried out, e.g. Rabiner et.al. (5),(6).

Every pitch detector will produce occasional erroneous results. Depending
on the nature of the error, we can classify a particular pitch error as
belonging to a certain class of errors. This paper describes a qualitative
study, using trained listeners, on how certain classes of pitch errors
influence our perception of LPC synthesized speech.

PROBLEMS IN PITCH DETECTION

There are many reasons why a pitch estimation algorithm might fail to give
accurate results (7). The glottal excitation signal never displays perfect
periodicity but has a variation both in period and in pulse shape. Formant
influence can, sometimes dramatically, obscure the quasi-periodic structure
of the glottal waveform. As mentioned above, it is also not always clear
which features of the waveform should be used for an interval measurement.
Such interval measurements obtained from different "significant features" of
the waveform (e.g. using peaks versus using the zero crossings that precede
the peaks) often lead to quite different results.

Another problem is associated with speech that has been transmitted through
a telephone system. The fundamental frequency and some of its lower harmonics
can then be severely attenuated.

PITCH REFERENCE DATA AND CLASSES OF PITCH ERRORS

The initial pitch data was obtained using a user-interactive method (8) that, in addition to user-selectable listening and display modes, allows the user to choose a particular mode of pitch analysis. Examples of such user-defined analysis conditions are (i) the choice of inverse filtering or no inverse filtering before autocorrelation function (ACF) analysis and peak picking and (ii) the choice of a weighting function to eliminate the fall-off of the ACF function that occurs with increasing lags.

This reference data base was then modified to contain pitch errors of four different types:

(i)   unvoiced-to-voiced errors

(ii)   voiced-to-unvoiced errors

(iii)   fine pitch errors where the pitch frequency error is between 10% and 33% of the "true" pitch frequency

(iv)   gross pitch errors where the pitch frequency error is greater than 33% of the "true" pitch frequency

The choice of limits in (iii) and (iv) is somewhat arbitrary and other definitions are possible (5).

To examplify the error categories, a pitch algorithm using LPC inverse filtering, ACF calculation and peak picking typically generates 1% each of unvoiced-to-voiced errors, voiced-to-unvoiced errors and fine pitch errors and .5-1% gross pitch errors.

The user-controlled parameters when modifying the pitch reference data are:

(i)   the percentage of pitch errors of each category in frames which form part of a voiced-to-unvoiced or unvoiced-to-voiced transition.

(ii)   the percentage of pitch errors of each category in other frames.

LPC ANALYSIS AND SYNTHESIS CONDITION

The conditions under which LPC analysis and synthesis can be expected to give good results have been thoroughly investigated (9),(10) and are quite well understood.

For this investigation, speech was sampled at 8 kHz and analyzed using the LPC autocorrelation method of order 12 with a first-order adaptive preemphasis to insure spectral balance. A 384-point Hamming window was applied to each 3-frame speech segment, each frame being 128 samples, and from this windowed sequence the 12 LPC parameters and the prediction error energy were found.

Synthesis from the (distorted) pitch data and the LPC parameters was then carried out, using interpolation of the LPC parameters in the reflection coefficient domain to simplify stability control. The analysis/synthesis scheme is shown in Fig. 1.

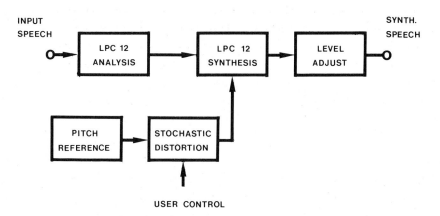

Fig. 1. Analysis/synthesis scheme

SPEECH DATA BASE

The data base was chosen so as to include different pitch ranges as well as various recording conditions. Three different recordings were used:

(i)   a 13-second segment consisting of a telephone conversation in English between a male and a female (DAT1). The frequency range is 100-3400 Hz.

(ii)   a 48-second segment consisting of a low-pitched male voice reading a text in Swedish (DAT2). It was recorded using a close-talking microphone, sampled at 16 kHz, low-pass filtered to 4 kHz and finally sampled down to 8 kHz.

(iii)   a 16-second segment consisting of a male voice talking in Swedish (DAT3). It was recorded from a radio broadcast, sampled at 16 kHz, low-pass filtered to 4 kHz and finally sampled down to 8 kHz.

SUBJECTIVE LISTENING TESTS

Subjective listening tests were conducted over the data base by 3-6 different listeners. The tests included the following two categories:

(i)   the listener was asked to describe, in his/her own words, the impression given by synthesized speech containing a large amount (typically 10-30%) of pitch distortion of each of the four categories described above.

(ii)   the listener was subjected to an A/B-comparison test and had to show preference for either A or B. The two choices were LPC synthesized speech containing the pitch errors described above versus an error-free LPC synthesis.

For both (i) and (ii), two separate cases were singled out: one with the pitch errors distributed over all frames and one with the pitch errors located only in frames that formed part of a voiced-to-unvoiced or unvoiced-to voiced transition.

RESULTS

The listeners' reactions to synthesized speech containing large amounts of pitch errors are summarized in Table 1. The error rates were chosen high enough to cause substantial distortion: 70% unvoiced-to-voiced errors and 30% of the remaining categories.

TABLE 1

LISTENERS' REACTIONS TO SPEECH CONTAINING LARGE AMOUNTS OF PITCH ERRORS

Pitch Error Category	Reactions
Unvoiced-to-voiced	Background buzz, chirps
Voiced-to-unvoiced	Cracked voice, "severe cold"
Fine errors	Very unpleasant, vibrating, speaker "very weak, half-dead"
Gross errors	Cracked voice, creaky

Restricting the pitch errors to transition regions caused the synthesized speech to be quite similar to an error-free synthesis for all classes of pitch errors. In this case the reactions mentioned above were not present.

The results of the A/B-comparison test are shown in Table 2. The numbers indicate the amount of pitch errors necessary (in % of the total number of unvoiced or voiced frames) to cause the speech to be perceived as being of inferior quality compared to an error-free synthesis. There is a separate column for the case where the pitch errors are in transition regions only.

TABLE 2

AMOUNT OF PITCH ERRORS NECESSARY (IN%) TO CAUSE PERCEIVABLE DEGRADATION

Pitch Error Category	All Frames	Transitions Only
Unvoiced-to-unvoiced	20-30	> 10*
Voiced-to-unvoiced	0	0
Fine errors	2-5	6-8
Gross errors	0	0

* No perceivable degradation with errors in every transition frame.

DISCUSSION

Some general conclusions can be drawn from the results in Table 1. The unvoiced-to-voiced errors were not found to be very disturbing. This is to be expected since the unvoiced frames are low level sounds where it is hard to separate voiced synthesis from unvoiced. One listener even preferred these errors over an error-free synthesis, maybe because the chirping background noise they cause tends to camouflage the buzzing sound that is usually obtained from a LPC synthesis.

The voiced-to-unvoiced errors and the gross pitch errors were both perceived as discontinuities (sudden jumps) in an otherwise smooth pitch contour. The fine pitch errors seemed to give the synthesis a vibrating, but still continuous quality. This vibrating quality was found by some listeners to be extremely unpleasant.

In Table 2, lower limits on the number of voiced-to-unvoiced errors and gross pitch errors are not meaningful. This is so because one single frame in a synthesis with any of these errors can be quite noticable.

The entries for the fine pitch errors shows the camouflaging effects of the transients that have been discussed by other authors (7).

The results were fairly consistent among the different listeners and using the different speech data.

REFERENCES

1. Noll, A.M., "Cepstrum Pitch Determination", J.Acoust.Soc.Am., Vol.41, pp. 293-309, February 1967.

246

2. Sondhi, M.M., "New Methods of Pitch Extraction", IEEE Trans.Audio and Electroacoustics, Vol. AU-16, No. 2, pp. 262-266, June 1968.

3. Gold, B., Rabiner, L.R., "Parallel Processing Techniques for Estimating Pitch Periods of Speech in the Time Domain", J.Acoust.Soc.Am., Vol. 46, No. 2, Pt. 2, pp. 442-448, August 1969.

4. Ross, M.J., Shaffer, H.L., Cohen, A., Freudberg, R., Manley, H.J., "Average Magnitude Difference Function Pitch Extractor", IEEE Trans. Acoust., Speech and Signal Proc., Vol. ASSP-22, pp. 353-362, October 1974.

5. Rabiner, L.R., Cheng, M.J., Rosenberg, A.E., McGonegal, C.A., "A Comparative Performance Study of Several Pitch Detection Algorithms", IEEE Trans. on ASSP, Vol. ASSP-24, No. 5, October, 1976.

6. McGonegal, C.A., Rabiner, L.R., Rosenberg, A.E., "A Subjective Evaluation of Pitch Detection Methods Using LPC Synthesized Speech", IEEE Trans. on ASSP, Vol. ASSP-25, No. 3, June, 1977.

7. Flanagan, J.L., "Speech Analysis, Synthesis, and Perceptions", Springer-Verlag, New York, 1972.

8. Hedelin, P., "Manual for Manpit - A Pitch Editor", Internal Memo, Dept. of Information Theory, Chalmers University, Göteborg, Sweden, January, 1982.

9. Markel, J.D., Gray, Jr., A.H., "Linear Prediction of Speech", Springer-Verlag, New York, 1976.

10. Rabiner, L.R., Schafer, R.W., "Digital Processing of Speech Signals", Prentice-Hall, Englewood Cliffs, 1978.

© 1982 Elsevier Biomedical Press
The Representation of Speech in the Peripheral
Auditory System, R. Carlson and B. Granström eds.

A REPRESENTATION OF SPEECH WITH PARTIALS

PER HEDELIN

Chalmers University of Technology, S-412 96 Gothenburg, Sweden

INTRODUCTION

   Traditional speech models are based on a separation of speech production
into a glottal source and a vocal tract filter (1). In particular, the
conventional LPC-model (2), makes use of a simplified description where
the voiced source is an impulse generator (supplemented with some shaping
filter). This model has been used extensively for over 10 years in both
speech coding and speech synthesis and is known to give good but somewhat
distorted quality.

   One obvious shortcoming of the LPC-model is the assumption of a quasi-
periodic white impulse source. Recently there has been some interest (4)
(5) and (6) in extending the glottal model to essentially include the
partials. Hopefully this should give improved synthesis by relaxing the
assumption of perfectly harmonic and white partials in the excitation.

   This paper discusses some alternatives when formulating an extended model
and presents a few experimental results.

MODEL

   The works reported in (5)(6) and (7) provide a few examples of different
frameworks for introducing partials in a speech model. Here we briefly review
the description used in (7). Let the sampled speech signal $y(k)$ be described
by the sum

$$y(k) = \sum_{i=1}^{n} a_i(k) \sin[\psi_i(k)]$$

where
   - $a_i(k)$ is the time-varying amplitude of tone i.
   - $\psi_i(k)$ is the instantaneous phase of tone i. We shall think of $\psi_i(k)$
     as being the integral of an instantaneous frequency $\varphi_i(k)$, related by
     $\psi_i(k) = \psi_i(k-1) + 2\pi/f_s \, \varphi_i(k)$.

We shall not necessarily invoke an assumption of perfectly harmonic tones. However, a harmonic model as in (6) can be seen as a special case when $\varphi_i(k) = i\, f_o(k)$ (f_o being the fundamental frequency).

THE NUMBER OF TONES

Most important is the number of partials included in the model. Obviously with a fixed bandwidth the number of tones will vary considerably depending on the fundamental frequency of the speaker and even more with different speakers. For a 4 kHz bandwidth and a "worst case" with a low pitched male something like 100 parameters are necessary (50 harmonics with individual amplitude and frequency).

Now, several simplifications are possible. One convenient approach is to let the tones be perfect harmonics. Another is to describe the amplitudes by a LPC-model retaining only individual phase/frequency for the tones (5).

Furthermore perceptual aspects can be included when choosing a suitable representation. It is well known that the formant regions dominates the "phonemic" perception. Moreover the low-frequency region dominates the perception of pitch and of "voice quality" whereas the high-frequency region typically exhibits a less clear harmonic pattern.

Making use of these properties another approach would be to "highlight" a subset of the tones in the model. Obviously this subset must be dynamically adapted to the speech spectra. The remaining tones can either be left out or represented in a simplified fashion (perfect harmonics with amplitudes from a LPC-model).

EXPERIMENTAL RESULTS

Software for analysis and synthesis in terms of the parameters of the suggested model has been developed. For the analysis a FFT-based scheme has been used. Parameters have been extracted once every 16 ms corresponding to standard frame-sizes used in speech coding.

A number of experiments have been undertaken to investigate the synthesis quality and its relation to various analysis conditions. In particular the degradation when leaving out partials has been studied. Some findings are summarized below.

- A formant requires 2-3 partials. In practice one or two additional partials should be included to ensure high quality during fast transitions.

- The first few harmonics - "the voice formant" - should be included to give faithful reproduction of "voice quality".

- Accurate analysis is required giving frequency with an error well below 1%. Amplitude requires a precision of 2-3 dB.

- Synthesis quality is well above traditional pitch-excited LPC-synthesis.

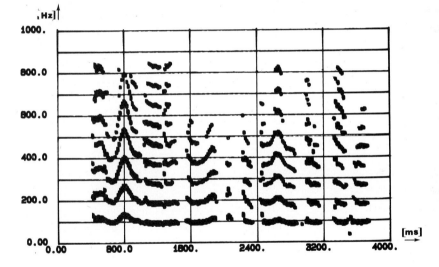

Fig. 1. Analysis of 4 seconds of male speech. 10 tones used. Frequency-band 50-850 Hertz.

SUMMARY

Speech models based on partials offer some advantages as compared to traditional models such as LPC, the main feature being improved speech quality. Low distortion is possible with a reduced number of partials only if the formant regions are well preserved. Intra-formant regions play little or no perceptual role.

The speech models discussed are of importance both for low- and medium-band voice-coding as well as for constructive speech synthesis.

REFERENCES

1. G. Fant, ACOUSTIC THEORY OF SPEECH PRODUCTION, Mouton, The Hague, 1960.

2. J.D. Markel and A.H. Gray, LINEAR PREDICTION OF SPEECH, New York: Springer-Verlag, 1976.

3. P. Hedelin, "A Base-Band Vocoder with Extended-Kalman Coding", EUSIPCO-80 proc, 1980.

4. P. Hedelin, "A Tone-Oriented Voice-Excited Vocoder", ICASSP-81 proc, 1981.

5. L.B. Almeida, J.M. Tribolet, "A Spectral Model for Nonstationary Voiced Speech", ICASSP-82 proc, 1982.

6. V. Viswanathan, A.L. Higgins, et.al, "A Harmonic Deviations Linear Prediction Vocoder for Improved Narrowband Speech Transmission", ICASSP-82 proc, 1982.

7. P. Hedelin, "Models for Non-linear Estimation of Speech", Chalmers, 1979.

© 1982 Elsevier Biomedical Press
The Representation of Speech in the Peripheral
Auditory System, R. Carlson and B. Granström eds.

MECHANISMS OF SPEECH AND MUSICAL SOUND PERCEPTION

HANS M. BORCHGREVINK
Institute of Aviation Medicine, P.O. Box 281 Blindern,
Oslo 3 NORWAY

INTRODUCTION

When a pure tone is presented to the mammal ear, it creates a
"travelling wave" motion of the basilar membrane in the cochlea.
The point of maximal membrane displacement is located at a certain
distance from the stapes depending upon the tone frequency
(Bekesy 1960, Johnstone & Taylor 1970). The relative width of the
basilar membrane from base to apex and the structure of the
cochlear partition determine the tonotopic frequency analysis in
the cochlea (Spoendlin 1970).

Electrophysiological registrations from primary afferent nerve
fibers (running from the cochlear hair cells to the cochlear
nucleus) show that each nerve fiber is sharply "tuned" to a certain best frequency, to which it is most sensitive and responds
with high discharge rate even to low intensity stimulation
(Kiang 1965). Upon slight alteration of sound stimulus frequency,
the corresponding nerve fiber discharge rate can only be obtained
with considerably higher stimulus intensities. Recent results
indicate that the sharply tuned fiber response reflects a
correspondingly sharp "tuning" of the basilar membrane motion
(Johnstone & al. 1982).

The central auditory nervous system is strictly cochleotopically
organised, which means that any given section of the basilar
membrane projects to one specific section in the auditory pathway
nuclei and auditory cortex. There are complex, spatially convergent
highly-ordered fiber projections from lower to higher levels
(Merzenich & al. 1977). This fiber arrangement may be regarded to
give the auditory cortex an "overview" of the pattern of
simultaneously present frequencies in the sound stimulus, in good
agreement with the (spatially coded?) central auditory pattern
analyser indicated by psycho-acoustical experiments (e.g. Houtsma
& Goldstein 1972).

The auditory pathways are largely crossed: nerve fibers from the
right cochlea project to the right (ipsilateral) cochlear nucleus,

from where the majority of neurons end more or less directly in the left (contralateral) auditory nuclei/cortex -- and vice versa. Extensive exchange of information between the right and left sides may take place at the oliva and inferior colliculus level (Whitfield 1967, Peele 1977).

CEREBRAL HEMISPHERE SPECIALISATION FOR SPEECH AND MUSICAL FUNCTION

Speech and language function are controlled by the left hemisphere in practically all righthanders (~85% of the population) and in about 2/3 of lefthanders (~7% of the population). 1/3 of the lefthanders (~3% of the population) control speech and language in their right hemisphere (for review, see Steffens 1975). Accordingly, most people control speech/language and their preferred hand in the same hemisphere. Handedness and the cerebral lateralisation of speech/language are genetically determined, but may be affected by unilateral cerebral lesion in early life (Annett 1976, Chi & al. 1977, Entus 1977, Molfese 1977). The more direct projections to the temporal cortex from the contralateral ear is believed to be the neuroanatomical base for the characteristic ear preferences for speech and non-speech stimuli recorded in dichotic listening experiments.

Musical functions were earlier assumed to be controlled by the right (non-speech) hemisphere in righthanders (e.g. Kimura 1964). However, examining speech/language and musical functions in epilepsy patients during diagnostic selective hemisphere amytal anaesthesia, the author demonstrated the following pattern of cerebral lateralisation:

In righthanders, the left hemisphere generally controls speech perception, speech production, counting, musical rhythm and prosody/intonation/local dialect -- as well as the onset of the act of singing. The right hemisphere controls pitch and tonality in singing. Cerebral pathology may alter this pattern of lateralisation. Speech may suppress pitch control when both are controlled by the same hemisphere. Singing may facilitate speech, and vice versa, during recovery from left (speech) hemisphere anaesthesia. Memory is normally represented in both hemispheres, but may be unilaterally controlled in case of cerebral pathology. Consciousness and attention are normally preserved throughout.

Carotid angiography showed no x-ray contrast medium in the contralateral hemisphere (Borchgrevink 1977, 1979, 1980, 1982).

  The results were presented to the Symposium by real-time tape
recorded example of a righthanded patient's performance before,
during and after anaesthesia of the right and left hemisphere.
  When counting 1.2.3.4.5.6.7 instead of lyrics to a well-known
tune during selective right intracarotid amytal injection, the
patient lost control of pitch and tonality - counting monotonously
with preserved musical rhythm. Tonal control was gradually regained
during recovery. Consciousness and normal speech comprehension
and -production including dialect (stress, prosody, intonation)
were preserved throughout. Corresponding left hemisphere anaesthesia produced abrupt loss of speech comprehension, -production and
singing ability, normal functions being as suddenly regained
("let through") at a certain stage of recovery.

  One might argue that since the examinations is performed on
epileptic patients, their cerebral lateralisation pattern might be
deviating from the normal pattern due to the cerebral pathology
that causes the epilepsy. However, as the above lateralisation
pattern is seen in (so far) 13 out of 15 patients (two patients
had all functions controlled by the right hemisphere due to
left temporal lobe agenesia and left childhood epilepsy), and all
but two (other) patients were intelligent people going to normal
school/work, the chances of having the cerebral lateralisation
pattern shifted in the same direction in so many individuals must
be regarded negligible. The above lateralisation pattern must
therefore be regarded to reflect the organisation of the normal
brain in righthanders.
  Losing control of musical pitch in singing while at the same
time preserving pitch accuracy in speech (normal prosody) during
right hemisphere anaesthesia, indicates that physically rather
similar complex sounds will be controlled by different hemispheres
and thus different analysing units depending upon context: whether
the sound is a signal referring to a symbol or concept, as in
speech -- or whether the sound is analysed as non-symbolic "sound
as such". In another experiment, patients with right (non-speech)
temporal lobe pathology without aphasia were able to perform the
linguistic discrimination of the Norwegian words SIL and SYL, but
failed to discriminate between the same vowels I and Y removed from
linguistic context. They also failed to discriminate between

major/minor/diminished triads (Borchgrevink & Reinvang IN PREP).
Studies that investigate auditory perception phenomena by psychoacoustical methods, using sounds and phonemes presented in isolation or outside normal context, may accordingly fail to activate
the appropriate cerebral analysing units responsible for the
complex sound analysis from which the stimulus is isolated. The
results may then be unexpected and/or be irrelevant for the
perceptive functions intended to be illuminated by the study.
Pols' investigation of the discrimination of rapid tone sweeps
(this volume) where people failed to perceive changes in frequency
that obviously are discriminated in normal speech perception,
might be explained by the above reasoning.

HOW DOES THE BRAIN READ THE NEURAL INFORMATION FROM THE INNER EAR?
   Musical sounds (tones and intervals/chords) represent a well
defined system of sound classification and as such offers a struc-
tured approach to the study of (non-speech) sound perception. By
means of tone combinations one can cover the range from simple
tonal sound to noise by varying the number of simulataneously
sounding tones and their frequency relations. The rather delicate
problem of investigating perceptive quality might be solved by
transforming the individual's subjective qualitative impression of
the percept to the definite task of quantitatively registering the
number of tones perceived to be present in a stimulus. Through
systematic variation of the number of tones in each presented
stimulus, and their frequency relations, asking a skilled musician
(solfeggio teacher) to mark "How many tones do you hear in this
chord?" in a scheme (non-verbal procedure, forced choice 1.2.3.4.5
or more tones in each chord), one would get a psychoacoustical
mapping of man's optimal ability to analyse complex sound into its
elements. Such data would necessarily contain information concerning the nature of perceptive quality - and thus: from the eventu-
ally arising pattern of errors and correct analyses, the principal
features of the sound perceptive mechanism by be derived.
   12 skilled solfeggio teachers, 6 had absolute pitch, individually
judged the number of tones present in each of 69 different, randomly presented chords. Each chord consisted of 1,2,3 or 4 sinus tones.
The results showed that sound analysis was poor when the presented

tone combinations coindided with harmonic series (the overtone row),
analysing faculty increasing with deviation from harmonic series
of the lowest frequency presented, both for non-harmonic tone
combinations and for combinations of harmonic intervals deviating
from the overtone pattern (e.g. fifth+fifth, fourth+fourth). There
was an overall tendency to judge the chords to contain less than
the actual number of tones present, indicating considerable fusion.
Fusion was greatest for the chords with tones coinciding with the
harmonics of the lowest frequency. The brain thus seems to act as
a sound pattern analyser, using harmonic frequency relations as a
"template" for sound analysis. Fusion at the perceptive level indicates signal similarity for the brain between the actual and the
assumed (perceived) stimulus. Fusion must be involved when complex,
harmonic tones from a musical instrument are perceived as one
pitch. Consonant chords consist of harmonic frequency combinations.
Consonance and tone pitch might accordingly represent different
degrees of perceptive fusion along the same dimension, caused by
the harmonic template for sound analysis. The neuroanatomical base
for perceptive fusion might be nerve fiber convergence, shown to
be present in the auditory pathways (Merzenich & al. 1977). The
study will be more thoroughly reported elsewhere (Borchgrevink1982).

If the brain has a central auditory pattern analyser working with
harmonic frequencies/series as a template for sound analysis, the
pan-cultural presence of harmonic chords and intervals in most
(if not all)music traditions might be a perceptual, aesthetic
consequence of the influence of acoustical laws on the mammal
auditory system, consonance preference thus being inherited. Harmonic chord preference was found experimentally in naive rats,
using an operant choice paradigm in which the rat could freely
choose to press either of two identical levers to obtain consonance
(major triad) and dissonance (of corresponding frequencies),
respectively (Borchgrevink 1982). No pretraining or reward apart
from the obtained sounds were involved. Different music traditions
might therefore reflect different degrees of deviation (stimulus
variation?) from the inherited special percept of harmonic frequency relations. The existence of atonal music should not question
the concept of inherited consonance preference to a greater extent
than the presence of non-figurative art questions the existence of
naturalistic form.

256

CONCEPT - REFERENCE COHERENCE INFLUENCES SPEECH COMPREHENSION

Simple Norwegian and English sentences were read by a bilingual adult, taperecorded and presented individually to bilingual adults with English or Norwegian as their first language and good command of the other. Each sentence was first presented in so strong background noise that it could not be perceived, and was repeated with the noise level progressively reduced in 2 dB steps until the sentence was adequately repeated by the subject. For both groups the first (native) language sentences were correctly repeated/ comprehended after fewer presentations, that is at (~3 dB) lower signal-to-noise ratio, than the second language sentences. One thus needs fewer acoustical cues to comprehend messages in the first language, presumably because of better established concept - reference (word) coherence giving better access to the brain's semantic association network (Borchgrevink 1981).

CONCLUSIONS CONCERNING THE REPRESENTATION OF SPEECH IN THE PERIPHERAL AUDITORY SYSTEM

Central cerebral processing, presentation mode and context will influence the psycho-acoustical analysis of any sound stimulus. Presenting stimuli that are fragments of some complex sound system may activate other analysing systems in the brain than those relevant for the complex sound analysis which one intended to study a part of.

ooOoo

REFERENCES

Annett, M. (1976) Handedness and the Cerebral Representation of Speech, Ann. Human Biol. 3 (4), pp. 317-28.

Bekesy, G. von (1960) Experiments in Hearing, McGraw-Hill, N.Y.

Borchgrevink, H. M. (1977) Cerebral lateralisation of speech and singing after intracarotid amytal injection, Int. Symp. Aphasia, Gothenburg, Sweden.

Borchgrevink, H. M. (1979) Speech, singing, object identification and memory investigated during intracarotid hemisphere anaesthesia, 2. Conf. Int. Neuropsychol. Soc., Noordwijkerhout, the Netherlands. Abstract in INS-Bull. June 1979 p. 14.

Borchgrevink, H. M. (1980) Cerebral lateralisation of speech and singing after intracarotid amytal injection, in Sarno, M. T. and Høøk, O. (eds.): Aphasia. Assessment and Treatment, pp. 186-91, Almqvist & Wicksell, Stockholm, Sweden.

Borchgrevink, H. M. (1981) Second language speech comprehension in noise - a hazard to aviation safety, AGARD Conf. Proceed. No. 311

Aural Communication in Aviation, pp. 15-(1-5) from conf. at TNO, Soesterberg, the Netherlands April 1981.

Borchgrevink, H. M. (1982) Musical chord preferences in man elucidated by animal experiments, accepted by J. Acoust. Soc. Am.

Borchgrevink, H. M. (1982) Perception of complex sound I, paper prepared for submittance to J. Acoust. Soc. Am.

Borchgrevink, H. M. (1982) Prosody and musical rhythm are controlled by the speech hemisphere, in Clynes, M. (ed.): Music, Mind and Brain: The Neuropsychology of Music, Plenum Publ. Corp., New York.

Borchgrevink, H. M. & Reinvang, I. (IN PREP) The correlation between speech and musical functions in adult aphasics.

Chi, J. G., Dooling, E. C. & Gilles, F. H. (1977) Left-right asymmetries of the temporal speech areas of the human fetus, Arch. Neurol. 34, pp. 346-8.

Entus, A. K. (1977) Hemispheric asymmetry in processing of dichotically presented speech and non-speech stimuli by infants, in Segalowitz, S. J. & Gruber, F. A. (eds.): Language Development and Neurological Theory, Acad. Press, London.

Houtsma, A.J.M. & Goldstein, J.L. (1972) The central origin of the pitch of complex tones: Evidence from musical interval recognition, J. Acoust. Soc. Am., 51(2), pp. 520-29.

Johnstone, B.M. & Taylor, K. (1970)Mechanical aspects of cochlear function, in Plomp, R. & Smoorenburg, G.F. (eds.): Frequency analysis and periodocity detection in hearing, Sijthoff, Leiden.

Johnstone, B.M., Robertson, D. & Cody, A. (1982) Basilar membrane motion and hearing loss, in Borchgrevink, H.M. (ed.):Effects of noise on hearing, Proceedings from the Oslo Int. Symp. Effects of Noise on Hearing, Scand. Audiol. Suppl.(IN PRINT).

Kiang, N.Y.-S. (1965) Discharge patterns of single fibers in the cat's auditory nerve, Research Monograph No. 35, M.I.T. Press, Cambridge, Mass.

Kimura, D. (1964)Left-right differences in the perception of melodies,Quart.J.Exp.Psychol. 16, pp. 355-8.

Merzenich, M.M., Roth, G.L., Andersen, R.A., Knight, P.L. & Colwell, S.A. (1977) Some basic features of organization of the central auditory nervous system, in Evans, E.F. & Wilson, J.P. (eds.): Psychophysics and Physiology of Hearing, Acad. Press, Lond.

Molfese, D.L. (1977) Infant cerebral asymmetry, in Segalowitz, S.J. & Gruber, F.A. (eds.):Language Development and Neurological Theory, Acad. Press, London

Peele, T.L. (1977) The auditory pathways and the temporal lobe, in Peele, T.L. The Neuroanatomical Bases for Clinical Neurology, 3.ed. McGraw-Hill, New York

Spoendlin, H. (1970) Structural beasis of peripheral frequency analysis, in Plomp, R. & Smoorenburg, G.F. (eds.):Frequency analysis and periodicity detection in hearing, Sijthoff, Leiden.

Steffen, H. (1975) Cerebral Dominance: The development of handedness and speech, Acta Paedopsychiat. 41 (6), pp. 223-235.

Whitfield, I.C. (1967) The auditory pathway, Edw. Arnold, London.

SIMULATION AND SPECIFICATION OF PERIPHERAL HEARING IMPAIRMENT

MARK P. HAGGARD
MRC Institute of Hearing Research, University Park, Nottingham NG7 2RD,
England.

What is Simulation?

I should explain first that the 'simulation' of my title does not refer
to models whose input-output functions may be reconciled with, or derived
from, physiological data as are represented elsewhere in this volume. Rather
it is a set of transformations which, when presented with an input waveform
such as speech, produces another, degraded, waveform. In some sense -
elaborated below - this second waveform represents to the normal-hearing
person how the speech would sound to a hearing-impaired person. The justi-
fications for designing such a device are threefold. Firstly such a demonstration has considerable educational and public relations value. Secondly,
once implemented in a generally accepted fashion, and related in its parameters to average data from real patients, different versions of the device
could constitute laboratory standards by reference to which given hearing
impairments could be judged. This presupposes that it is possible to have
a person adjust parameters of the simulation to give a measure of whether
the effective degradation by each parameter is not so bad as, or is worse
than, that residing in his auditory system. The standard would thus be an
aspect of a measurement technique, which is the second justification. Thirdly
the standard could provide a laboratory tool to economise on testing with
real patients - for example in the development of new hearing aids for
particular classes of patient.

The idea of a simulation of impairment is not particularly new. It
occurs in the audiological literature implicitly in conceptions of impairments - eg. the conception as a mere attenuation that made the phenomenon
of recruitment seem so interesting in the 1930's and 1940's. It also occurs
explicitly but tangentially in many investigations where patterns of performance of normal listeners under the simple electronic distortions are
compared with or are used as a simple surrogate for patterns in hearing-
impaired listeners. But despite frequent emergence of such a concept there
has only been one serious attempt to incorporate psychoacoustical or
physiological findings in the nature of impairment into a simulation, that
of Villchur (4) and even that was not pushed as far into application as its

interest warranted. A possible reason for this abstention from applying the classical approach of modelling to impairment may have been that any simulation which is to be radical will also become complex and have too many parameters for convenient application. A review of how this difficulty may be circumvented, as well as a partial review of the literature is given in Haggard (1). Another deterrent may have been the lack, until the 1970's of psychoacoustic and physiological specifications of hearing disorders.

ASPECTS OF A SIMULATION

1.	L.P.	Filter	(U) H
2.	H.P.	Noise	(R) H
3.	Modulated Noise (H.P.)		(R) (U)
4.	Smeared Spectrum		D U
5.	Expanding Non-linearity		R H
6.	L.P. Modulation Transfer		T

R = Recruitment ; U = Upward spread of masking ;
D = Degraded frequency resolution ;
T = Temporal distortion ; H = Hearing loss

Table 1 lists six aspects of the degradation of speech quality beyond overall attenuation that have been implicitly incorporated into or suggested for simulations. It also lists some of the salient phenomena of senorineurally impaired hearing that a comprehensive simulation must generate, and details those phenomena which, to a first approximation, each aspect is capable of generating. The point is made that no single class of transformation so far suggested can generate all the phenomena. If all the phenomena are to be generated then either a fundamental and economical physiological model is required (giving nerve impulses, not waveforms as an output) or else a multi-stage and rather complex simulation must result. However complex systems demand complex models and the effort should not be abandoned.

Disabling aspects of impairment

While a partial simulation may be useful for a particular purpose, in general a simulation should heed the aspects of impairment that have been established in clinical psychoacoustics, and especially those known to relate closely to aspects of disability such as difficulty in understanding speech. Tyler et al. (3) performed a correlational study in which, as well as thresholds, various aspects of sensory resolution were measured on normal and impaired listeners: frequency resolution, temporal integration, and three measures of temporal resolution, to assess the degree of temporal smear in the impaired auditory system. All measures showed differences between the groups but they did not all correlate equally well with a disability measure across the combined group. The measure used was the ability to identify spoken words in a background masking noise. Specifically, the introduction of frequency resolution in addition to thresholds did not add significantly to the predictability of speech perception; however, incorporating temporal resolution and particularly the threshold for detecting a temporal gap in a narrow-band noise did add significantly. This does not deny that frequency resolution (measured here by psychoacoustic tuning curves) is an important aspect of disability; rather it happened to be closely correlated with thresholds within the population in question. But temporal resolution is clearly an important separate variable.

This leaves an ambiguity as to the patho-physiological origins of temporal smear. Animal models so far do not lead us to expect abnormalities of the temporal microstructure of neural excitation accompanying raised thresholds or broadened tuning curves in single auditory nerve fibres. More complicated temporal assets of excitation such as after-discharge have not yet been examined in pathology and could repay investigation. On the other hand, temporal acuity also suffers in damage to the central nervous system and the degraded temporal resolution could, for example, be a central correlate of diffuse cardiovascular pathology that also happens to affect hearing; its effect is not however removed by partialling out age. Even if the temporal factor does not turn out to be of central origin the fact that it increases the proportion of explicable variance in word identification scores indicates that it is appropriate to take it into account while focusing on peripheral variables.

A demonstration by Summerfield et al (2) shows how purely temporal factors (this time with a well-established physiological base) can play a role in speech perception. Figure 1 shows 3-Dimensional spectrotemporal

262

graphic plots of a gated vowel, and of a flat spectrum preceded and followed
by the spectrum complementary to the vowel.

Fig. 1
(see text)

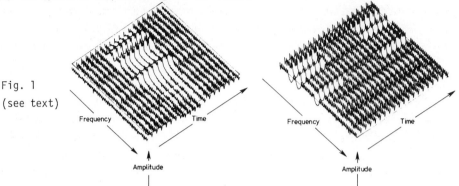

    In the variants of the latter case, provided that the complement pre-
cedes the flat spectrum presented to the same ear, perception of the appropriate vowel results from presentation of the flat spectrum, even though no
true formant structure is ever presented. The effect is also observed if
broad rectangular-band approximations to the vowel complements are used.
Obviously this depends upon the well-known physiological effect of adaptation.
More importantly it also shows that in the mapping of spectro-temporal information onto a linguistic response the analysis of temporal patterning is not
necessarily secondary to the analysis of spectral patterns, but rather that
the spectro-temporal pattern is analysed as such. Although we do not know
whether or not the underlying adaptation mechanism suffers particularly in
hearing impairment, the demonstration serves to remind us that there are other
ways of looking at speech than as spectral cross-sections with formant peaks.
And it suggests a general mechanism by which temporal smearing in impairment
could influence speech perception beyond those phonetic feature distinctions
known to depend primarily on contrasts of temporal interval. Tyler et al
show that such contrasts are generally robust enough to survive the temporal
smearing experienced in hearing impairment.

Aiding need not be the inverse of simulation
    In designing new types of aid the third application of simulation
mentioned in the introduction would be most useful. The time and tolerance of
the necessarily cooperative and motivated hearing-impaired listeners would
not be used until a new scheme had shown preliminary promise with normal-
hearing listeners in preprocessing speech prior to a simulation. What then

is the appropriate relationship between the transformations in the simulation
and the transformations in the preprocessing? Two types of argument follow
to the effect that this need not necessarily be an inverse relationship. The
denial of an inverse relationship realistically limits the benefit we may
expect from signal-processing, but it by no means exhausts the possibilities
for preprocessing the signal in ways that may make it more analysable by the
impaired ear.

The first argument against simplistic inverse aiding comes purely from
precedent. Generally, the chosen gain values in an aid are not equal to the
average hearing loss, but are more like one half that loss. Likewise optimal
frequency responses can with some tedium be found for individuals but when
found are not simply the inverse of the audiogram. Finally multiband compression can be made to restore equal loudness contours, but there is no very
good evidence that the (restricted) benefits of compression systems are
related to this property.

PHYSICAL
REPRESENTATION

INTERNAL
REPRESENTATION

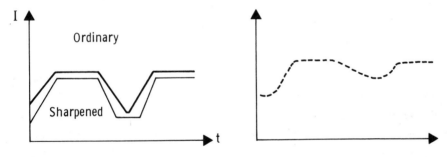

Fig.2

The second argument is illustrated in Fig 2 which attempts to show how
in a gap-detection paradigm, the expected remedial effect of signal preprocessing depends critically upon assumptions about the detailed parameters
of the impairment. The argument was derived as a rationalisation of the
failure of an enhanced spectrum (reduced bandwidth) to augment intelligibility
for the hearing-impaired. It is couched here in terms of temporal resolution,
in view of the foregoing discussion of the importance of that parameter. If
temporal smear in hearing has the quality of an after-discharge, with post-
masking, then the most intense portion of the signal just before its intensity
drops will control the extent of the temporal smear represented on the right
of the figure. Only if the rate of decay of the signal is already in a range

slower than the rate of decay of the auditory sensation, will enhancing that
rate show a differential effect. This may not be the case for important
classes of sounds. Thus the inverse transformation will only constitute a
valid principle of aiding where the impairment is slight by comparison with
the resolution requirements of the stimulus and hence where it is unlikely to
constitute an important obstacle in the first place! In addition, the processing suggested by the figure to be of a remedial nature increases the
dynamic range of the input sound. For some particular speech feature this
might be appropriate, but at the general level it conflicts with the notion
that the effective reduced dynamic range in a (recruiting) hearing impairment
has to be compensated. For that aspect of impairment it should theoretically
compress - not expand - the stimulus.

Thus we have an intriguing parallel with the earlier observation that
no single transformation simulating an impairment encompasses all the
phenomena. We now find that a single inverse will not remedy one degraded
aspect of the hypothetical internal representation without also making some
other aspect worse. This conclusion has been reached by a Gedanken-
experiment without the cost of implementation. However selective implementation of more sophisticated simulations and preprocessing schemes for aids
may still be worthwhile provided it is realised that highly flexible software will be required to recoup the investment in the research, because the
characteristics and the requirements among the more severely hearing-impaired
are highly idiosyncratic.

REFERENCES

1. Haggard, M.P. (1982). In Preparation

2. Summerfield, A.Q., Foster, J., Gray, S. and Haggard, M.P. (1981).
    J. Acoust. Soc. Amer., 69, S116.

3. Tyler, R.S., Summerfield, A.Q., Wood, L., and Fernandes, M. (1982).
    J. Acoust. Soc. Amer. In Press.

4. Villchur, E. (1977). J. Acoust. Soc. Amer., 62, 665.

*The Representation of Speech in the Peripheral
Auditory System*, R. Carlson and B. Granström eds.

WHAT INFORMATION CAN BE GAINED FROM THE AUDITORY BRAIN STEM RESPONSE WITH RESPECT TO DISCRIMINATION OF SPEECH?

ERIK BORG, ELIS PETTERSSON, ANITA HIRSCH AND JOHAN BERGENIUS
Department of Audiology, Karolinska Hospital, Box 60 500, 104 01 Stockholm 60,
(Sweden)

INTRODUCTION

Bioelectric activity in groups of neurons in the ascending auditory system induces electric fields that can be sensed by electrodes placed on the skull surface. Generation of distinct and reproducible farfield potentials presupposes a precise time-locking and synchrony of a large number of neural elements in response to an external stimulus, e.g. a transient sound (1). These requirements form a basis for using farfield potentials, as with the auditory brain stem response (ABR) in studies of timing processes in the lower auditory system. Although the ABR, which is generated in the inner ear and lower brain stem pathways, has gained considerable clinical interest, it has seldom been related to the sound analysing capacity of the auditory nervous system. The main clinical use of ABR is in the diagnosis of eighth nerve and brain stem disorders and in the determination of auditory thresholds, particularly in children. To what extent ABR can be used as a measure of the signal analysing capacity of the auditory system is not known (such as its relation to pure tone and speech discrimination test results in hearing loss). Pure tone thresholds provide no information about temporal resolution of the auditory system, and the ABR may therefore significally extend the description of the analysis performed by the deafened ear.

The conventional clinical methods for estimating the ears' analysing capacity are based on discriminating words from standardized word lists. Speech reception thresholds and speech discrimination scores can be ascertained with these methods which have a fairly good reproducibility and are easily applied to adults. Their obvious drawback, however, is with pre-lingual children. The deterioration of speech discrimination seems to be related to the etiology of the hearing loss in a systematic way. In conductive loss, maximal discrimination usually reaches 100%; in cochlear hearing loss, discrimination deteriorates roughly in proportion to the decay of auditory sensitivity, whereas in eighth nerve disorders discrimination is often remarkably poor in spite of normal or near normal thresholds for pure tones. The dissociation between hearing of pure tones and discrimination of speech in eighth nerve lesions can not at present be explained.

We designed a series of experiments to study whether the ABR can give information of value in assessing the analysing capacity of the lower auditory system, in particular with regard to discrimination of speech in subjects with hearing loss. In the first series on subjects with inner ear deafness, ABR features and threshold were compared with pure tone thresholds and maximal speech discrimination scores. The second series of experiments, on patients with acoustic nerve lesions (acoustic neurinoma) related ABR features to maximal speech discrimination and pure tone thresholds.

METHODS

The investigation was performed on 2 groups of subjects: 21 pupils (42 ears) at Alvik's school for hearing handicapped children with hearing loss classified as being of cochlear origin and 14 patients (15 ears) with radiologically verified acoustic neurinoma (one case of Mb Recklinghausen with bilateral tumors) having pure tone thresholds not exceeding 60 dB in the frequency range 0.5-2.0 kHz and reproducible ABR.

Pure tone audiograms and maximal speech discrimination were determined according to Lidén (2). The auditory brain stem response (ABR) was picked up by surface electrodes on the vertex and ipsilateral mastoid, with ground on the forehead. The signals were routed to a Medelec M-6 system. The filter band pass was set to 32 Hz and 3200 Hz. The sampling interval was 30 μs. The stimulus used was a 2 kHz haversine wave presented at a rate of 20 stimuli per second by a magnetically shielded TDH-49 ear phone. For the group with acoustic neurinoma the ABR features were only determined at a high stimulus level (75 dB nHL), i.e. the latency, amplitude and duration of wave V. For the group with cochlear hearing loss the electrophysiological threshold was also determined.

RESULTS

Cochlear group. The electrophysiological ABR thresholds were highly correlated both to mean hearing thresholds at 0.5, 1.0, and 2.0 kHz, and to maximal speech discrimination (Fig. 1 A and B). In fact, the correlation between ABR and speech discrimination was slightly better than the correlation between mean hearing level and speech discrimination. At 75 dB nHL the latency and amplitude of ABR-wave V were only sligntly altered in comparison to normal subjects. In this cochlear group latency, amplitude, and duration of the main wave of ABR were nearly totally uncorrelated both to speech discrimination (r=-0.24, 0.23, and -0.12, respectively) and hearing threshold (r=0.22, -0.28, and -0.66, Spearman rank order correlation).

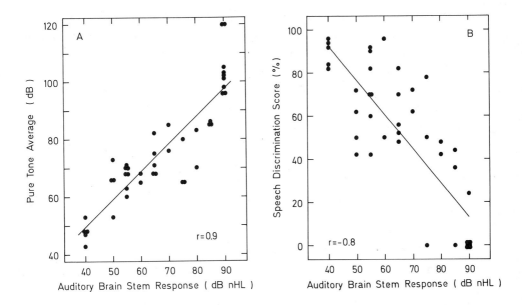

Fig. 1 A. Relation between ABR threshold and average pure tone threshold (0.5, 1.0, and 2.0 kHz) in 21 subjects with inner ear lesions.

B. Relation between ABR thresholds and maximal speech discrimination. (Reproduced from Borg et al. 1982: Scand Audiol)

The ABR does give an estimate of the sensitivity in the speech frequency range, but measurement of its amplitude, latency and duration does not give significant information about the analyses of speech.

Acoustic neurinoma. In these patients the ABR wave V was regularly observed with a reduced amplitude and a prolonged latency at a stimulus level of 75 dB nHL. The ABR latency and amplitude as a function of maximal speech discrimination as well as the relation between hearing threshold and maximal speech discrimination are shown in Fig. 2. It can be seen from Fig. 2 C that speech discrimination is not related to hearing threshold whereas it is significantly correlated to ABR latency (Fig. 2 A, p<0.05) and amplitude (Fig. 2 C, p<0.01, Spearman rank order correlation.

268

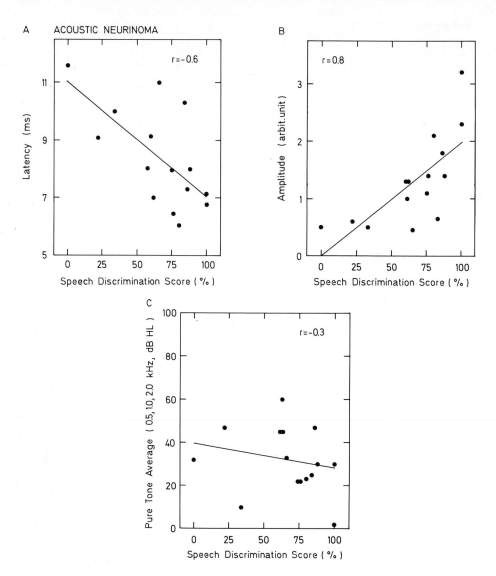

Fig. 2. Correlation between maximal speech discrimination and ABR-wave V latency (A), amplitude (B), and mean hearing threshold (C). 14 subjects (15 ears) with acoustic neurinoma. Stimulus: 2 kHz haversine wave, 75 dB nHL. (Reproduced from Borg, 1982: Scand Audiol)

DISCUSSION

In subjects with inner ear lesions the ABR wave form at suprathreshold level is only sligntly affected. This is compatible with the assumption that the temporal precision in the firing of action potentials is unaffected. However, while ABR does not reveal any significant information about (abnormal) signal processing in excess of that given by the pure tone audiogram, the ABR threshold does seem to be as equally good estimate of speech discrimination as the psychophysically determined pure tone thresholds (mean 0.5, 1.0, and 2.0 kHz). This information supports using the 2 kHz haversine wave ABR threshold as a crude estimate of auditory analysis, e.g. in children.

The subjects with acoustic neurinoma show the well known pattern of poor correlation of speech discrimination and pure tone average combined with an abnormal ABR, e.g. a prolonged latency (3). The amplitude of the ABR wave V is on the other hand highly correlated to speech discrimination which is compatible with the assumption that the pressure exerted on the eighth nerve by the tumor causes a temporal disorganisation of the nerve impulses. Since the pure tone threshold is insensitive to temporal accuity it is resistant to this type of pathology. However, speech discrimination and ABR rely on temporal precision and are therefore both affected.

In acoustic neurinoma (and probably in other eighth nerve disorders) ABR can be used to provide a different type of information about auditory signal processing and to reveal more relevant features of speech analysis than that of pure tone thresholds.

ACKNOWLEDGEMENT

This study was supported by grants from Stiftelsen Tysta Skolan, Torsten Söderbergs and Ragnar Söderbergs Stiftelse and Riksföreningen Förstamajblomman.

REFERENCES

1. Huang, C-M. and Buchwald, J.S. (1977) Interpretation of the vertex short-latency acoustic response: A study of single neurons in the brain stem. Brain Res 137, 291.

2. Lidén, G. (1954) Speech audiometry, an experimental and clinical study with Swedish language material. Acta Otolaryngol (Stockh) Suppl 114, 1-143.

3. Selters, W.A. and Brackmann, D.E. (1977) Acoustic tumor detection with brain stem electric response audiometry. Arch Otolaryngol 103, 181.

© 1982 Elsevier Biomedical Press
The Representation of Speech in the Peripheral
Auditory System, R. Carlson and B. Granström eds.

ELECTRIC AND BIOMAGNETIC RESPONSES TO FREQUENCY GLIDES
RECORDED FROM SUBJECTS WITH NORMAL AND IMPAIRED HEARING

STIG ARLINGER

Dept. of Audiology, University Hospital, S-581 85 Linköping (Sweden)

INTRODUCTION

In the speech signal, dynamic events of relatively short duration carry a
considerable part of the information. As a first approximation, modulated pure
tone signals should provide a possibility for evaluating how the auditory system analyzes such acoustic events. Dynamic stimuli of this kind may provide a
functionally relevant description of hearing (1).

Responses to modulated tone stimuli can be determined either in psychoacoustic tests, e.g. detection or discrimination experiments (2-5), or by recording
some physiological reaction caused by the auditory stimulus (6-7), which may
then be well above detection threshold.

One kind of physiological reaction is the electrophysiological response originating in the human cortex after stimulation. The stimulation gives rise to
a synchronized electric activity in the auditory pathways, and this can be
recorded as *potential differences* between surface electrodes placed on the
scalp. In addition, the electric currents across synchronously activated nerve
cell membranes also produce *magnetic fields*. By means of extremely sensitive
magnetometers, such neuromagnetic fields can be recorded outside the human
skull. This report will present such magnetic field data together with electric
potentials recorded from subjects with different auditory functional status,
using frequency glides as stimulation. From this variety of data some conclusions on the auditory analysis of frequency glides can be drawn.

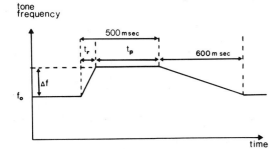

Fig.1
Temporal characteristics of
the stimulus signal.

METHOD

Stimulation made use of a pure tone, presented monaurally through a TDH39 earphone at 60dB HL to normal ears and at most comfortable level (usually in the range 60-90dB HL) to ears with hearing loss. The base frequency of this tone was 1kHz (f_o in Fig.1), and the actual stimulus was a glide in frequency of duration t_r=20ms and magnitude Δf (values up to 500Hz were studied). The frequency returned slowly to f_o after a plateau. This stimulus in the frequency domain was repeated with intervals varying randomly from 2s and up (mean interval 4s).

Electric scalp potentials were recorded by means of surface electrodes on the vertex and left mastoid with a ground electrode on the right mastoid. Details are described in (6). The latency of the N1-component, i.e. the vertex-negative peak in the latency range 100-200ms after the frequency glide onset, is the characteristic of the response that shows the best stability (6), and is therefore used as the quantitative descriptor of the response.

Magnetic fields were recorded by means of a SQUID (Superconducting Quantum Interference Device), a device where the detector is based on the Josephson effect. It attains an extremely high sensitivity for magnetic fields, which is still further enhanced by the use of signal averaging techniques in the same way as for the electric potentials. Placed close to the skull, the magnetometer can record the magnetic field component perpendicular to the skull surface as generated by electric currents in the brain tissue within a few centimeters from the tip of the magnetometer. Specifically, magnetic fields can be recorded over the temporal lobe in response to auditory stimulation (8). Fig.2 shows a set of magnetic fields recorded with the magnetometer in different positions.

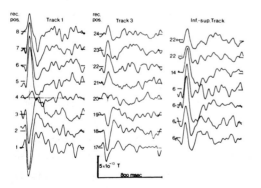

Fig.2
Set of magnetic field recordings obtained in different positions over the left hemisphere of one subject in response to 200Hz glides, presented contralaterally.

It can be shown (9) that this field is determined only by the neuronal currents with negligible influence from volume currents through the skull, in contrast to evoked electric potentials, which are influenced to a very large extent by volume currents. Therefore, as a first approximation the magnetic field
can be described as generated by a current dipole, whose strength and location
can be calculated from measurements at the skull surface (10).

Subjects. Ten subjects with normal hearing were evaluated extensively with
regard to electric responses together with ten subjects having a cochlear
hearing loss. Further, 39 subjects with hearing loss of retrocochlear type,
mainly verified tumours of the auditory nerve, have been studied by means of
electric responses. Finally, magnetic fields were recorded on a group of five
normal-hearing subjects.

RESULTS AND DISCUSSION

Normal-hearing subjects. The electric potentials recorded in normal-hearing
subjects have been described in detail in (6). In Fig.3 are shown the N1-laten-
cies for these responses as a function of the magnitude of the frequency glide
(filled circles joined by the dashed line).

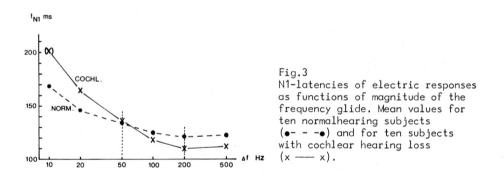

Fig.3
N1-latencies of electric responses
as functions of magnitude of the
frequency glide. Mean values for
ten normalhearing subjects
(●- - -●) and for ten subjects
with cochlear hearing loss
(x —— x).

The general waveform of these responses and their qualitative dependence on
stimulus magnitude is very similar to that of electric responses to simple
tone bursts or clicks. The question of whether these electric responses to
frequency glides and those to tone bursts or clicks are generated by the same
or different parts of the brain cannot be easily answered through analysis of
electric recordings, because of the complicated spread of current inside the
volume conducting human skull.

However, the magnetic field data can illuminate this question. From the detailed results, reported in (11), we can summarize that the location of the equivalent current dipole in response to frequency glides was found to be very close to that previously found for tone burst stimulation (8). A difference of the order of 10mm may exist but the material is too small to allow any definite conclusion.

Comparing latencies in magnetic field data obtained over the left and the right hemisphere with tone burst stimulation, Elberling et al. (12) found no side difference. However, with frequency glide stimulation a statistically significant difference was found. The magnetic responses recorded over the left hemisphere showed a mean latency 6ms shorter than that from the right hemisphere using contralateral stimulation. This result indicates a difference in the neural processing of frequency glides that does not exist for tone burst stimulation.

A comparison between magnetic and electric responses of response amplitudes and latencies as functions of stimulus magnitude indicates that at least the major contributions to the two types of response are produced by the same generator in the temporal lobe of the human cortex.

Subjects with cochlear hearing loss. In Fig.3 are shown also the latencies obtained from this group of subjects (crosses and fully drawn line). Small frequency glides gave rise to longer latencies than in the normal group, while for larger glides similar or even shorter latencies were recorded. This shows clearly that the peripheral lesion, the disturbed cochlear function, has a significant influence on the processing of small frequency glides, in agreement with results from psychoacoustic detection experiment (13).

Subjects with retrocochlear hearing loss. Electric responses to frequency glides of 50 and 200Hz magnitude have been recorded from these subjects, which with the exception of one person had unilateral hearing loss. Results show significantly prolonged latencies for these stimuli when presented to the tumour side as compared to the better ear. Fig. 4 shows the results for 50Hz glides. In 33 out of 40 tested tumour ears the latency was significantly longer than that found in the cochlear group, while stimulation on the other usually produced results within normal range. Remember that no significant difference in latency was found between normal-hearing subjects and the group with cochlear hearing loss for 50 and 200Hz glides (Fig.3).

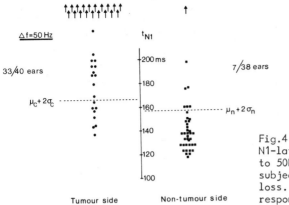

Fig.4
N1-latencies of electric responses
to 50Hz glides obtained from 39
subjects with retrocochlear hearing
loss. Arrows indicate that no
response could be identified.

In addition to. frequency glides, two other types of stimuli were used. Tone
burst stimulation, applied to 33 of the subjects, gave rise to somewhat longer
mean latency when stimulating the tumour side (12ms mean difference). This is,
however, much less than when stimulating with frequency glides. Further, on 8
of the subjects also amplitude glides were tested. On these, no significant
difference between the ears was found in mean latency. Frequency glides, on
the other hand, gave rise to mean latency differences on these 8 subjects that
were statistically highly significant ($p < 0.5\%$). These results taken together
indicate that the latency change found for frequency glides is a specific
effect for this particular stimulus caused by the disturbed function of the
auditory nerve.

Speech discrimination scores for these subjects with retrocochlear lesions
varied between 0 and 100%. Looking at the possible correlation between these
scores (determined by means of phonetically balanced lists of monosyllabic
test words) and N1-latency to 200Hz frequency glides, the data were found to
fall into three categories of about equal size: A) fairly good speech discrimination with the majority having scores above 70%; B) poor speech discrimination with most scores below 20%; C) no identifiable cortical response to
frequency glides. In both A and B, the response latency varied over equally
large ranges. Group A showed a statistically significant correlation between
speech discrimination and N1-latency ($r = -0.48$; $p < 10\%$) while in group B with
the very poor discrimination data no such correlation was found. Also in

another unpublished study, on approx. 50 old subjects with presbyacusis, such relations have been seen: regression analysis indicating a significant correlation between a speech discrimination score and N1-latency in electric response to frequency glide stimulation.

CONCLUSION

In conclusion, our experience supports the idea that frequency glides of a tone have some relation with the complex speech signal. By the use of electric and magnetic response recording on groups of subjects with different peripheral auditory function we have found evidence for a specific analysis of frequency glides which starts already at the most peripheral level of the auditory system and which may show side differences at higher levels.

ACKNOWLEDGEMENT

These studies have been supported by grants from Swedish National Board for Technical Development.

REFERENCES
1. Tyler, R.S. (1979). Br. J. Audiol., 13, 29.
2. Nabelek, I.V. (1978). J. Acoust. Soc. Am., 64, 751.
3. Arlinger, S.D., Jerlvall, L.B., Ahrén, T. and Holmgren, E.C. (1977). Acta Otolaryngol., 83, 317.
4. Small, A.M. (1978). J. Acoust. Soc. Am., 61, 1293.
5. Jerlvall, L.B., Arlinger, S.D. and Holmgren, E.C. (1978). Scand. Audiol., 7, 207.
6. Arlinger, S.D., Jerlvall, L.B., Ahrén, T. and Holmgren, E.C. (1976). Acta Physiol. Scand., 98, 412.
7. Kohn, M., Lifshitz, K. and Litchfield, D. (1978). Electroenceph. Clin. Neurophysiol., 45, 236.
8. Elberling, C., Bak, C., Kofoed, B., Lebech, J. and Saermark, K. (1982). Scand. Audiol., 11, 59.
9. Cuffin, B.N. and Cohen, D. (1977). IEEE Trans. Biom. Eng., 24, 372.
10. Bak, C., Kofoed, B., Lebech, J., Saermark, K. and Elberling, C. (1981). Physics Letters, 82A, 57.
11. Arlinger, S., Elberling, C., Bak, C., Kofoed, B., Lebech, J. and Saermark,K. (1982). (in preparation).
12. Elberling, C., Bak, C., Kofoed, B., Lebech, J. and Saermark, K. (1981). Scand. Audiol., 10, 203.
13. Arlinger, S.D., Jerlvall, L.B., Ahrén, T. and Holmgren, E.C. (1977). Acta Otolaryngol., 83, 310.

© 1982 Elsevier Biomedical Press
The Representation of Speech in the Peripheral
Auditory System, R. Carlson and B. Granström eds.

AUDITORY PERCEPTION IN CHILDREN WITH LEARNING DISABILITIES:
Pilot studies

Gunnar Aniansson[1] and Annalena Lindhe[2]
[1]Department of Otolaryngology, Sahlgren's Hospital, S-413 45
Göteborg (Sweden) and [2]Högabergsvägen 20, S-436 00 Askim (Sweden)

There are several causes of learning disabilities in primary
school (1,2). Auditive perception appears to be one of the most
significant known factors (3). In particular deficits in auditory
sequential processing and auditory serial memory in children with
delayed language development or reading skills or both have been
noted repeatedly, i.e. (4). It is desirable that test methods be
developed which both reveal, before school age, which children
risk having learning disabilities, and also provide indications
of the underlying cause. This would make it possible to provide
the child with suitable adapted teaching methods in an appropriate
group.

It is evident that this type of testing method would have to
include, for example, psychological, neurological, linquistic,
visual and auditive tests. It should be possible, after carrying
out a number of different tests on 4 - 500 preschoolers, and then
making a subsequent follow-up study of these children after 2 - 3
years in the present school system, to evaluate the best possible
combination for such a battery of tests.

The following is a description, in terms of appropriate auditive
tests, of pilot studies of two testing methods used in the
examination of children with learning disabilities in primary
school. In addition to these two tests, the children are subjected
to tone audiometry and speech intelligibility measurements in a
quiet environment and a classroom environment.

Method I

A revised version of the pitch patterns test originally developed by Pinheiro (5) has been used. Briefly, this test includes
a presentation of sequences of sinus tone bursts with a duration
of 200 msec at intervals of 150 msec. Two different frequencies,
800 Hz and 1200 Hz were used. The task of the subjects is,
first, to practice distinguishing between low and high tones.

Then the children are taught that a low tone is symbolized, for example, by an earser, while a high tone is symbolized by a pencil. When it is clear that the child can distinguish between, and correctly indicate, the pencil and the earser when the tones are presented first individually and then in slow succession, a rapid pace should be practiced. When it is perfectly clear that the child has understood the instructions and had sufficient practice, the test is performed. It is comprised of a presentation of 12 sequences of 2 and 3 tone bursts respectively (i.e. di-do or di-do-do) in varied order according to a given pattern.

Method II

A slightly revised test of Tallal (6) has been used. This method allows for variation of the interval between two tone bursts (75 msec). Two complex tones are used, presented at varying intervals (150, 305, 428 and 947 msec). The tones differ in their fundamental frequencies, 100 and 305 Hz, but have the same formants (497, 750 and 1500 Hz). Presentation takes place, in principle, according to the general description given above under Method I.

Subjects I

All ten children who received remedial instruction in Swedish in one school in Gothenburg were tested. These children came from four classes with a total of 120 pupils. Thus they comprise 1/12 of the fourth graders at that school. The ten children in one of the fourth grade classes whose results on a spelling test were best, were selected as a control group.

Subjects II

From the same school district as above, ten children were selected from five classes in the second grade. These children were known to have spelling and reading disabilities. Ten children in the same grade who did not need remedial instruction in Swedish were used as a control group.

RESULTS

The following tables indicate the individual results in each group of ten children with learning disabilities, and ten children with no disabilities, tested according to methods I and II above, respectively.

TABLE I

Individual results in children with and without learning disabilities according to Method I. Number of wrong answers.

Disabilities				No disabilities		
2-tone	3-tone	Total		2-tone	3-tone	Total
4	11	15		1	2	3
5	7	12		0	0	0
11	9	20		0	2	2
8	10	18		1	4	5
4	8	12		1	0	1
5	7	12		0	0	0
8	8	16		0	2	2
6	9	15		0	0	0
0	0	0		0	3	3
1	5	6		0	0	0

TABLE II

Individual results in 10 children with and without learning disabilities, according to method II. The figures with which the columns are headed indicate intervals in msec. Number of wrong answers are given.

Disabilities					No disabilities				
947	428	305	150	Total	947	428	305	150	Total
10	7	4	4	25	0	0	1	3	4
6	7	6	10	29	0	1	1	1	3
4	5	4	6	19	0	2	3	7	12
6	6	6	7	25	1	2	4	7	14
3	7	3	6	19	2	4	0	0	6
10	7	8	7	32	0	0	1	4	5
2	3	6	9	20	0	1	0	1	2
7	6	4	9	26	3	3	3	5	14
2	2	4	3	17	0	2	0	5	7
2	1	3	6	12	2	1	3	6	12

DISCUSSION

It is obvious that comparisons between the groups would reveal significant differences. But the aim of these pilot studies was to find test methods which, at an individual level, could distinguish the child with potential learning disabilities from his peers.

Using method I, children with no learning disabilities were found to make a total of five of fewer mistakes, while eight of the ten children with learning disabilities made at least twelve mistakes.

Using method II, children with no learning disabilities were found to make fourteen or fewer mistakes, while eight of the ten children with learning disabilities made at least nineteen mistakes.

The results of these pilot studies, then, indicate that the two tests used here are promising for distinguishing children with learning disabilities, and motivate further examination of their potential.

REFERENCES

1. Gjessing, H.-J. (1978) Specifika läs- och skrivsvårigheter, dyslexi. AWE/Gebers STockholm.

2. Auditory perception in children with learning disabilities: Handbook of clinical audiology (1972) William & Wilkins Baltimore.

3. Central auditory dysfunction (1979) Keith, R.J. (Ed.) Grune & Stratton New York, New York.

4. Bakker, A. (1971) Temporal Order in Disturbed Reading: Developmental and Neuropsychological Aspects in Normal and Reading Retarded Children. Rotterdam: Rotterdam Univ. Press.

5. Pinheiro, M.L. (1977) Auditory pattern perception in patients with left and right hemisphere lesions. Ohio J Speech and Hearing, 12.

6. Tallal, P. (1976) Rapid auditory processing in normal and disordered language development. J Speech Hearing Research, 19, p 561-571.

© 1982 Elsevier Biomedical Press
The Representation of Speech in the Peripheral
Auditory System, R. Carlson and B. Granström eds.

DEVELOPMENT OF SPEECH AUDIOMETRIC TEST MATERIAL

KOLBJÖRN SLETHEI
Department of Linguistics and Phonetics, University of Bergen, Sydnesplass 9,
N-5000 Bergen. (Norway)

INTRODUCTION

Sinusoid waves are easy to produce, measure, describe and manipulate.
They are therefore ideal as stimuli in audiometric testing - and consequently
their use is widespread. Furthermore, sinusoids are - at least in our types
of societies - "culture-fair", although some groups of the population are
more exposed to sinusoids than others.

Exactly the opposite may be said about speech. It is difficult to measure,
and hard to describe in physical terms; it is closely knit to a culture in
a given community and it is practically impossible to produce and to manipulate in an organised, controlled manner. In addition it is an unstable
phenomenon. It varies from one person to another, it varies from one age
group to another, and the meaning it carries may vary with time.

Nevertheless, because listening to speech is far more important than sine
waves, and because pure tone audiometry does not always give the data
necessary to decide type and/or method of treatment, speech audiometry is now
generally regarded as a valuable supplement to pure tone audiometry. In Norway, speech audiometry is compulsory if a hearing aid is to be paid for by
the National Insurance.

"SPEECH" IN SPEECH AUDIOMETRY

Balance. In the available literature we frequently find linguistically
naive notions about speech when this concept is applied to audiometry. It
takes only little more than basic knowledge to see that the concept "phonetic
balance", "PB", is in fact a *phonemic balance,* relating to the structural
units of the language in question, not to speech as an acoustic signal.

Carrier phrase. The Americal W-1 test is being distributed together with
instructions from which the following is taken: (1) "To facilitate the construction of the tests, this carrier phrase was recorded separately from the
words, and therefore the carrier phrases do not have exactly the same quality
as the words". As early as in 1957 Ladefoged and Broadbent (2) demonstrated
that the identification of the test word to a large extent is determined by
the vowel qualities of the carrier phrase.

Speech and meaning. The results obtained by speech audiometry are supposed
to have some relation to speech in our everyday discourse. Normally, speech
is the unproblematic vehicle of meaning; we chose our words because of their
meaning, not because of their phonetic or phonemic structure. Listening to
isolated words, with or without a carrier phrase and at regular intervals -
words which have the same phonotactic structure being read in a monotonous
voice - is far from using speech for communication purposes. The patient is
not supposed to have any meaningful relation to the *content* of the test word,
he is supposed to *repeat* it to the person administrating the test.

  This, I think, is the most important difference between speech and speech
audiometry.

TEST DEVELOPMENT

  Several years ago the Department of Linguistics and Phonetics, University
of Bergen, was approached by the Department of Oto-Rhino-Laryngology, who reported that the speech audiometric test they had in use, which was developed
in Oslo, seemed to induce hearing deficiencies in elderly people from rural
Western Norway.

  We assumed the responsibility of participating in the development of a
speech audiometric test aiming at the population of Western Norway as its target group.

  Linguistic sensitizing. The group working on this wished to avoid sensitizing the test by filtering, peak or center clipping, temporal splitting or
similar methods. Instead we sensitized the test linguistically by means of
two methods: (i) by using only CVC-words, thus reducing the inherent redundancy
of the individual words, (ii) by selecting words where either one of the consonants or the vowel was crucial to identify the word, i.e. all the words were
easy to misunderstand if all the linguistic elements were not properly identified.

  Test Organisation.   The test was organised in 24 well-defined lists of 10
words, without a carrier phrase, but with the "heading" *"List number ..."*
audibly recorded. This phrase was included to allow the patient to adapt to
the voice and resonance qualities of the speaker. The *list* is the test unit,
and reliability was controlled on list level; i.e. one list may replace any
other at any level of presentation.

  Regional Considerations. The phoneme inventory from which consonants and
vowels were selected was carefully established as that common to the majority
of the target group. This inventory differs somewhat from that of Eastern
Norway.

The reader was a phonetically trained person, fully aware of all the considerations embedded in the test, and a native speaker of a Western dialect.

Validity. This test (3) focused on the *predictive* validity instead of the
content validity. Instead of asking: "How can the qualities of speech be embedded in the test?" we asked: "How should this test look and sound in order
to provide the answers needed in clinical practice?"

Implementation. After a test period where inter-list reliability was controlled, the test was implemented as a standard clinical test at Haukeland
Hospital, Bergen, in autumn 1975. It is now implemented in the majority of
audiological wards in Western Norway.

FURTHER DEVELOPMENT

A new challenge has recently turned up. A considerable proportion of all
hearing aids are paid for by the patients themselves. Frequently a patient
may wish to buy only one hearing aid, and the pure-tone audiometry does not
give any indications of which ear to supply with the instrument. The majority
of these patients are elderly people suffering from presbyacusis, and the test
just described cannot provide good advice of whether the right of left ear
should be fitted with a hearing aid. The standard test is too difficult, i.e.
it contains too little redundancy for this group of patients.

A new test development is now in progress as an interdisciplinary project between the two departments mentioned earlier. We are confident that a suitable
test will result, once again demonstrating that speech audiometry is a field
where knowledge from widely separated disciplines come together, where interdisciplinary cooperation is very fruitful and, last but not least, very useful
for the patients who depend on the results of an audiometric testing.

REFERENCES

1. Central Institute for the Deaf. Auditory Tests W1 and W2. Description and
   Instructions for Use. CID, St. Louis.

2. Ladefoged, P. and Broadbent, G. E. (1956) Information Conveyed by Vowels.
   Journal of the Acoustical Society of America 31, pp. 280-286.

3. Slethei, K. (1975) HS24. En taleaudiometrisk test på fonetisk grunnlag.
   Dept. of Linguistics and Phonetics, Univ. of Bergen, Bergen.

© 1982 Elsevier Biomedical Press
The Representation of Speech in the Peripheral
Auditory System, R. Carlson and B. Granström eds.

AUDITORY MODELS IN HEARING AID FITTING

ARNE LEIJON

Dept of Audiology, ENT- Clinic, Sahlgren's Hospital, S-413 45 Gothenburg

INTRODUCTION

In the future each hearing aid type will probably be much more flexible than today's aids, through the use of digital signal processing or digitally controlled analogue processing. To help utilizing the flexibility of such programmable hearing aids (9, 10) and to simplify the use of conventional aids, an obvious method is using a computerized "fitting system", containing a semi-automatic measuring unit, which collects the audiological data relevant for hearing aid fitting. The same system also contains a program which generates a preliminary recommendation for the hearing aid characteristics to be used. If a programmable hearing aid is being fitted, the recommended characteristics are automatically programmed into the aid by a coding unit also contained in the fitting system. Then the hearing aid is evaluated and the fitting system is used interactively in the further optimization of hearing aid sound processing.

As part of an interdisciplinary project aimed at realizing such a scheme in routine clinical hearing rehabilitation, the present work is concentrated on the mathematical basis for an algorithm producing the preliminary hearing aid recommendation.

This paper is intended to present a critical summary of some theories that can be used as such a basis.

ARTICULATION THEORY

Formulation

An articulation index can be defined as

$$AI = P \cdot SUM(i=1, N: BI(i) \cdot BE(i)), \quad where$$

i is a frequency band index,
BI is a weight factor for each band, reflecting the relative importance of that band in speech perception,
BE is the proportion of amplified speech dynamic range in each band, which is below the listener's discomfort level and above the equivalent noise level in that band, i e the highest among the following: hearing threshold in quiet,

the actual noise level within the band, and the equivalent masking level caused by spread of masking from speech and noise in other bands.

Discussion

Using the factor P as a free parameter with one value for each individual, Dugal et al (4) were able to fit theoretical AI values to experimental results with relatively good correlation.

A problem with this type of theory is that different hearing aid character- istics may give similar AI and also speech test scores not significantly different from each other. But the hearing aid user may have a very clear subjective opinion as to which hearing aid is the best, even for small diff- erences, and the choice may be based on other factors than speech perception.

LOUDNESS DENSITY SPECTRUM

Figure 1 shows an example of the transformation of two vowel spectra to the sone/bark plane, accounting for sensorineural hearing loss and for the amount of hearing aid gain preferred by the patient.

Formulation (example)

For each frequency, transformation was done in the following steps:

1. Spectral energy summation within one critical band, using the formula given by Schröder et al (14).

2. Convolution of the critical band density spectrum by a filter function, assumed to describe spread of masking. A level dependent filter function suggested by Karnickaya et al (6) was used.

3. To simulate an assumed loss of frequency selectivity, caused by the cochlear impairment, the resulting spectrum was convolved with a triangular filter function, one critical band wide for the normal ear. For the impaired ear the width was made linearly proportional to hearing loss, using a band- width 4 times the normal for a hearing loss of 80 dB. Of course this is a very crude representation of the loss of frequency selectivity in an impaired ear, although it may be qualitatively reasonable in the light of data given by Pick et al (11).

4. Transformation to the sone scale taking the abnormal threshold into account. The formula proposed by Zwicker et al (16) was used.

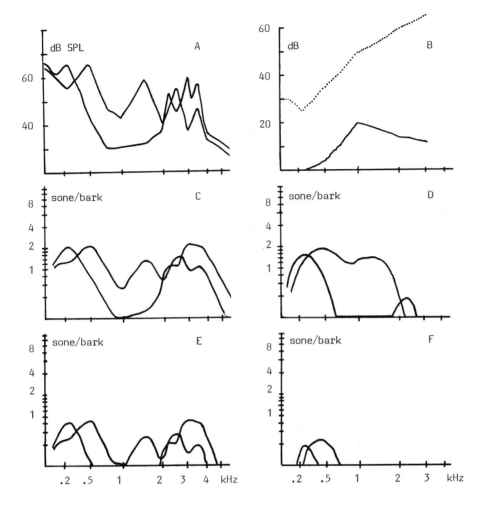

Fig 1. A. Power density spectra for two vowels at 70 dB SPL overall level.
B. Hearing threshold (dotted) and hearing aid gain (full line) for one patient.
C. Computed loudness density spectra for the vowels in A for a normal ear.
D. Computed loudness density spectra for the vowels in A for the patient data
   shown in B.
E, F. Same as C and D, but for the same vowels at 55 dB SPL overall level.

Discussion

   In experiments summarized by Klatt (7) the response by listeners judging the
phonetic difference between vowels could not be correlated to a distance
measure based on a model similar to this one (but not including a hearing
impairment model). But the model gave a fairly good correlation with experimental data for the case when listeners were asked to judge timbre differences

288

between vowels, as reported by Bladon, Lindblom (3).

As shown in fig 1, C–D, the patient actually preferred an amount of gain which gave approximately the same overall loudness for a conversational level vowel as the loudness perceived by an unaided normal ear. This is a typical result.

Thus a model of this type gives some insight into the sound quality perceived by a normal ear, and presumably to some extent also by an impaired ear.

Loudness density patterns for the long- term speech spectrum or for noise spectra can be quickly computed even in a small micro- computer, including only steps 1 and 4 mentioned above. A program which produces a preliminary hearing aid recommendation based on this type of computation is presently being tested clinically. In this pilot test, the algorithm calculates the frequency response needed to restore loudness density of the long- term speech spectrum, preferrably the 90% cumulative level, to the same loudness as for a normal ear. A simple formula was included to account for the binaural loudness summation. If binaural amplification is used, the algorithm matches the loudness in the two ears.

For other sound spectra than that on which the recommendation is based, the hearing aid will give loudness density patterns very different from the normal situation. A display of such patterns helps the clinician to interpret the user's comments on the sound quality of various amplified sounds.

PHYSICAL MODEL COMPONENTS

Physiological changes in the impaired cochlea and their consequences in hearing aid fitting can be modeled only qualitatively using the above mentioned model types. A more realistic model for this purpose must include the following parts:

Mechanics

For the representation of transient speech sounds, and to account for nonlinearities, cochlear mechanics models working in the time domain would be preferred to the otherwise powerful WKB- methods used e g in Taber's (15) detailed work.

One- dimensional models, like the one explored by Hall (5), can be made computationally efficient, but apparently lack some accuracy near the BM resonance. Allen's et al (1,2) two-dimensional time domain model seems to be a step towards a reasonable compromise between the demands on physical realism and computational efficiency.

By "physical realism" is meant e g that the model should not just assume som function describing BM compliance, but should compute each parameter directly from the geometry and mechanical properties of the moving tissues. Then e g the consequences of a 90% loss of ciliar stiffness in one cochlear region can be directly modeled.

Transduction

A simple but powerful model for this stage is the one proposed by Schröder, Hall (13), relating neural firing probability to mechanical stimulation through a first order differential equation.

Acoustical pattern decoding

The place- time pattern of firing probabilities, produced by the transduction model, has to be decoded in different ways, depending on which psychoacoustical task the model is related to. As for loudness perception, e g Lachs, Teich (8) tested a simple method to predict loudness from a calculated firing pattern. Features related to phonetical perception can be extracted, as shown by Sachs, Young (12) using an interval histogram computation for neighbouring groups of fibres.

CONCLUSION

Mathematical models can contribute to the prediction of optimal hearing aid characteristics and improve our understanding of user performance. Such models must attempt to describe not only overall speech perception but also, and maybe above all, the subjective loudness and timbre of various other sounds, which are of interest for the hearing aid user.

Theories for the preliminary fitting of hearing aids must be developed and tested in two parallel approaches:

1. For practical implementation in clinical work, rather simple procedures are used, like matching the aided loudness density spectrum of som sound to that of the same sound for the normal ear. Other sounds will give loudness densities very different from the normal situation, and these discrepancies, displayed by the model calculation, may help us interpret the user's comments on hearing aid sound quality.

2. The implementation is checked using information obtained from physically more realistic models. Such models should be able to predict patient performance with and without hearing aid, given a specific hypothesis on cochlear impairment. Since these models are already partly developed in basic research, they can now be applied in the practical problems of hearing aid fitting.

ACKNOWLEDGEMENT

The present work is supported by the Swedish National Board for Technical Development.

REFERENCES

1. Allen, J.B., Sondhi, M.M. (1979) Cochlear macromechanics: Time domain solutions. JASA 66, pp 123- 132.

2. Allen, J.B. (1980) Cochlear micromechanics: A physical model of transduction. JASA 68, pp 1660- 1670.

3. Bladon, R.A.W., Lindblom, B. (1981) Modeling the judgment of vowel quality differences. JASA 69, pp 1414- 1422.

4. Dugal, R.L., Braida, L.D., Durlach, N.I. (1980) Implications of previous research for the selection of frequency- gain characteristics. In Studebaker, Hochberg (eds): Acoustical factors affecting hearing aid performance, Univ Park Press, Baltimore, pp 379- 403.

5. Hall, J.L. (1974) Two-tone distortion products in a nonlinear model of the basilar membrane. JASA 56, pp 1818- 1828.

6. Karnickaya, E.G., Mushnikov, V.N., Slepokurova, N.A., Zhukov, S.Ja. (1975) Auditory processing of steady state vowels. In Fant, Tatham (eds): Auditory analysis and perception of speech, Acad Press, London, pp 37- 53.

7. Klatt, D.H. (1982) Prediction of perceived phonetic distance from critical-band spectra: a first step. ICASSP 82 (IEEE), Paris, pp 1278- 1281.

8. Lachs, G., Teich, M.C. (1981) A neural- counting model incorporating refractoriness and spread of excitation. II. Application to loudness estimation. JASA 69, pp 774- 782.

9. Mangold, S., Leijon, A. (1979) Programmable hearing aid with multichannel compression. Scand Aud 8, pp 121- 126.

10. Mangold, S., Leijon, A. (1981) Multichannel compression in a portable programmable hearing aid. Hearing Aid J, April 1981, pp 6, 29-32.

11. Pick, G.F., Evans, E.F., Wilson, J.P. (1977) Frequency resolution in patients with hearing loss of cochlear origin. In Evans, Wilson (eds): Psychophysics and physiology of hearing, Acad Press, London, pp 273- 281.

12. Sachs, M.B., Young, E.D. (1980) Effects of nonlinearities on speech encoding in the auditory nerve. JASA 68, pp 858- 875.

13. Schröder, M.R., Hall, J.L. (1974) Model for mechanical to neural transduction in the auditory receptor. JASA 55, pp 1055- 1060.

14. Schröder, M.R., Atal, B.S., Hall, J.L. (1979) Objective measures of certain speech signal degradation based on masking properties of human auditory perception. In Lindblom, Öhman (eds): Frontiers of speech communication research, Acad Press, London, pp 217- 229.

15. Taber, L.A. (1979) An analytic study of realistic cochlear models including three- dimensional fluid motion. Ph. D. Diss., Stanford University.

16. Zwicker, E., Feldtkeller, R. (1967) Das Ohr als Nachrichtenempfänger. S Hirzel Verlag, Stuttgart, p 138.

AUTHOR INDEX